# The Literature of
# Spiritual Values
# and Catholic Fiction

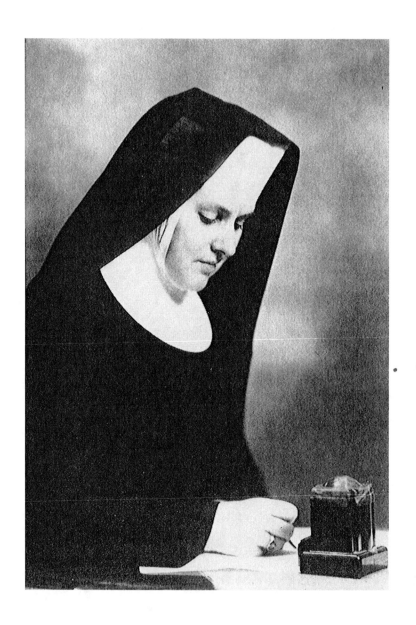

# THE LITERATURE OF SPIRITUAL VALUES AND CATHOLIC FICTION

Mariella Gable, O.S.B.

Edited and with an Introduction by

Nancy Hynes, O.S.B.

University Press of America, Inc.
Lanham • New York • London

Copyright © 1996 by
**University Press of America,® Inc.**
4720 Boston Way
Lanham, Maryland 20706

3 Henrietta Street
London, WC2E 8LU England

**Library of Congress Cataloging-in-Publication Data**

Gable, Mariella, 1898-1985.
The literature of spiritual values and Catholic fiction / Mariella Gable
  : edited and with an introduction by Nancy Hynes.
        p.      cm.
  Includes bibliographical references and index.
  1. American fiction--Catholic authors--History and criticism. 2.
English fiction--Catholic authors--History and criticism. 3. French
fiction--Catholic authors--History and criticism. 4. Christian fiction--
History and criticism. 5. Fiction--Religious aspects--Christianity. 6.
Christian ethics in literature. 7. Spiritual life in literature. 8.
Catholics--Intellectual life. 9. Christianity and literature. 10. Values
in literature. I. Hynes, Nancy. II. Title.
  PS153.C3G33    1996    813'.54099222--dc20    96-14164 CIP

ISBN 0-7618-0343-2 (cloth: alk. ppr.)

⊖™The paper used in this publication meets the minimum
requirements of American National Standard for information
Sciences—Permanence of Paper for Printed Library Materials,
ANSI Z39.48—1984

"Edification at the expense of truth
is always a doubtful good."

*Mariella Gable, O.S.B.*

"The Kingdom of heaven is like to leaven which a woman took and
hid in three measures of meal, enough to leaven the whole batch."

*Matthew 13:33*

# Contents

# List of Illustrations

# Preface

In the words of Meridel LeSueur, this book is for "the continuous matriarchal root"—my grandmother, Rose Mulcahey Cram, and my mother, Charlotte Cram Hynes, and their daughters and their daughter's daughters.

This book is what LeSueur calls a "collective" book. Like a tree made by a communal movement of root, stem, flower and seed, this book "grew." Below are a few of the collaborators.

I thank my English teachers, especially Sisters Mariella Gable, Kristin Malloy, Linnea Welter, and Andre Marthaler, mentors who needle, instruct, and inspire me daily; Sister Imogene Blatz who meticulously indexed 135 file folders of the Gable papers in an eleven-page bibliography; my Benedictine family, both the College of St. Benedict and St. Benedict's Monastery. Without their financial and psychological support I could not have completed this book.

Two writing groups gave me encouragement and helpful argument: St. Benedict's and St. John's English faculty—Ozzie Mayers, Charles Thornbury, Cynthia Malone; and Studium of St. Benedict's Monastery—Sisters Mara Faulkner, Anne Patrick, and Ephrem Hollermann.

Special, special thanks to Beverly Radaich, the computer whiz of the English department, for her sharp editor's eye and her fleet of ably-trained, competent student workers: Anna Klein, Constance Fernholz, Kristin Wendling, Tracey Kieser, Julie Olsem, Jodi Wallace.

I am deeply grateful to Sister Kristin Malloy and J.F. Powers for their interviews and counsel; to Rita Tobin for her air conditioner; to Robert Spaeth for the idea to publish this book; to Sister Thomasette Scheeler for photo layout; and to cheerful proofreaders—Sally Melton, Sisters Sheila Rausch, Hilda Keller, Mary Gerald Maiers, Mary Anthony Wagner, and Michelle Schumacher.

Finally, this book is for all the intelligent, capable women of St. Benedict's Monastery and the College of St. Benedict, who have already caught the torch that Sister Mariella Gable had to lay down and whose "gifts of mind and heart will keep it burning brightly" (Gable's tribute to Sister Kristin Malloy).

# Acknowledgments

I gratefully acknowledge permission to reprint the following material:

From *The Divine Comedy* by Dante Alighieri. Trans. Carlyle-Wicksteed. Copyright ©1932 by Modern Library. Reprinted by permission of Modern Library/Random House.

From "Loss of Faith" by Alfred Barrett in *Mint By Night*. Reprinted with the permission of America Press, Inc., 106 West 56th Street, New York, NY 10019, in the absence of Alfred Barrett. Copyright © 1938 All Rights Reserved.

From *Joy* (trans. Louise Varese) and *Plea for Liberty* (trans. Harry Binsse) by Georges Bernanos. Copyright © 1946, © 1944 by Pantheon. Reprinted by permission of Random House, Inc.

From definitions of ecumenism by Yves Congar quoted in *American Benedictine Review*. Copyright © 1964. Reprinted by permission of *American Benedictine Review*, Assumption Abbey, Richardton, North Dakota 58652.

## Essays by Mariella Gable, O.S.B.

"Prose Satire and the Modern Christian Temper," "Ecumenic Core in Flannery O'Connor's Fiction," "The Concept of Fame in Teilhard de Chardin and Dante" by Mariella Gable, O.S.B. Copyright © 1960, 1965, 1964 by *American Benedictine Review*. Reprinted by permission of *American Benedictine Review*, Assumption Abbey, Richardton, North Dakota 58652.

Review by Mariella Gable O.S.B., of *Everything That Rises Must Converge*, by Flannery O'Connor. Copyright © 1965 by *The Critic*. Reprinted by permission of *The Critic*, 205 W. Madison, Chicago, Illinois 60606.

Reprinted by permission of HarperCollins Publishers, Inc., Mrs. Laura Huxley, and Chatto & Windus, London.

From *Viper's Tangle* by Francois Mauriac. Copyright © 1932 by Éditions Bernard Grasset. Reprinted by permission of Georges Borchardt, Inc.

From *The Idea of a University* by John Henry Newman. Copyright © 1921 by Longmans Green. Reprinted by permission of Random House.

Excerpts from *The Complete Stories* by Flannery O'Connor. Copyright © 1971 by the Estate of Mary Flannery O'Connor. Excerpts from *The Habit of Being: Letters of Flannery O'Connor*, edited by Sally Fitzgerald. Copyright © 1979 by Regina O'Connor. Excerpts from *The Violent Shall Bear in Away* by Flannery O'Connor. Copyright © 1960 by Flannery O'Connor. Copyright renewed © 1988 by Regina O'Connor. Excerpts from *Wise Blood* by Flannery O'Connor. Copyright © 1962 by Flannery O'Connor. Copyright renewed © 1990 by Regina O'Connor. Reprinted by permission of Farrar, Straus & Giroux, Inc. Copyright © renewed by the Estate of Mary Flannery O'Connor. Reprinted by permission of Harold Matson Company Inc.

From interview with Flannery O'Connor by C. Ross Mullins in *Jubilee*. Copyright © 1963. Reprinted by permission of *U.S. Catholic/Claretian Publications*, 205 W. Monroe St., Chicago, Illinois 60606.

From interview with Flannery O'Connor by Joel Wells in *The Critic*. Copyright © 1962. Reprinted by permission of *The Critic*, 205 W. Madison, Chicago, Illinois 60606.

From "No Man Can Stay" by Jessica Powers in *The House at Rest*. Copyright © 1984 by The Carmelite Monastery. Reprinted by permission of The Pewaukee Carmelite Monastery.

From "The Forks" and "The Valiant Woman" in *The Prince of Darkness* by J.F. Powers. Copyright © 1947 by Doubleday. Letter on *Prince of Darkness* by J.F. Powers. Reprinted by permission of the author.

Photographs, courtesy of Sisters of St. Benedict Archives.

Acknowledgments are continued at the back of the book on page 259.

# Introduction

## Nancy Hynes, O.S.B.

Prophet and pioneer—Sister Mariella Gable, O.S.B., was both. "Some made her a pariah, but if she was by *anyone's* measure a pariah, it was as a consequence of her work as pioneer and prophet," said Sister Kristin Malloy, O.S.B., her student and friend.[1]

**Pariah.** In 1958, after thirty-seven years of teaching and chairing the English department, this Benedictine nun was ousted from the College of St. Benedict, a small liberal arts college in St. Joseph, Minnesota, by Bishop Bartholome of St. Cloud. The issue was J.D. Salinger's *The Catcher in the Rye* on a reading list in a contemporary American literature course taught by Sister Kristin Malloy, O.S.B. Father Jerome Doherty, O.S.B., objected to the book because of its "obscene language" and brought it to the attention of the bishop. Both Malloy, the teacher, and Gable, the chair of the English department, were held accountable. Gable spent four years in what she called "assassination and exile," teaching in colleges outside Minnesota.[2] This dramatic and telling incident, unreported in newspapers and rarely discussed within Gable's own religious community, marks both the nadir and the zenith of her remarkable career as teacher, editor, and definer of Catholic fiction from the 1940s to the 1960s. It is the nadir because she was silenced for four years. It is the zenith because she refused to compromise her principles and carried on her work elsewhere.

**Prophet.** As early as 1942 Gable published an anthology containing a short story on abortion and several stories on race relations—two of the most controversial issues of twentieth-century America. She also searched for stories on labor relations, apologizing for having only one story on that timely topic for her collection, *Many-Colored Fleece* (1950). She urged seminaries to offer literature courses as a way to seek truth and define values. One reviewer of her pamphlet, *This is Catholic Fiction* (1948), praised it as a book "rich in ideas and expression," but cautioned against literature courses in seminaries.[3] In 1993, however, Richard Sipe, consultant to the Interfaith Sexual Trauma Institute located at St. John's Abbey, urged seminaries to adopt literature courses to deal with issues of sexuality.[4]

Finally, she tirelessly promoted the cause of two then little known authors—J.F. Powers and Flannery O'Connor.

**Pioneer.** A brilliant and meticulous scholar, she helped to shape artistic standards for Catholic fiction in Catholic secondary schools and colleges across the country. The three anthologies she edited were also daring and exposed her to criticism.

Gable's major essays on fiction are collected for the first time in this book, essays that insist that Catholic fiction rise above the usual didactic and sweetly pious fiction of rosary beads and crucifixes. *Today* magazine, a weekly Catholic publication for Catholic students of the 1940s and 1950s, noted that Gable's first collection of short stories, *Great Modern Catholic Short Stories*, gave an "electric shock to those Catholic readers who were raised on the sentimental pap which had passed for Catholic fiction for so many years. Sister Mariella gave literary-minded Catholics a chance to lift their heads."[5] Gable urged writers to avoid the pious and hortatory and to strive instead for the "new realism" defined by Chekhov. Gable added that Chekhov defends his "ordinary" stories by pointing out that real persons rarely go to the North Pole and fall off icebergs; most go to offices, quarrel with their wives, and eat cabbage soup. The "new realism," she said, portrays the lives of "the sister, the priest, the brother, and the monk as normal, intelligent persons doing normal, intelligent work" and "they teach rapid addition to children in parochial schools, drink the proverbially bad coffee brewed in monastery kitchens, and are occasionally jealous of each other."[6]

Gable broadened her selection of short stories in her next two volumes, including authors from Russia, Ireland, Great Britain, Australia, and America. Furthermore, she did not limit the subject matter to clerical life, but sought to represent Catholic life in general and to raise the standards of Catholic fiction. In his history of the Catholic Literary Revival and American Catholicism from 1920-1960, Arnold Sparr credits Riley Hughes and Mariella Gable as leaders in the "search for the American Catholic novel."[7] Writing in the London *Tablet* in 1989, John Harriott also pays tribute "forty years overdue" to Gable's contribution. Prompted by a friend's discussion and his memories of Gable's collections, he revisited them to see if they were as good as he had remembered. He found them "superb." According to Harriott, her legacy is not only her selection of well-written and memorable stories but also "her shrewd observation that bad art makes for bad religion and that the non-believing artist may often strike a note of truth beyond the incompetent religious artist."[8]

Several contemporary Catholic writers have commented on Gable's influence, judgement, and critical insight. Irish fiction writer Bryan MacMahon told Kristin Malloy: "Sister Mariella Gable and her religious community can never know what that woman did for all Irish writers."[9] He referred to the many Irish writers she anthologized and thus made them known to the United States and Great Britain. Among them are Frank O'Connor, Sean O'Faolain, Mary Lavin, Michael McLaverty, and Bryan MacMahon himself. Describing Gable's introduction to *Many Colored Fleece* (1950), MacMahon says: ". . .it was one of the finest—let's say, expositions—of the short story I have ever read."[10] Flannery O'Connor paid high praise to Gable's article, "Ecumenic Core in the Fiction of Flannery O'Connor": "I do very much appreciate what you've put into the essay and I shall learn from it myself. And save my breath by referring other people to it."[11] Arnold Sparr also notes that Gable "did more than any other Catholic critic to bring [J.F.] Powers to the attention of the Catholic American reading public."[12] Powers comments that while Gable is a critic who raised the standard for Catholic fiction, "I'd have to say that she expected too much. If she were here, she'd probably say, 'No, Jim, I didn't expect too much. I expected more than we have had.' That's true."[13]

Yet she was well known and influential, and her writings are a record of over forty years of persistent and passionate teaching, writing, editing, which helped shape high standards for Catholic fiction here and abroad.

\*\*\*\*\*\*\*\*\*\*\*\*\*\*\*\*\*\*\*\*\*\*\*\*\*\*\*\*\*

Mary Margaret Gable was born in 1898 in St. Croix Falls, Wisconsin, to Joseph Gable and Mary Marzolf Gable, and within two years moved to Marine-on-St. Croix where Joseph operated a flour and feed mill.  A close friendship with her younger brother, John, and their mutual love of the natural beauty around them marked her early childhood and teenage years.  Together they waded in icy rivers, built dams, and enjoyed winter sports.  They explored the countryside, enjoying the "dogtooth violets on the Wisconsin cliffs, a luna moth pursued a whole summer afternoon along the riverbanks, partridge berries under pine needles, a new cave under tumbled rocks."[14] Gable's lifelong love of nature is captured in her book of poetry, *Blind Man's Stick* (1938), especially in "The Spy" where she celebrates stars and "a filigree of apple boughs/Against a satin sky" as signs of supernatural mystery.[15]  She did not read many books in these early years, but she brought extraordinary emotion to those she read.  Her fear that Tom Sawyer would be lost in the cave was so great that by her own account, she "could not breathe without pain" and was forced to read the book in short sections.[16]

When at age fifteen she entered St. Benedict's Academy, St. Joseph, Minnesota, a new world opened to her.  She responded wholeheartedly to daily Mass, the warmth of the Benedictine nuns, and the friendships of girls her own age.  A month after her graduation from the academy in her seventeenth year, she entered the novitiate of St. Benedict's Convent and received the name, Sister Mariella, O.S.B. (Order of St. Benedict).  Her autobiographical sketch devotes a terse line to this novitiate year: "To one so young, so high-spirited, and so accustomed to the free run of woods, hills, and streams, the discipline of the novitiate was difficult."[17]

As a young nun, she helped open St. Mary's High School, Bismarck, North Dakota, in 1918, teaching all subjects on the first two levels, including Latin, English, algebra, geometry, history, typing, and shorthand.  She also taught a year at Melrose, Minnesota, and then at St. Benedict's Academy, St. Joseph, Minnesota. Meanwhile she attended the College of St. Benedict until she earned her B.A. in English in 1925.[18]  Despite this full schedule, she wrote poetry which was published in *America, The Commonweal,* and *Spirit.*  Francis X. Talbot, S.J., literary editor for *America,* wrote to her: "I feel that I have discovered you as a real, authentic poet."[19]

Later the poems were collected in *Blind Man's Stick* (1938), and twelve of Gable's poems also appeared in *Our Lady's Choir*, a collection of poetry by religious sisters.[20]

Studying for her Master's degree at the University of Minnesota (1925-29) was exciting and challenging since she took summer courses and some correspondence courses while she taught at the College of St. Benedict. Her M.A. thesis was "A Study of the Influence of Rossetti's Paintings and Art on his Poetry." Later she confessed misgivings that perhaps she should not have minored in creative writing because she spent all that time expressing herself instead of putting information into her head.[21] Yet surely from that subject she learned the craft of writing, its form and rhythm. Her feel for language carried over to her students who won *Atlantic Monthly* prizes in the 1940s.

Her year at Columbia University from 1931 to 1932 introduced her to European literature and sharpened her technical and historical insights into the English language. She delighted in having the *New York Times* delivered to her door every morning for one cent a day, a cost which she and another Sister shared. She was also reading Cather's *Shadows on the Rock* and Hilaire Belloc, and she enjoyed long walks along the Hudson. At Columbia she had her first glimmer of a dissertation topic—the Oxford movement and the Catholic literary revival. The literature from this movement later became the yardstick with which she judged her selection of short stories.[22] She also began her love affair with Dante, the benefits of which countless students received later in her courses.

She transferred to Cornell to study with Dante scholar, Dr. Lane Cooper. His demands on her time were discouraging, and more than once, she considered dropping his Dante class because of the time it took away from her dissertation, a rhetorical analysis of Cardinal Newman's Anglican sermons.[23] Nonetheless, by spring, 1934, she had completed all requirements for her Ph.D. She returned to the College of St. Benedict to chair the English department until 1958. She taught courses in Dante, Shakespeare, Chaucer, and creative writing, advised the student publication, *The Quarterly*, edited three anthologies destined to shape and define Catholic fiction, reviewed many books for Catholic periodicals and newspapers, and published articles on Catholic writers. She was a charter member of Delta Epsilon Sigma, a Catholic intellectual society. In 1937 she wrote a pageant, *So Let Your Light Shine,* celebrating Benedictine history and initiating the first-year students into the academic community of the college.  An outdoor ceremony which celebrated fourteen centuries of Benedictine culture in dance, song, and choral reading, it was performed every year until the mid-1960s.[24]

She did not accomplish these things without a price, however. Weighing just ninety-eight pounds when she went to Bismarck, North Dakota in 1918, she suffered all her life from bouts of fever and stomach pain on her left side, much later diagnosed as diverticulitis. She also suffered from exhaustion, nerves, and depression, especially in the 1940s and 1950s, a decade marked with Gable's butting heads with bishops and at the same time forging new standards in Catholic fiction.

Her relationships with two bishops of St. Cloud—Joseph Busch (1915-1953) and Peter Bartholome (1953-1968)—were rocky, though Busch appears to have been more understanding than Bartholome. Both questioned her literary judgment and delayed crucial decisions concerning her books.  Three major incidents mark Gable's relationship with these bishops between 1941 and 1958: Busch's public silence about Father E.B. Scallan's attack on *Great Modern Catholic Short Stories* (1943); Bartholome's censorship of the second anthology, *Our Father's House* (1943-44); and Bartholome's ousting of Gable over Salinger's *The Catcher in the Rye* (1958).

Gable's first encounter in 1941 with Bishop Busch and Mother Rosamond Pratschner, O.S.B., prioress of St. Benedict's Convent, was amicable.  After approving her plan and selection of stories for her first anthology, Bishop Busch called in his assistant, Father Michael Kremer, to witness his giving permission to publish the book.[25]   Trouble came from a censorious priest, Father E.B. Scallan whose pamphlet, *A Competent Censorship or Else Chaos* (1943), pronounced: "*Great Modern Catholic Short Stories* is not a Catholic book."  Sent to 116 bishops in the United States, his pamphlet attacked Gable's criticism of sentimental pap in Catholic newspapers and magazines.  Since these publications were often edited by Catholic priests and approved by Catholic bishops, Gable was in effect putting the Catholic press on trial.  Furthermore, Scallan added, this woman is dangerous: "Believe it, if the accusations made by Sister Mariella, O.S.B., in her book *Great Modern Catholic Short Stories* were made by a most violent anti-Catholic, it would be cause for alarm.  That they were made by a Catholic nun and that Catholics were found who would assist and abet her in publishing the unjust slanders is a matter of far greater import."[26]

Because her book had been chosen as Catholic Book of the Month by Sheed and Ward, Scallan warned that many readers would be misled. He also attacked Ernest Hemingway, one of Gable's selected writers, as a threat to Catholic faith and American democracy. None of Hemingway's stories could be Catholic, Scallan insisted, because he wrote *For Whom the Bell Tolls*, a book in which "the hero glorifies the cause of Godless Communism." Finally, Scallan criticized Gable's statement that Hemingway's "The Gambler, the Nun, and the Radio" is morally indifferent: "No story that speaks of nuns in a frivolous manner concerned more about batty baseball games than the reconciliation of a dying Catholic with his Creator in Sacramental Confession, we repeat, no such story is an indifferent story."[27] Later Frank Sheed, Gable's publisher, described Scallan as a renegade priest who defied ecclesiastical authority, left his own diocese, and was living in New Orleans without permission to offer Mass.[28]

Most people scoffed at Scallan's attack, but his criticism caused Gable "many sleepless nights."[29] The situation was later complicated by Bishop Busch's remark to several priests that he "had not seen the manuscript," giving a false impression that Gable had not received his permission to publish the book. In fact, she and Mother Rosamond had secured permission from him in 1941. Nonetheless, the damage was done. Bishop Busch's silence in response to Gable's request that he clarify the situation allowed the story to spread among St. Cloud priests, to Gable's own sisters in her religious community, and to Gable's friends at the College of St. Thomas. She found herself forced to explain her innocence even to her trusted friends.[30]

Some of the trouble stemmed from Sheed's choice for the title of the book, *Great Modern Catholic Short Stories*, against which Gable had argued vehemently because it was misleading. Had the title been different, it might not have come to Scallan's attention. Gable had written to Frank Sheed in a final attempt to change his mind:

> Can't we compromise? *Three Measures of Meal* is an intelligent title. The stories are intelligent. There aren't many intelligent readers. I haven't faith in trying to catch the *hoi polloi* by a flashy cover-jacket. You can't possibly use *Great Modern Catholic Short Stories* because the book isn't that. It is just one small section of the whole.[31]

Later she wrote to Bishop Busch: "By my own definition the stories in my first book are not Catholic. By my own protest to Sheed you can see that I never regarded them as such."[32] Her first choice of a title was *They Are People*, which emphasized her call for Chekovian realism in portraying nuns, priests, and monks as human beings. When the second edition came out in 1944, she finally got her wish.

Privately, Bishop Busch observed to Gable that "the Scallan attack called forth nothing but sympathy" for Gable,[33] and six months later he apologized for any hurt he might have caused by his silence regarding the false impression that Gable published her anthology without his permission.[34] Yet he expressed strong reservations about some stories in the anthology as "caricatures which gave the wrong impression about *normal* priests, monks, and nuns," and wondered if Gable could not have chosen more stories with happy endings.[35] A postscript on one of her letters to Busch gives the flavor of their sometimes heated, always civil, debates. She writes in response to his praise of the film, *The Song of Bernadette*:

> You like *The Song of Bernadette*. But if that were fiction you would cry out against the ridiculous slobbering father, the girl clawing the earth in the cave, the mean and critical clergy, the abuse given the girl. Truth has a way of not being as nice as the insipid pink and white fiction we used to call Catholic. Edification at the expense of truth is a terribly doubtful good.[36]

Certainly, this is a strong statement in defense of her goal: to fight shoddy sentimentalism in literature and to challenge Catholic writers to neither glorify nor vilify Catholic life. In the same letter quoted above, she asked Bishop Busch for permission to pursue her second book, *Our Father's House*, which would include a full discussion of Catholic fiction:

> Some of the stories for the new collection *are* Catholic. Many are not. You can very well ask why I want to edit them, this being true. I want to edit them because the general literary level of Catholic fiction is deplorably low. Great Catholic things have not as yet been written. There is not a single Catholic magazine (except *The Commonweal* which seldom publishes a story) that prints stories of quality. But fiction is a tremendous power in molding lives. If we could get Catholics to write truly Catholic fiction well, we could set the world on fire.[37]

She reaffirmed her promise to revise as he directed and asked that their correspondence be kept confidential and that she be able to work with him and not Busch's coadjutor, Bishop Bartholome, who already judged her anticlerical because of her insistence on realism.[38]

Nonetheless, by fall, 1943, Bishop Bartholome was the one from whom Gable was to get the imprimatur for the plan of her second book, and this proved difficult. After a stormy interview, she wrote a list of Bishop Bartholome's objections to her plan for her second book, *Our Father's House*. What follows is the author's summary of that list: literature should be about the average person, and these stories do not deal with the average person; confession should not be written about because it is confidential [on Frank O'Connor's classic "First Confession"]; "Polack" in one of the stories would infuriate his Polish priests; people do not expect Sisters to know anything about sex, so to include a story about birth control is unbecoming for a Sister; in fact, stories collected by laypersons might be fine and good, but the same stories might be inappropriate for Sisters to publish; a story should *not* be judged by what it is, but by whether it has been written by a good person. This summary illustrates Bartholome's inadequate standards for judging literature and his bias against women, especially Sisters, as authorities; yet despite his objections, he then conceded that all but three stories were acceptable for the new book.[39] This troublesome interview between Gable and Bartholome began seventeen months of delays before Gable received permission for her new volume.

By May, 1944, she had revised the manuscript. Wanting to insure that she was on the right course, she asked for suggestions from Father Vincent J. Flynn, who had published her essay on Catholic fiction in his college text, *Prose Readings* (1943). Flynn had also asked two other priests—Father John Louis Bonn and classics professor, Father Fred Bieter—to review the manuscript. Upon receiving Mother Rosamond Pratschner's enthusiastic support for the new book, Gable sent the revised manuscript plus Flynn's report to Bishop Bartholome. Perhaps irked over Gable's asking for outside advice, Bartholome sent her a curt letter insisting on yet another evaluator of his choosing: Father Basil Stegmann, O.S.B., the Diocesan Censor at St. John's Abbey. The bishop's crushing postscript implied that Gable was telling him what to do: "I am also requesting you to allow the Bishop full liberty in the manner in which he is to deal with Sisters and the people of the Diocese."[40]

In her letter of response to Bishop Bartholome, Gable said she wept bitterly over his displeasure and continued: "I am incomparably more concerned to render willing and whole-hearted obedience to my superiors, particularly to my bishop, than to get any book whatsoever into print."[41] She took the manuscript to Stegmann and by February 13, 1945, she rejoiced to Flynn: "After seventeen months of grief not a syllable to be changed."[42] Bonn's evaluation of Gable's book, which Gable sent to the Bishop, provides some perspective on the bishop's delay and disapproval. In his sermons to the Benedictine nuns, Bishop Bartholome often warned them against intellectual pride.[43] He may have felt that Bonn's praise of Gable's "common sense" and sound educational approach would go to her head. Then, again, the bishop may have felt threatened by this intelligent woman. Bonn wrote to Flynn:

> I like Sister Mariella's approach which is full of definite common sense, and I think that such a book would go far, educationally, toward battering down the accusation, which is too often well founded, that our nuns do not teach literature in relation to life, but only as a kind of religious propaganda—in other words that they do not teach contemporary letters at all. Therefore, I think this book is important, and particularly important that it is written by a nun. Self-appointed moralists will attack it, and the counter-attacks upon them will help to break down the Jansenism so destructive of our Catholic life. This is a brave, good book.[44]

This positive evaluation plus the recommendations of Flynn and Bieter may have convinced Bishop Bartholome that Gable's book was worthy; yet he delayed the manuscript further to get it approved by another reader designated by himself, a move which clearly demonstrated his authority. In fact, Bartholome delayed so long that Frank Sheed, eager to publish the book, suggested to Gable that he get the imprimatur from Archbishop Spellman. Gable agreed, a move which angered Bartholome and which returned to haunt her in 1958.[45]

In the decade between 1941 and 1951, Gable's vitality and productivity were remarkable. In addition to living a disciplined religious community life, she chaired the English department, taught college courses each semester, and published four books and twenty-four articles, some of which were reviews of books. Her writing students consistently placed in *The Atlantic Monthly* writing contest, two of them winning the top prizes in 1942 and 1944.[46] The 1942 prize sent her student, Bernadette Loosbroek, and Gable, to the Breadloaf School of Writing in Vermont that summer. During this decade she read voraciously, keeping up on the new writers, and hailing a young, then unknown American, J.F. Powers, in her article, "Catholic Fiction Arrives in America"[47]

Her introduction to *Our Father's House*, a landmark article in that it developed her literary bull's-eye theory, received wide circulation through *The Catholic Digest* in February, 1946. It defined Catholic fiction, citing Bernanos and Tolstoy as models and arguing against Catholic "pulps" which turned out miracles, three for a cent. In 1948 she gave a prophetic speech, "This is the New Pentecost," at St. Joseph's College, Hartford, Connecticut, which was reprinted in *The Catholic Messenger* and *The Catholic Digest*.[48] The speech was stunning in its foresight and acumen. In it she hailed six signs of a spiritual awakening in the United States: the liturgical movement, education of lay people in theology, renewed interest in spiritual reading, the Catholic literary revival, rediscovery of contemplation, and Catholic Action.[49] All of these have developed and some are still developing, especially the growing number of educated laity in theology and the modern interest in meditation and contemplation. As a tribute to her work, she was honored by "Toast of the Month" in *The Marianist* magazine and was lauded as poet, anthologist, critic, and "a real pioneer in the rich forest of Catholic fiction."[50]

Gable demonstrated her breadth of vision in her choice of a wide variety of writers. *Great Modern Catholic Short Stories* included well known writers such as Katherine Mansfield, Ernest Hemingway, and F. Scott Fitzgerald. *Our Father's House* included writers from Great Britain, Scandinavia, Russia, and America, including Leo Tolstoy, Stephen V. Benet, J.F. Powers, and Abigail Quigley (later to become McCarthy and author of *Private Faces, Public Places*). Long before the women's movement in the sixties, Gable included women writers in her anthologies—Antonia White, Elizabeth Madox Roberts, and Betty Wahl [Powers], for example. Of the seventy-eight stories represented in her three anthologies, one-third are written by women.

Gable's anthologies were widely and favorably reviewed in the religious and secular press. When her first anthology, *Great Modern Catholic Short Stories*, came out in 1942, Francis X. Connelly, S.J., chair of Fordham University English department, described her introduction as "provocative" and "peppery," explosive enough "to

blow up many a peaceful parish circle."[51]  John Erskine of the
Chicago *Sun* praised her "breadth of vision which is none too
common in secular editors, and which is extraordinary in one devoted
to the life with which these stories deal."[52]  *The New York Times*
called the book "significant of the new Catholicism which makes no
pretence to be perfect but claims to be actual in its human relations."[53]
Only seven of the twenty-four reviewers made negative comments and
those were minor: two noted what Gable herself had insisted—that the
first title of the book was a misnomer—and three disagreed with
Gable's "literary bracketings."  *Our Father's House* (1945), stories by
Catholic and non-Catholic writers from Russia, Ireland, Great Britain,
America, and Scandinavia, was the most favorably received and sold
the most copies.[54]  Thirty-five reviewers selected vastly different
stories as the best, illustrating Gable's broad, varied, and
discriminating taste, and they frequently recommended the book as
required reading for Catholic students in both secondary schools and
colleges.  Nearly all reviewers commended the discriminating choice
of stories, "varied enough to appeal to many tastes"[55] and "alive with
human meaning, with the radiance of the divine often showing
through."[56]

Gable's next publication did not receive wide reviewing.  *This is
Catholic Fiction* (1948), a collection of five previously published
essays on Catholic fiction, was published in response to teachers'
requests for use in the classroom.  Generally, the eight reviewers
supported Gable's attempt to define Catholic fiction and applauded
her incisive mind.  Some, however, quarreled with what they
considered her restrictive definition—at this early point, she still
defined Catholic fiction with a capital "C," yet she also said it was a
"re-ordering of love"; others wondered if Catholic fiction could ever
be defined.

Her last book, *Many-Colored Fleece* (1950), had almost as many
reviews as *Our Father's House*, but it did not get as much
international attention.  Twenty-three of the thirty reviews praised
Gable as anthologist, teacher, and critic, affirming John Cogley's
view that she had "probably done more than anyone else to show
people what decent Catholic fiction looks like and to hint at what it
might be."[57]  Gable's strong influence is demonstrated by the fact that
five of these reviews are retrospectives, summarizing her other works
and placing this book in the context of her overall achievement in
defining Catholic fiction.[58]  Another sign of her influence is that

Thomas More Bookshop, a new and influential Catholic bookstore in Chicago, chose just two people to speak at its tenth-year anniversary in 1949: J.F. Powers and Mariella Gable.

Considering her many duties of chairing the English department, teaching college classes, publishing books, and living religious community life, it is not surprising that Gable's health often gave out. As early as 1935, references to her hopitalizations appear in her letters. When she was at Breadloaf in 1942, she was hospitalized with a mysterious fever and stomach pain. Later that year she was hospitalized for pleurisy, dysentery, and a broken rib; the end of the year found her "sedated" at St. Cloud Hospital. She was absent most of the school year (1942-43), suffering a nervous breakdown. In summer, 1944, she was under a doctor's care for "nervous trouble" and she begged Bishop Busch not to add to it.[59] Kristin Malloy sums up Gable's life as a constant battle between her poor health and her passion for work: "She was always frail and often flat on her back."[60]

Her zest for learning and understanding never faltered, however. In 1944 when she was at St. Joseph's Hospital, St. Paul, Minnesota, she had to wait all day for tests. She sneaked into the nearby public library and found a wonderful *New Yorker* story [Brendan Gill's "The Knife"] for her book [*Many-Colored Fleece*].[61] Five months later she wrote: "If I never exhaust myself, I need never get these attacks. . . The doctor says to keep my sugar up and stay within my limitations."[62] However, in June, 1950, she was at St. Benedict's Hospital, Ogden, Utah, staffed by Minnesota Benedictines. Suffering from depression and insomnia, she was under the care of Dr. O'Gorman. She underwent a series of shock treatments, first by insulin, later electric, and when they did not work, a lobotomy was performed.[63] No one can know fully the extent of her suffering, but for three months she was kept in isolation, locked in her room, and was not told that her third book, *Many-Colored Fleece*, had been published. True, the English department at the College of St. Benedict sent her a congratulatory telegram, but no one at Ogden mentioned that her third book had been published. Her plight was similar to that of the narrator in Charlotte Perkins Gilman's "The Yellow Wallpaper." Isolated, lonely, longing for the intellectual stimulation of a Jacques Maritain who had just been a speaker at the College of St. Benedict, she must have found her isolation unbearably painful.[64] She returned to Minnesota in April, 1951, and resumed teaching in the fall at the College of St. Benedict. She also chaired the English department, advised the student *Quarterly*, and lectured on Catholic fiction in summer sessions across the country. In 1957 she edited *Harvest*, a pictorial history of St. Benedict's Convent which celebrated her Benedictine religious community's centennial year in the United States.

A significant event affecting convent-diocesan relationships had been brewing since 1939 when Pope Pius XI requested that all Benedictine houses belong to a congregation and be approved by the Holy See. The reasons for a union were to strengthen religious houses following the same rule and to share in one another's good works. When Bishop Busch denied Mother Rosamond's requests to start this process in 1939 and again in 1941, she appealed to Abbot Primate Fidelis von Stotzingen, the official Benedictine connection to the Holy See. In 1942 he succeeded in petitioning Rome to establish the Congregation of St. Benedict. By 1956 St. Benedict's Convent, having undergone a nine-year probation period, became a pontifical institute, which meant that the local bishop, now Bishop Bartholome, no longer had jurisdiction over matters relating to the convent.[65]

However, a new convent and college chaplain, Jerome Doherty, O.S.B., influenced this delicate political situation between the bishop and the convent. An Australian priest living at St. John's Abbey, he was told by Bishop Bartholome to "watch out for Sister Mariella Gable because she is famous for being anticlerical and for furthering pornographic literature."[66] Bartholome got the ammunition he wanted when Doherty objected to the "filthy and obscene" language in Salinger's *The Catcher in the Rye,* a book on the college's suggested reading list for contemporary American literature. Doherty called a meeting in March, 1958, with college officials and Mother Richarda Peters, O.S.B., then prioress of St. Benedict's Convent, and the two nuns—Kristin Malloy, teacher of American literature and Mariella Gable, chair of the English department. Not reading the whole novel, Doherty paged through it, counting the number of times God's name was taken in vain. At the meeting he read only those "blasphemous" parts to the group and insisted that the two nuns should be barred from receiving the sacraments until two conditions were met: they must make a public apology to the college students and the religious community, and they must gather all copies of the offending book and turn them in at that assembly.

Such extreme public measures were not taken, but the priest had given Bishop Bartholome the evidence he sought, and the bishop insisted that the two nuns leave the College of St. Benedict. The bishop had not checked the facts. Neither nun had taught the book; as everyone now knows, the book itself is a sensitive portrayal of a confused and idealistic teenager; moreover, censorship does not belong in an academic institution.[67] Perhaps Bartholome still chafed from his disagreement with Gable concerning *Our Father's House* and seized this opportunity to humiliate her. Perhaps he was also piqued because St. Benedict's Convent had recently become a papal institute and, therefore, was not under his jurisdiction. The truth is that it was common knowledge that he had little love for Benedictines. He was convinced that "the world was creeping onto the campus at St. Benedict's," and he was going to clean it up.[68] He insisted that Gable leave the diocese. A year later he wrote to Gable: "I again want to assure you that there are no personalities involved, that the action was thoroughly objective on the evidence presented [by Jerome Doherty], and that I felt duty-bound to act not against you but against your work."[69]

Heartsick at what had happened, Gable wrote three months later to Mother Richarda from Loretto College, Colorado, where she was teaching a summer course in Catholic fiction. It reveals both her pain and her courage.

> The trouble with the Bishop is so serious I must humbly appeal to you to permit me to move to another priory outside the jurisdiction of Bishop Bartholome. . . . I know my teaching days are over [at St. Benedict's]. . . . I cannot tell you how much this decision has cost me. I love St. Benedict's, I love teaching, I love all that I must leave. God knows why He has permitted this most heavy cross to fall on me. I pray for only one thing and that is that I shall be able to know what God's will is in carrying it and that God will give me the strength to carry out that will.[70]

Mother Richarda did not transfer her to another priory, nor did she forbid her to teach, but she sent her to Mt. Angel College, Salem, Oregon. Before returning to the College of St. Benedict, Gable spent a year at Mt. Angel and three years at Marillac College, the national sister formation college, Normandy, Missouri. Kristin Malloy was sent to St. Cloud Cathedral High School and later Pierz Memorial High School, both in Minnesota, returning to the College ten years later.

Today it is difficult to believe that this event could ever have happened, that Gable could have been ousted without trial, without recourse, without substantial evidence.  However, convent discipline as perceived and taught in the 1950s often encouraged obedience to those in authority, especially the prioress and the bishop who take the place of Christ.  In 1959 Gable wrote to Bishop Bartholome, whose authority as her bishop meant Christ's authority: ". . .the purpose of this letter is to beg your pardon for all that I have done amiss.  I am so grief-stricken because you are the voice of Christ for us here in your diocese. . . .  Exile is a cruel punishment. . . .  If you wish to let your recommendation to the council stand [that she teach out-of-state] so that this punishment shall stand the rest of my life, so be it."[71]

Also painful was the silence after the March, 1958, incident.  No one discussed it, and when Gable went to teach a summer course in Catholic fiction at Loretto College, Colorado, she still did not know what would happen.  Father Harold C. Gardiner, S.J., Jesuit author and critic and one of her guest lecturers that summer, urged protest, but she did not feel she could.  She did talk with him about her banishment, however, and took great comfort in his support.[72]

Gardiner responded to Gable's plight in an editorial in *America*, defending the study of literature as a way to clarify values.[73]  The same issue of *America* published an article by Michael Boyle, S.J., "Teaching 'Dirty Books' in College."  Boyle discussed Graham Greene, James Joyce, J.F. Powers, and J.D. Salinger as genuine artists and their novels as portraying truth—the genuine goal of a liberal arts education.[74]  Neither writer mentions Gable directly, but Gardiner makes clear in a letter to Gable that her situation spurred the articles:

> . . .keep your eyes open for our issue of December 13, which will contain an article by Father Boyle of Regis College in Denver, which tackles head-on the problem which caused you such difficulty.  I will say that I am in great admiration of the spirit in which you took a very mortifying and disappointing experience.  We will keep up the good fight, and I am sure the atmosphere in our colleges will change, where such a change is vitally necessary.[75]

During this exile her letters to friends give insight into her sense of humor, irony, and pain.  Early in 1958 she wrote to her former

student and friend, Sister Thomas Egan, O.S.B.,: "I have been
expelled from the college. After thirty-seven years of faithful service
to the department of English this is a very hard thing to bear in my
sixtieth year of age. One strikes deep roots." And her postscript
adds: "Kristin is expelled, too. Only the Puritans remain."[76] In 1959
her wry humor shows when she writes: "Wouldn't life be grand if
there were no Puritans and all Jesuits?"[77] Later that year Gable
attended the dedication of Thomas Aquinas Hall at St. John's
University, Collegeville, Minnesota. She wrote again to Egan:
"Bishop Bartholome kept eying modern crucifixes a hundred times
more violent than Sister Thomas Carey's lovely ones. Could be the
monks will hear more about them. But it isn't as easy to shove men
around as women."[78] Her letter to Sister Remberta Westkaemper,
O.S.B., sums up her feeling of injustice:

> The gravest injustices are: That after thirty-seven years of faithful
> service I was given no warning of a new policy. That I was
> never warned by any superior. That the best Catholic colleges in
> the country (St. Teresa's, Rosary etc.) were doing what we were
> doing and that I felt safe in accepting the standards that prevailed.
> Even the Bishop admitted to Mother that he knew the standards at
> St. Benedict's were the prevailing standards. That he holds it
> against me for getting an imprimatur through my
> publisher—which is one of the three ways permitted by Canon
> Law. [79]

Finally, a letter from a former student, Mary Thomes [Locke]
expresses her distress over Gable's situation and pays tribute to the
College of St. Benedict and Gable:

> Having contact with the warm, Christian humanism which was so
> evidently your philosophy made it possible for my Catholicism to
> grow up along with the rest of my mind. . . . And this
> humanistic point of view, this deep respect for the integrity of the
> human personality always has seemed to be characteristic of St.
> Ben's. For me, and for many, many others who knew you well,
> as I did, you were the touchstone of expression of this
> philosophy.[80]

What did the College of St. Benedict lose as a result of this
incident? Two superb English teachers, Kristin Malloy and Mariella

Gable. Malloy's scholarly and professional life in the college was interrupted for ten years. Gable was prevented, for the time being, from coordinating the Tri-College program with St. Benedict's, St. John's, and St. Cloud State College [now University]. The paper on Christian satire she was scheduled to give at the American Benedictine Academy (ABA) was turned down. Father Roland Behrendt, O.S.B., Chair of Languages and Literature of the ABA, wrote to her: "Mother Richarda and I agreed that it is advisable to conduct next year's meeting without your paper."[81] But her productivity was not halted during her four-year exile. Despite recurring stomach pains, despite ill health, despite profound depression at being treated unfairly, she taught classes in Catholic fiction, gave lectures at Marylhurst College, Marylhurst, Oregon, and elsewhere, wrote her definitive article on the Catholic novel, polished her paper on Christian satire, wrote a pageant for Marillac College, and started Delta Epsilon Sigma at Marillac. She also travelled to Europe with her dear friend, Sister Remberta Westkaemper, and studied at Oxford University, England, during the summer of 1961 at the Institute of International Education. Finally, she began significant work on Flannery O'Connor and Pierre Teilhard de Chardin which later influenced all who attended her retreats for adults, college and high school students.

A new prioress, Mother Henrita Osendorf, O.S.B., and new coadjutor bishop, George Speltz, helped to ease Gable's situation, and she returned to St. Benedict's in 1962. What had haunted her in 1958 was her fear that she may have been a shade "too liberal" in the English department.[82] Gardiner had eased her mind about that. Furthermore, her participation in the 1962 Twentieth Symposium in Literature at the College of St. Thomas (St. Thomas University) in St. Paul, Minnesota, restored her confidence that she was on track. Herbert Slusser, the organizer of the symposium, captured her contributions and her magnetic personality when he wrote a year later:

> I thank God that there are people like you—or, rather, that there *is you*—in the world, generous, spontaneous, fully articulate, whose every act and gesture, verbal and physical, bespeaks wholesomeness and intelligence. . . . I have always loved your ardor. . . . But it is much more attractive, even now. You have it in such beautiful control; and you direct it like an arrow from a bow. Your moderator's introduction and comments were instances in point, but one gets the best of your mind and heart

when in informal situations you see so sharply and respond so
honestly, so—I can only call it—lovingly.[83]

Slusser has aptly expressed Gable's ability to speak honestly,
directing her remarks "like an arrow from a bow," her own metaphor
for the bull's eye of Catholic fiction.

Recognition and acceptance abroad did not mean acceptance at
home, however. The new prioress, Mother Henrita Osendorf,
O.S.B., rejected Gable's suggestion that an open panel discussion on
literature, similar to the one at St. Thomas, be held at St. Benedict's.
Osendorf gently discouraged her from "overeagerness to defend your
stand" and urged her to "come home willing to let others champion
the cause of certain kinds of literature. Rather than bring up the old
problem, it is better to let the matter rest in silence; can you agree
with me on this?"[84] Written in the margins of this letter are Gable's
responses: "Rubbish" and "Nuts." Yet to the question, "Can you
agree with me on this?" she writes: "Of course," and to Osendorf's
plea that she not "bear a grudge," she writes: "Not the least
[grudge]." To Gable's credit, she kept her word.

Upon her return she had the satisfaction of chairing the
Literature section of the American Benedictine Academy (ABA) from
1965 to 1968, delivering her paper on Christian satire at the ABA,
and chairing the committee for the Tri-College Program at the
invitation of CSB academic dean, Sister Firmin Escher, O.S.B.

She set to work, teaching Chaucer, Dante, and contemporary
fiction in the college, studying Flannery O'Connor and Pierre
Teilhard de Chardin, and publishing her articles on them. An expert
on O'Connor by O'Connor's own admission, she published a key
article, "Ecumenic Core in Flannery O'Connor's Fiction," and a
tribute to O'Connor on the occasion of her death.[85] Dr. Nathan A.
Scott, a noted professor of theology and literature at the University of
Chicago, wrote to thank her for her "fine essay" on Flannery
O'Connor which would help him prepare his own paper for a
symposium.[86] Gable also accepted speaking engagements.

She wrote to Sister Thomas Egan that she represented St.
Benedict's at a panel on liberal education at St. John's University: " I
was able to underline with vigor the idea that *protection is no part of
education.* I got terrific response. It was so good I felt as if I had
drunk champaign" [sic].[87] In response to Egan's news reports on
Gable's lectures on Teilhard de Chardin in Crookston, Minnesota,

Gable wrote: "I marvel that you could produce such a long news report of 'The New Optimism' without ever mentioning *evolution*. The fearful looking for trouble cannot find a syllable to blame. You are wonderful. Prudent. Wise."[88] At this same time Gable had the satisfaction of presenting three sessions on Teilhard's "New Optimism" to students at Cathedral High School, the diocesan school of Bishop Bartholome. In another letter to Egan, Gable refers to praise of Teilhard by the coadjutor, Bishop Speltz. "Could be I can soon crawl out from under a cloud."[89]

Crawl out from under a cloud she did. She was visiting professor on Newman and Dante and Catholic fiction at Marygrove College, Detroit, Michigan, in 1967 and St. Martin's College, Olympia, Washington, in 1969. Building on her ten years of personal study of Teilhard with special courses at Fordham University in 1964, and the University of San Francisco in 1972, she inspired those who heard her. Reflecting her interest in ecumenism, she gave eight-session retreats on Teilhard to a variety of ecumenical groups in Minneapolis and St. Paul in 1972-73. *The Central Minnesota Counsellor Newsletter* named Gable "counsellor of the month" because she taught Teilhard at the Minnesota State Reformatory, St. Cloud, with Dr. Gelbmann, clinical psychologist, at the reformatory.[90] Her manuscript for a book describing this prison program, "Reshape," is in the St. Benedict's Convent Archives. During this time she continued reviewing books, the last three revealing her current and future interests: Robert Giroux's *Flannery O'Connor, The Complete Stories*; Ivan Illich's *De-Schooling Society*; and Pierre Teilhard de Chardin's *The Heart of the Matter*.[91] Two other creative artists she studied and taught were Aleksandr Solzhenitsyn and Buckminster Fuller.

In 1971 she was presented with the President's Medal by the College of St. Benedict for her pioneering scholarship and excellence in teaching. Retiring as Professor Emerita in 1973, she was still teaching her beloved Dante course to St. Benedict's alumnae in 1978. Gable celebrated her Diamond Jubilee, sixty years of professed religious life, in 1977, and she died at St. Scholastica Convent, St. Cloud, Minnesota, in 1985.

Gable's former student and friend, Sister Bernetta Quinn, O.S.F., wrote a sonnet in tribute to her in 1946, unconsciously predicting Gable's future trials. This poem expresses her dynamism and dedication, her courage and clear-sightedness.

Who Dare Take Christ at His Word

(For Sister Mariella Gable, O.S.B.)

Because you are unafraid and no half-giver
Because you are drunk with the liquid light of prayer,
You can pour love out of your heart like a flaming river;
You can stand head high and in loneliness who dare
Take Christ at His word, though it means the steepest mountain
Though it means renouncing life and death to lead
The uninspired and the weak to His secret fountain
Where flourishes even the bruised and broken reed.

"For they shall possess the land": thus humility
Was given as legacy all of Paradise.
O this is the meaning we cannot miss who see
A silver courage gleam out of gray-blue eyes,
Who listen to tidings flower upon the air
As fearless as those of a saint in camel's hair.[92]

\*\*\*\*\*\*\*\*\*\*\*\*\*\*\*\*\*\*\*\*\*\*\*\*\*\*\*\*\*\*\*\*\*\*\*

    Gable's essays are organized chronologically in this book, from "Catholic Life and Catholic Fiction" (1940) to the review of Flannery O'Connor's *Complete Stories* (1972).   Part One comprises five general essays in which Gable defines and re-defines Catholic fiction. Part Two contains eight essays on twenty-one authors, ranging from Francois Mauriac and Georges Bernanos to John Updike, Flannery O'Connor, and Muriel Spark.   These essays make concrete—Gable's favorite word—her general definition of Catholic fiction.   Humanities teachers and readers will find Gable's list of seventy-one authors and 306 titles  in "The Novel" especially valuable.   Her insights into individual authors are keen, her analysis of what the Catholic historical novel should be is sharp, and some of her wry comments are downright delightful.   Although the essay on philosopher Pierre Teilhard de Chardin and poet Dante Alighieri focuses more on philosophy than on literature, it is appropriate because Chardin's optimism permeated the last thirty years of Gable's life, and Dante's

"In His Will is our peace" informed her whole adult life. The Appendix includes primary material about two well-recognized Catholic writers: J.F. Powers and Flannery O'Connor. Finally, a note on language is in order. Gable's use of "man" and masculine pronouns, as if they included both men and women was the accepted terminology of the 1940s and 1950s. If she were alive and writing today, she would be using current and inclusive language. In that spirit I have changed the few references in her essays from "man" and "mankind" to "humanity" or "human being."

Gable unflaggingly challenged, defined, and redefined the idea of Catholic fiction. Her first essay, "Catholic Life and Catholic Fiction," celebrates Mauriac's *Viper's Tangle*, Undset's *Kristin Lavransdatter*, Bernanos' *Star of Satan*, Dante's *Divine Comedy*, Joyce's *Portrait of the Artist as a Young Man*, and Leon Bloy's *The Woman Who Was Poor* as models of Catholic fiction.[93] Next she argues for Chekhovian realism in portraying monastery and convent life (*Great Modern Catholic Short Stories*).[94] In a seminal essay in *Our Father's House*, she creates the literary "bull's eye," arguing for Catholic fiction with a capital "C." The fiction at the center of the bull's eye portrays saints, the "little people" who struggle daily to make appropriate choices between values. Next to the center are concentric circles of fiction dealing with various Church teachings on the race problem or birth control, for example. Finally, there is peripheral fiction, strong in local color, but not Catholic fiction. She bases her literary bull's-eye theory on Dietrich von Hildebrand's *Liturgy and Personality* and its definition of the classic personality which regards human love and friendship as the highest gifts in the world. Therefore, the "reeducation of love" is the main life work of human beings. They struggle to give appropriate responses to values. "[They} never mistake a door for a house. And the house is our Father's [God's]." Hence, the title, *Our Father's House*.[95] Picking up on this theme in *Many-Colored Fleece* (1950), she reaffirms this reordering of love, calling it three-dimensional "literature of spiritual affirmation": the individual in relationship with others and with God. In this same essay she points out the importance of the anthologist as "salvager and critic," reclaiming literature that might otherwise be lost and setting standards for true art.[96]

Her groundbreaking article on the Catholic novel in 1962 outlines her broadest definition of Catholic fiction: art which portrays the "spiritual and moral mystery of the human condition."[97] She arrives at this conclusion by arguing for two contradictory definitions and then rejecting them for a third. First, she argues that, *strictly speaking, Catholic fiction doesn't exist.* Fiction is a story which gives pleasure, and human beings' highest pleasure "comes from knowing—specifically, from knowing *through vision*—something of the mystery of life."[98] By its very definition, fiction portrays the whole of human experience—religious experience being the highest of these whether it is Buddhist, Mohammedan, Mormon, Jansenist, Jewish, Protestant, Catholic, or others. Therefore, because fiction portrays all of human experience, Catholic fiction is simply fiction; there's no such thing as Catholic fiction.

This conclusion leads to her second definition: *all the great fiction in the world is Catholic fiction.* She argues that subconsciously, writers have two views of the world: either the world is material and nothing more, or it is a "sense-observed world" in which human beings subconsciously realize that they are creatures of God. If writers subscribe to this second view, they are Catholic; if they subscribe to the first view, they are materialistic or secular. She quotes a non-Catholic critic, Arthur Machen, to support her own assertion that if artists are not sensitive to spiritual realities, what they write will not be literature. Hence, since secular fiction does not always deal with spiritual realities, it is circumscribed; and Catholic fiction, since it does deal with spiritual realities, is all-inclusive.

Rejecting these two contradictory definitions, she comes to a third: *Catholic fiction communicates artistically through Catholic symbols the spiritual and moral mystery of the human condition.* However, she insists that Catholic local color alone does not make a Catholic novel. Essential in her definition is not the subject matter, nor the special symbolism of artists, but the "depth and insight of their spiritual vision."[99] This spiritual vision involves the "reordering of love" on a three-dimensional plane—the individual, others, and God. Clearly, defining the Catholic novel as the artistic communication of the "spiritual and moral mystery of the human condition" is a broader definition than her previous ones.

A resurgence of interest in Catholic fiction is evident in the publications of the last eight years: a bibliography by Albert Menendez and a biographical dictionary by Daniel Tynan; five books of criticism by Malcolm Scott, Thomas Woodman, Anita Gandolfo, Arnold Sparr, Paul Giles, a chapter by Mary Gerhart, and articles by John Desmond and Andrew Greeley.[100] *Commonweal* is running a series of articles on individual Catholic writers in 1995-96. (For example, see Joseph Hynes' article on Jon Hassler, 3 November 1995). Anita Gandolfo's *Testing the Faith* (1992) argues that the Catholic novel need not promote Catholic dogma or be written by Catholic authors but it is "informed by a concern for the experience of being Catholic in the United States."[101] She identifies "patterns of vision" in novels from "Days of Innocence" (1900-50) to the "New Catholic Novel after Vatican II," the latter emphasizing "personal experience and knowledge rather than the acceptance of the authoritative and absolute." What is interesting is that Gandolfo describes the Catholic novel of pre-Vatican II as a "contradiction in terms" from a literary standpoint since it limits art to didacticism, and the result is what Flannery O'Connor calls "pious trash."[102] This "pious trash" was what Gable fought hardest against, and her anthologies demonstrated what she hoped was a union of art and values.

Mary Gerhart's chapter on "Whatever Happened to the Catholic Novel?" also discusses the Catholic novel before and after Vatican II, and suggests at the end that Catholic novels today are not locked into immutable Catholic doctrine, but their mainspring for action is located in foundational principles: "Sacramental vision and a conception of human beings as themselves sacred before God."[103] This last description is close to Gable's "spiritual and moral mystery of the human condition"[104] and what both Flannery O'Connor and Gable call the incarnational view of the universe.

What is amazing is that forty years ago, Gable's vision of the Catholic novel foreshadowed the present discussions mentioned here. Before the radical changes in the Church following Vatican II and before the ecumenical movement developed, she pioneered a broad definition of Catholic fiction, one which saw Catholic local color as peripheral and which cited as essential the moral and spiritual struggle of human beings. She wrote in 1962: "In the wake of the promising ecumenical movement alive in the world, one wonders sometimes if one ought not be talking of Christian fiction rather than of Catholic fiction."[105] Today she would suggest an even broader category: the literature of spiritual values. Her willingness to pay the price of her vision is clearly evident in her life of scholarship and teaching.

# NOTES

1. Kristin Malloy, O.S.B., interview by the author, St. Benedict's Convent, St. Joseph, Minnesota, 7 July 1995.
2. Mariella Gable, O.S.B. to Thomas Egan, O.S.B., 15 May 1964, Gable Collection, St. Benedict's Convent Archives, St. Joseph, Minnesota. Unless otherwise indicated, the following abbreviation is: GC (Gable Collection in the St. Benedict's Convent Archives).
3. H.R., review of *This is Catholic Fiction*, by Mariella Gable, *Friar's Bookshelf* (September 1949): 247.
4. Richard Sipe and Arleen Hynes, O.S.B., taught this pioneering course to seminarians at St. John's Seminary, Collegeville, Minnesota, in January, 1995.
5. Ruth Casey, review of *They Are People* and *Our Father's House*, ed. Mariella Gable, *Today*, May 1946, 8-9.
6. Mariella Gable, "Introduction" to *Great Modern Catholic Short Stories*, (New York: Sheed & Ward, 1942). Reprinted in *The Literature of Spiritual Values*, 11.
7. Arnold Sparr, *To Promote, Defend, and Redeem* (New York: Greenwood, 1990), 145.
8. John X. Harriott, "The Nun's Tales," *The Tablet*, 12 August 1989, 1.
9. Bryan MacMahon, quoted by Kristin Malloy in her interview notes, Tralee, County Kerry, Ireland, May 1983.
10. Quoted by Kristin Malloy in funeral eulogy for Mariella Gable, 24 March 1985, GC.
11. Flannery O'Connor to Mariella Gable, 5 July 1964, *The Habit of Being: Letters of Flannery O'Connor*, ed. Sally Fitzgerald (New York: Vintage, 1980), 591.
12. Sparr, *To Promote*, 160.
13. J.F. Powers, interview by the author, 29 June 1994, Collegeville, Minnesota, tape recording.
14. Mariella Gable, autobiographical essay, 1940, GC, 1.
15. Mariella Gable, "The Spy," *Blind Man's Stick* (Boston: Bruce Humphries, 1938), 12.
16. Mariella Gable, autobiographical essay, 2.
17. Ibid., 3.
18. Mariella Gable to Andriette Rohrenbach, O.S.B., 18 September 1975, GC.
19. Francis X. Talbot, S.J., to Mariella Gable, 22 March 1927, GC.

20. Both books were published in 1938 by Bruce Humphries, Boston. Brandon Press, Boston, reprinted *Blind Man's Stick* in 1966 without Gable's permission, much to her distress since she was unaware that the copyright had expired. A song was written for her poem, "To a Carrara Madonna," by Charles Repper (Trinity Court, Boston: Brashear Music Co., 1936). "The Sheep Herd" is also popular. Scholastic Magazine reprinted it in *Literary Cavalcade* (December 1949). The poem inspired a play by Gretchen Green which was performed as a Christmas service in Riverside Church, New York, in 1965. It was reprinted in *McCall's* (December 1976) and *A Christmas Feast*, ed. James Charlton and Barbara Gilson, (New York: Doubleday, 1976). Gable donated the money from this poem to the Mary Gable scholarship at the College of St. Benedict (Letter from Gable to Beverly Miller, College of St. Benedict college president, 12 April 1977, GC).

21. Mariella Gable to Marcine Schirber, O.S.B., February 1932, GC.

22. Mariella Gable to Marcine Schirber, May 1931, GC. Oxford movement is the name given to a movement begun at Oxford University in 1833 by certain Anglican clergymen to bring Catholic doctrine and ritual into the Anglican Church in opposition to the liberal movement in religion (*Webster's New World Dictionary*). Later with Cardinal John Henry Newman's conversion from Anglicanism to Catholicism in 1845, there developed the English Catholic literary revival, touting such writers as G.K. Chesterton, Hilaire Belloc, Agnes Repplier, Coventry Patmore, and, later, Gerard Manley Hopkins. In the United States an organized movement of the Catholic literary revival began with a series of articles on Newman in 1933 by *The Queen's Work* edited by Daniel A. Lord (Sparr, *To Promote*, 31). Finally Gable credits the translations of Mauriac, Bernanos, et al. with sparking the Catholic literary revival in the United States. (*The Literature of Spiritual Values*, 5-6).

23. Mariella Gable to Marcine Schirber, Fall, 1933, GC.

24. In 1980 St. Joseph Convent, Tulsa, Oklahoma, requested a copy of this pageant to celebrate the Benedictine sesquimillenium.

25. Mariella Gable to Bishop Busch, 4 November 1944, GC. In this letter Gable reminds the bishop of their agreement in 1941.

26. E.B. Scallan, *A Competent Censorship or Else Chaos* (New Orleans: Catholic Herald Press, 1943), 5-6.

27. Ibid., 12.

28. Frank Sheed to Mariella Gable, 12 May 1943, GC.

29. Mariella Gable to Bishop Busch, 12 May 1943, GC.

30. Mariella Gable to Bishop Busch, 4 November 1944, GC.

31. Mariella Gable to Frank Sheed, 25 July 1942, GC.

32. Mariella Gable to Bishop Busch, 12 May 1943, GC.

33. Bishop Busch to Mariella Gable, [undated, but context indicates sometime between 12 & 21 May 1943], GC.

34. Bishop Busch to Mariella Gable, 8 November 1944, GC.

35. Bishop Busch to Mariella Gable, [between 12 & 21 May 1943], GC.

36. Mariella Gable to Bishop Busch, 12 May 1943, GC.

37. Ibid.

38. Vincent A. Yzermans' laconic comment is accurate in *Journeys*, (Waite Park, Minnesota: Park Press, 1994): "His [Bishop Bartholome's] relationships with the Sisters of St. Benedict often left much to be desired," 147. Gable begged Bishop Busch again and again not to tell Bartholome about her negotiations with Busch.

39. Mariella Gable memoradum, Fall, 1943, GC.

40. Bishop Bartholome to Mariella Gable, 26 May 1944, GC.

41. Mariella Gable to Bishop Bartholome, 29 May 1944, GC.

42. Mariella Gable to Vincent Flynn, 13 February 1945, GC.

43. As a college student and later as a young nun, the author sat through similar exhortations from Bishop Bartholome.

44. John Louis Bonn to Vincent Flynn, 27 April 1944, GC.

45. Bartholome's pique is puzzling, especially since none of Gable's books had imprimaturs from bishops in the St. Cloud Diocese. *Blind Man's Stick, Great Modern Catholic Short Stories* and *This is Catholic Fiction* do not have an imprimatur. Archbishop Spellman granted the imprimatur for *Our Father's House*, and Cardinal Cushing gave the imprimatur for *Many-Colored Fleece*.

46. *The Atlantic Monthly* first prizes were for short story, "The Hanky and the Sins" by Bernadette Loosbroek (1942) and essay, "These Gentle Communists," by Mary Thomes (1944). Other honorable mentions: top twenty essays, "Emily Post to the Contrary Notwithstanding" by Betty Wahl and "That One Talent" by Genevieve Powers (1942); third honorable mention, short story, "Novice in the Cellar," and story of merit, "They Also Serve," both by Elizabeth Zwilling (1944); honorable mention, essay, "Dante Loves Beatrice," by Betty Wahl and top twenty essays, "My Father and Eric Gill," by Mary Martin (1945).

47. Mariella Gable, "Catholic Fiction Comes to America," *Today*, 30 April 1947,12. The other connection between Powers and Gable is that she introduced him to her prize writing student, Betty Wahl, who later married him. Wahl published several stories in *The New Yorker, McCall's*, and

others, and a novel, *Rafferty*.

48. Mariella Gable, "This is the New Pentecost," *The Catholic Messenger*, 29 July 1948; *The Catholic Digest* (October 1948).

49. Sparr, *To Promote*, 136. Catholic Action is a term popular in the 1930s and 40s; it stressed the responsibility of Catholic intellectuals to think, reflect, and act in making their influence felt in a secular world.

50. Kristin Malloy, "Toast of the Month," *The Marianist* (October 1950).

51. Francis X. Connelly, S.J., review of *Great Modern Catholic Short Stories*, ed. by Mariella Gable, *Catholic Book Club Newsletter* (December 1942); *Catholic Mirror* (December 1942).

52. John Erskine, review of *Great Modern Catholic Short Stories*, ed. by Mariella Gable, Chicago *Sun*, vol. 1, no. 5, (1942).

53. *The New York Times*, 22 November 1942.

54. St. Benedict's archival records show the following sales: *Our Father's House*, 14,383 (six editions); *Great Modern Catholic Short Stories* [later re-titled *They Are People*], 8,631 (four editions); *This is Catholic Fiction*, 4,275; *Many-Colored Fleece*, 7,019. A Flemish translation of *They Are People* exists, and 2,000 copies of *Our Father's House* were distributed in Australia.

55. E.V.R. Wyatt, review of *Our Father's House*, ed. by Mariella Gable, *The Commonweal*, 23 November 1945, 146.

56. John S. Kennedy, review of *our Father's House*, ed. by Mariella Gable, *The New York Times*, 13 January 1946.

57. John Cogley, review of *Many-Colored Fleece*, ed. by Mariella Gable, *The Commonweal*, 22 December 1950.

58. Retrospectives in addition to John Cogley's are by Riley Hughes, *Renascence* (Spring 1950); Sister Frances Borgia, *Insight* (January 1951); Kristin Malloy, *St. Benedict's Quarterly* (Spring 1951); "Toast of the Month," *The Marianist* (October 1950). Riley Hughes commends all three of Gable's anthologies as showing sharp perception in purpose: that is, of calling on lay writers to come to terms with the wellsprings of holiness in the family and its conflict with secular values. John S. Kennedy says that Gable is "among the most discerning and exacting of our Catholic critics. Discerning, she really recognizes meaning and merit; exacting, she sets a high standard for substance and form in fiction," Los Angeles *Tidings*, 22 December 1950.

59. Mariella Gable to Bishop Busch, 8 November 1944, GC.

60. Kristin Malloy, interview by the author, St. Benedict's Convent, 7 July 1995.

61. Mariella Gable to Remberta Westkaemper, O.S.B., 3 March 1944, GC.

62. Mariella Gable to Remberta Westkaemper, August 1944, GC.

63. Mariella Gable to Remberta Westkaemper, 26 June 1950, GC, describes the insulin and shock treatments; Gable to Westkaemper, 20 March 1951 GC, shows in clearly legible script: "[The doctor] wanted me up on third floor (surgery) for a neurological examination. Since such an exam is part of the procedure for dismissal, I said O.K. But promptly on Friday morning, Mar. 16, he took me to the operating room and performed an intra-orbital lobotomy on me. That is, by lifting up the eyelid and severing certain nerves, he says he has my tenseness under control. He did not tell me until yesterday morning, Mar. 19!"

64. Mariella Gable to Remberta Westkaemper, 12 November 1950, GC. Gable says: "Solitary confinement constitutes the most terrible suffering in the world. I am a sane person now, completely myself, but a few more days of solitary confinement and I will be a stark, raving maniac." Regarding the electric shock treatment, she says: "[Dr. O'Gorman] said that the electric shock treatments sent me 'high as a kite.' In other words, the treatments made me crazy. I was terribly afraid of them. I do not think it is right to make any human being take any treatment of which she is so afraid." And of her sanity: "When Dr. O'G was in here today I asked him, just for the record, whether I am sane or insane now. He said 'You are sane, sane as you will ever be.' Then he went on shrewdly to outline some of my emotional problems. Some of what he said was right, & helpful. But am I not, being sane, a free agent with the right to refuse electric shock and solitary confinement? These methods will not help me. Of that I am sure." Finally, she describes the day her book came out when no one bothered to acknowledge it as "the most miserable day of my life." Another letter from Gable to Westkaemper, 19 November 1950, notes that when she mentioned that Jacques Maritain was to speak for Delta Epsilon Sigma at the College of St. Benedict, a Sister asked, "Who's Maritain?"

65. Grace McDonald, O.S.B., *With Lamps Burning* (St. Joseph, Minnesota: St. Benedict's Priory Press, 1957), 219-23.

66. Kristin Malloy, interview by the author, 7 July 1995, St. Benedict's Convent.

67. Kristin Malloy, summary of meeting, March 1958, GC.

68. Kristin Malloy, interview by the author, 7 July 1995. Doherty often quoted Bartholome to Malloy during his frequent interviews with her after that March session in which Doherty condemned *Catcher in the Rye.*

69. Bishop Bartholome to Mariella Gable, 15 July 1959, GC. Between

March and August, 1958, Mother Richarda tried to ease the situation by trying to replace Jerome Doherty, but she was unsuccessful; Kristin Malloy, interview by the author, 7 July 1995.

70. Mariella Gable to Richarda Peters, O.S.B., 29 June 1958, GC.

71. Mariella Gable to Bishop Bartholome, 6 July 1959, GC.

72. Mariella Gable to Remberta Westkaemper, 26 July 1958, GC. Gable writes: ". . .I cannot wait a whole week to tell you about my talk with Father Gardiner. I felt as if I had been born again. One of the worst things I have ever suffered was the thing communicated to me by Father Jerome [Doherty] last Palm Sunday and which has never left me one single moment since—the question in my own mind as to whether or not I might have been a shade too liberal in our English department. One cannot take so much beating without a great deal of soul searching. I knew that before God I was not accountable, because when one acts in good faith one's conscience is clear. But there would be the whole question of standards to be considered now with renewed diligence. Father Gardiner put my mind at rest. I cannot tell you what a relief it was."

73. Harold C. Gardiner, S.J.,"The 'Dangers' of Literature, *America*, 13 December 1958.

74. Michael Boyle, S.J.,"Teaching 'Dirty Books' in College," *America*, 13 December 1958.

75. Harold Gardiner to Mariella Gable, 25 November 1958, GC.

76. Mariella Gable to Thomas Egan, 14 August 1958, GC.

77. Mariella Gable to Thomas Egan, 10 January 1959, GC.

78. Mariella Gable to Thomas Egan, 12 August 1959, GC. Sister Thomas Carey's art, particularly her crucifixes, were banned as "too modern" by Bishop Bartholome.

79. Mariella Gable to Remberta Westkaemper, 4 November 1959, GC.

80. Mary Thomes [Locke] to Mariella Gable, 23 December 1958, GC.

81. Roland Behrendt to Mariella Gable, 27 October 1958, GC.

82. Mariella Gable to Remberta Westkaemper, 26 July 1958, GC.

83. Herbert Slusser to Mariella Gable, 20 April 1963, GC.

84. Henrita Osendorf, O.S.B., to Mariella Gable, 10 March 1962, GC.

85. Mariella Gable, "Ecumenic Core in Flannery O'Connor's Fiction, *American Benedictine Review* (June 1964); "Flannery O'Connor," *Esprit* (Scranton, PA, Winter 1964): 25-27.

86. Nathan Scott to Mariella Gable, 1 May 1965, GC.

87. Mariella Gable to Thomas Egan, 16 December 1963, GC.

88. Mariella Gable to Thomas Egan, 1 March 1966, GC.

89. Mariella Gable to Thomas Egan, undated letter, GC. This was

probably the late sixties. Bishop Bartholome retired in 1968, and Bishop Speltz took charge. Gable spoke at Cathedral High School at the invitation of Father James Rausch and Katherine [then Aquin] Kraft, O.S.B.

90. The preface to the manuscript states that the prison program was designed to "assist men who were dependent on drugs to overcome their need for chemical support." Gable lectured on Pierre Teilhard de Chardin's *The Phenomenon of Man* and showed five filmstrips in connection with the book; *The Central Minnesota Counsellor Newsletter* (May 1972).

91. Mariella Gable, review of *Flannery O'Connor, the Complete Stories*, ed. by Robert Giroux, *Sisters Today*, (April 1972); review of *Deschooling Society* by Ivan Illich, *Benedictines*, (Spring-Summer 1974); review of *The Heart of the Matter* by Pierre Teilhard de Chardin, *Spirituality Today* (March 1980).

92. Bernetta Quinn, O.S.F., (1946), GC.

93. Mariella Gable, "Catholic Life and Catholic Fiction," *The Literature of Spiritual Values*, 1-9.

94. Mariella Gable, Introduction to *Great Modern Catholic Short Stories*, *The Literature of Spiritual Values*, 11.

95. Mariella Gable, "Personality and Catholic Fiction" [introduction to *Our Father's House*], *The Literature of Spiritual Values*, 18-21.

96. Mariella Gable, introduction to *Many-Colored Fleece*, *The Literature of Spiritual Values*, 29-30.

97. Mariella Gable, "The Novel," *The Literature of Spiritual Values*, 56.

98. Ibid., 53.

99. Ibid., 56.

100. The definitions of Catholic fiction or Catholic writers run from narrow (Menendez) to unhelpful (Tynan). Albert J. Menendez, *The Catholic Novel: An Annotated Bibliography* (New York: Garland, 1988). Though Albert Menendez does not say that one must be Catholic to write Catholic fiction, he does insist that the Catholic novel reflect the "values, culture, and conflicts of the Roman Catholic faith and its community," thus excluding novels obviously Catholic in spirit, such as Rumer Godden and Flannery O'Connor (xvi).

Daniel Tynan, ed., *Biographical Dictionary of Contemporary Catholic American Writing* (New York: Greenwood, 1989). Tynan includes all baptized Catholics because, whether or not they have accepted Catholicism as the major influence in their lives, they are likely to share "a concern for the impact of a Catholic vision of the world upon them" (xii).

More inclusive definitions come from Thomas Woodman, Peter Giles, and John Desmond. Thomas Woodman, *Faithful Fictions* (Milton Keynes, PA:Open University Press, 1991), says Catholic fiction "deals with specifically Catholic themes or subject matter". . ."from a distinctly Catholic perspective and with a sufficient degree of inwardness" (ix). Peter Giles, *American Catholic Arts and Fictions* (Cambridge: Cambridge U Press, 1992), is not interested in defining the Catholic novel, but instead examines the "continuing significance of religion, and specifically Roman Catholicism as an ideological force, within modern American literature, film, and photography" (1). Andrew Greeley explains "The Catholic Novels of Jon Hassler," *America*, 17 November 1990, 366-67, 382. John Desmond, "Catholicism in Contemporary American Fiction," *America*, 14 May 1994, 7-11, cites Flannery O'Connor's assertion that Catholic fiction is concerned with three central truths—the fall of humanity, redemption, and judgment. He mentions ten major current writers of Catholic fiction and discusses briefly five more: Jon Hassler, Louise Erdrich, Andre Dubus, Richard Bausch, and Tobias Wolff. An interview with Mary Gordon by Patrick Samway is in the same issue of *America*.

101. Anita Gandolfo, *Testing the Faith* (New York: Greenwood, 1992), xii.

102. Ibid., 17-19.

103. Mary Gerhart, "What Ever Happened to the Catholic Novel?" in *Morphologies of Faith*, ed. Mary Gerhart and Anthony Yu (Atlanta, Georgia: Scholars Press, 1990), 200.

104. Mariella Gable, "The Novel," *The Literature of Spiritual Values*, 56.

105. Ibid., 57. The author was tempted to name this book, *The Literature of Ethical Values*, in Wayne Booth's sense of that term: "the entire range of effects on the 'character' or 'person' or 'self'" with moral judgments only a small part (Booth, *The Company We Keep*, Los Angeles: University of California, 1988, 8). Gable's definition, however, stresses the spiritual values of humanity and "ethical" doesn't quite suggest that.

# Part One: Catholic Fiction, A Developing Concept

# Chapter 1

## Catholic Life and Catholic Fiction[1]

The status of Catholic fiction at the present time reminds one of the three men from Cleveland who went to visit New York City. They procured rooms on the forty-fifth floor of a reputable hotel and went out to see the wonders of Manhattan. Returning shortly after midnight, they found their hotel in darkness. The clerk at the desk declared in dismay that something had gone wrong with the electric current. He could furnish candles, yes; but there was no elevator service. Did the gentlemen wish to walk up, or go to a different hotel? After some conference the three men decided to take the candle and toil up to bed. But to beguile the time they agreed to tell stories. The first man told romantic tales for the first fifteen flights, and they sighed and wept as they went. The second man told humorous stories for the next fifteen flights, and they roared with amusement in spite of being pretty much out of breath. The third man told tragedies as they ascended from floor thirty to forty-five. But just as they reached the top step, he sat down, pale with dismay, and announced, "But we haven't the key!"

During the last three decades our writers of fiction have gone up forty-five flights under almost incredible handicaps. All credit to them. The novel was born after the Protestant Revolt and had no Catholic tradition. Poetry, biography, apologetics, philosophy—all have forged ahead in the Catholic Revival to a perfection behind which fiction lags conspicuously. And this fact should give us pause. For the number of persons who read fiction is a few thousand times greater than the number of persons who read nonfiction or poetry. Furthermore, the tale or novel has a power to move people as the brilliant pages of Jacques Maritain's philosophy or the aspiration of Gertrude Von Le Fort's *Hymns* have not.

The peculiar and arresting thing, however, about the situation is this. We, not the writer of fiction, hold the key to final success. And unless we give the novel writers that key promptly, their amazing ascent against the present odds will be in vain.

Let us demonstrate by taking a look at one of the really fine novels already produced by the Catholic Revival—*Viper's Tangle*, by Francois Mauriac. The story is about a warped, morbid, miserly man, whose main ambition is to divert his millions from his wife and children. They are Catholics who go through all the motions of Catholic life—Sunday Mass, the sacraments, with quite impeccable regularity, and also pray daily so that dear papa will have the grace to come into the Catholic Church. But their burning ambition is to lay hold upon his money. Out of the depths of his heart he desires the love and magnificent spirituality the Church alone can give. But the materialistic lives of the Catholics in his own household are his greatest stumbling block in finding the light. He does ultimately find it, but not through them. His granddaughter, Janine, finally sums up the whole situation:

> . . . Except in the case of grandmother, our principles remained separate from our lives. Our thought, our desires, our actions struck no roots in that faith to which we adhered with our lips. With all our strength, we were devoted to material things, while grandfather. . . . Will you understand me if I tell you that, where his treasure was, there was not his heart also? (288)

And further, "It was the misfortune of all of us that he mistook us for exemplary Christians" (287).

The book is brilliantly executed. It embodies essential truth. It trumpets to the world the futility and shame of the materialistic Catholic. A negative message. But great art is always positive. The great Catholic novel will be the novel of grace, unfolding for the reader the magnificent reaches and depths of the life conscious of the indwelling of the Trinity.

To most of us, material comforts are the most important things in the world. Our lives are dedicated to being comfortable. And having sunk down into the depths of overstuffed davenports, our flabby spirits doze, only vaguely aware of the magnificent adventure open to those who live the life of grace.

In fact, the question has been raised whether the historical novel is not the only type which can yield the true Catholic novel. Before Sigrid Undset entered the Catholic Church, she steeped herself in the history, archaeology, and literature of the medieval period. She came to know the fourteenth century in the Scandinavian countries better than her own. *Kristin Lavransdatter* opened for the reader a door into the pre-Reformation past—a past vibrating with the life of faith. And though its author was not as yet a Catholic, the result of her honest portrayal of life in the Catholic centuries was a magnificent hymn in praise of the Church. Not an age without sin, mind you. But in spite of weakness and personal failure, a life that did believe to its utmost roots that heaven is our destination, not a V-8 or a Beautyrest mattress.

If it is true that only a novel portraying the ages of faith can be a Catholic novel in the fullest sense, this fact is a terrible indictment of our own age. Literature holds a mirror up to life. If we look into that mirror seriously, our hearts ought to be frozen with horror at the spectacle of our own failure.

But it is the spectacle of the beauty of the life of grace for which the world is sick at present. The most marked characteristic of secular fiction during the last six years is its turning away from filth. But to what? The Catholics have the full answer. But let us be honest. Let us not claim to have given that answer as yet. One of the best things Catholic critics could do for the novel would be to refrain from including as Catholic novels those which obviously do not measure up. Let us give our writers all due credit, but let us not call tinsel light. And let us not feel that skirting the circumference is the same as hitting the center of the circle.

And let us be a bit honest about our own responsibilities in these matters—about the leakage in the Church. The good writer for the "slicks" has a gift the Church needs. But why have some of these brilliant writers found their Catholic life so separate from their real living that the children of their imagination are utterly unregenerated in the waters of baptism? Somewhere, in a Catholic parish, they grew up without sufficient impact of Catholic life. Perhaps, if we have a number of half-baked Catholic writers, it is because *we* do not make the oven hot enough.

But there are certain indications that better things are at hand. After all, there has been a Catholic Revival. The Holy Spirit has been moving over the face of the dark waters in a marvelous way. We have had a liturgical revival, thanks to which millions have drunk more fully and understandingly at the fountain of grace. During the last decade we have begun to reap in our Catholic life the first harvest of this rich sowing.

And the younger novelists have been quick to catch the new spark in their books. They have been unperturbed by the timidity of Montgomery Carmichael, who declared:

> It must be admitted that the Life of Grace, as a subject, is an undoubted handicap to the writer of fiction, be his intentions as Catholic as may be. . . . The truth is that fiction is a faulty medium in which to convey these profound things of the spirit which most nearly concern a Catholic. The medium would break in the hands of even a Catholic genius who would assay the highest.

Incidentally, it was a spoiled Catholic, James Joyce, who demonstrated a long time ago that the problems of the life of grace, far from being a handicap to the writer of novels, are actually supercharged with dramatic interest. It would be difficult to find, in all the pages of English fiction, anything more gripping than the account of Stephan Dedalus struggling to make a good confession during a retreat, as Joyce has described it in *A Portrait of the Artist as a Young Man.* However, the whole episode is sprayed with a fine drench of poison, as any one can see who takes a little trouble to look closely at the sermons delivered by the Jesuit retreat master—though the average Catholic has perhaps listened to many sermons which take an equally unfair advantage of listeners, and not all by Jesuits, either. But in spite of all its faults, and not because of them, the episode remains a brilliant piece of writing, a kind of flaming monument to shame Catholics who have been blind to the possibilities of drama and suspense latent in the odyssey of a soul touched by grace.

But the young writers who are beginning to make use of this material have not come to it by way of Joyce. Which is all very well. A Catholic novel could never employ entirely the stream-of-consciousness technique. For the Catholic view of life supposes a mentor, a human choice, a power of will all opposed to an undisciplined flow of consciousness.

Thus far only one book of the first order artistically has hit the bull's eye squarely. It is a novel by the French writer, Georges Bernanos. *The Star of Satan* appeared in France in 1926 and an English translation was published by Macmillan in 1940. The Catholic critics fell foul of it, dismissing it as a morbid study. Yet the whole book is concerned with the struggle for sanctity of a peasant priest, in many respects like the Curé of Ars. This struggle articulates for the first time the exact center of the Catholic novel. Also, for the first time we see clearly the double force which will always modify the struggle and which will afford an infinite variety for the artist. Father Donissan's individuality colors strongly his pursuit of holiness. He is of stern, peasant stock, innately afraid of any softness whatsoever. Hence his sanctity is hard, unflinching. The second force molding his special form of struggle is the world around him. Bernanos thinks it is the devil's world. Unless one understands that Mouchette is possessed by a devil and is a symbol of the evil Father Donissan must fight against, the whole first part of the novel must appear to be excrescence. There are those who can look upon the catastrophe in the world today and think Bernanos has given an exaggerated interpretation of evil. There are delicate souls who would like their saints stamped with an individuality less hard than Father Donissan's. Any reader is permitted his personal preferences. Yet it is a pity that Catholic critics failed to recognize that in *The Star of Satan* Catholic fiction had finally come to rest precisely on the mark.

Encouraging as are many of these newer books, the fact remains obvious that novelists are often working under serious handicap. Unless we give them abundant material for positive work, they can never unlock the door to complete success. Sometimes it is asked: Which comes first, the egg or the chicken? It is not a frivolous question. Which comes first, the robust Catholic life or a great Catholic fiction? There is an analogous interdependence. Every layperson has the solemn obligation to write the books of tomorrow, not in ink, but in the flaming characters of the God-conscious life. The Catholic Literary Revival was begun and promoted largely by converts to Catholicism. It can be brought to its fullest blossom only by a landslide of converts from Babbitt-Rotarian Catholicism to the full living of the life of grace.

Outside the liturgy and the sacraments, the greatest help to this full blossoming of the Catholic life lies in the great Catholic classics of the past. The neglect of these, particularly in our Catholic colleges, is a matter for concern. The least one might expect would be a first-rate course in Dante's *Divine Comedy*, in translation, so that its magnificent interpretation of St. Thomas might be made accessible to every Catholic student. But you can count on the fingers of one hand the Catholic institutions offering such a course. Some heads of departments have looked down their noses in superior scorn at the idea of so unscholarly a course as one in translation. But the great nonsectarian universities have suffered no such pedantic inhibitions. For years Cornell has confided such a course to one of the greatest classical scholars in the country. And it is at Cornell that we have the greatest Dante library in the country—not at the Catholic University, or at Fordham, or at Notre Dame.

If one considers the neglect of the *Divine Comedy* merely from a cultural viewpoint, it is one of the lacunae in Catholic education over which tears might be shed. "The majority of poems one outgrows and outlives, as one outgrows and outlives the majority of human passions; Dante's is one of those which one can only just hope to grow up to at the end of life." But what if one turns from aesthetic to practical considerations? There the cause for grief goes still deeper. Nor does one apologize for making so great a poem a tool for improving the spiritual condition of its readers. Dante wrote it just for that, in his own words, "to remove those who are living in this life from the state of wretchedness to a state of blessedness." Behold, once and for all, the right use of propaganda! And literature did not suffer from it; it grew out of it.

Every adult owes it to himself, if he cannot master the whole *Divine Comedy*, to know well, at least, the last four cantos. Why? Because there is no other place in all literature that makes clear what the possession of God in heaven is like. Dante, with St. Bernard, stands in the center of the Eternal Rose and finally is able to look up to the Uncreated Light, flooding with glory the rows upon rows of blessed saints upon the petals of the flower. Here is "light intellectual full-charged with love, love of true good, full charged with gladness, gladness which transcendeth every sweetness." Let us make no mistake about its importance. It is the same doctrine as propounded by the Fathers through the centuries, the same philosophic interpretation as presented by the *Summa*. But philosophy is abstract.

Poetry is concrete. And we are so made that color and light and human emotions move us. I have seen students (the same who were dull clods in religion classes) struck silent with breath-held awe over the last canto, "which to my thinking," said T.S. Eliot, "is the highest point that poetry ever has reached or can reach."

Why insist that all adults know the last four cantos? Because only when they have some idea of what it means to possess God in heaven can they understand what the life of grace is—the possession here and now of that same heaven. "The life of grace and glory is the same." This is one simple little poem, and yet the most profound which has come out of the whole Catholic Literary Revival, concerned with precisely this link between heaven and the life of grace. The reader can find it in Alfred Barrett's volume *Mint by Night*, but it deserves to be quoted entirely here:

> The life of grace and glory is the same;
>   The life of grace is, by another name,
> Heaven and earth; and death is but a change
>   In range
> And nothing strange.
>
> There lies between our dreaming and our seeing
>   One pulsing continuity of being—
> Oh, when the life of glory we achieve
>   Why grieve?
> We only lose our having to believe.

It is only when readers have seen heaven in its heart-subduing awe and beauty that they can get excited about the pursuit of the life of grace here and now. Then suddenly the scales fall from their eyes. And for the first time they realize, by contrast, how low, despicable, and disgusting is the pursuit of mere comfort as a life dedication.

The first question is, but *how* can a poor beginner like myself achieve this wonderful thing? The answer lies in the great Catholic classics by St. Teresa and St. John of the Cross. They were written to tell in the most precise detail exactly how, beginning from the lowest and most inept stages, the soul might forge inward to the center of its own soul where the Blessed Trinity dwells—only awaiting human cooperation in order that the soul might begin its heaven on earth. To use the technical word, that the soul might begin contemplation. I see the reader shy away from the frightening word. It remained for the Protestant Revolt to put it into our heads that contemplation was something for Carmelites and Poor Clares. Our contemporary spiritual writers, Jaeger and Garrigou-Lagrange and Raoul Plus, particularly, are doing a fine work in rediscovering for us that contemplation is for everyone. Their books are excellent introductions to St. John of the Cross and St. Teresa, but no substitute for these magnificent classics of asceticism.

At large secular universities I have heard graduate students, dilettantes reading *about* mysticism, speak with complete ignorance of its real meaning. They were enjoying a kind of pseudo-intellectual delight in esoteric studies. *The Ascent of Mount Carmel* was not written to be quoted across seminar tables by young pedants as a means of complacent self-satisfaction. It was written to be used as a perfect tool in the pursuit of the life of grace. Our colleges have an obligation to introduce students to the great Catholic classics. Students are hungry for them. Why let students creep in rompers in their life of prayer, when in all their other abilities they are trained to pirouette on their toes with unimpeachable poise? Out of our Catholic colleges could come a powerful leaven that would change the whole consistency of Catholic life.

In 1897 Leon Bloy wrote *The Woman Who Was Poor.* Not long ago Sheed & Ward presented an English translation to the American public. The reception of the book proved two things: Readers are thrilled by the magnificence of the life of grace lived by the heroine. But they shy away from the incredibly fantastic, tortuous, sordid circumstances of her position. But authors have been constrained to take their heroes of grace from extraordinary circumstances lest their books seem unreal. What if the great mass of Catholics believed with the woman who was poor that "there is only one unhappiness, and that is—*not to be one of the saints?*"

### Notes

1. Mariella Gable, O.S.B., "'Catholic' Fiction," *The Catholic World* (December 1940). Also reprinted in Vincent J. Flynn, *Prose Readings: An Anthology for Catholic Colleges* (New York: Scribner's, 1942) and Mariella Gable, O.S.B., *This is Catholic Fiction* (New York: Sheed & Ward, 1948).

# Chapter 2

## Introduction to
### *Great Modern Catholic Short Stories*[1]

FOR THE FIRST TIME in the history of the short story, we have had in the recent past nuns, monks, brothers, and priests appearing as they are. A surprising number of the best short-story writers of our present decade have written about the cloistered and the consecrated: among others Paul Horgan, Ernest Hemingway, Elizabeth Madox Roberts, Sean O'Faolain, Frank O'Connor, L.A.G. Strong, Geoffrey Household, and Morley Callaghan. Curiously enough, these stories are among the best things they have written. These short stories, and others of comparable merit, have been gathered in the present volume as indicating something of a landmark. There has been nothing before quite like the distinguished realism of these descriptions of convents, monasteries, and the daily routine of parish duties.

How far we have come in the last few years may be appreciated if one places side by side two stories of Kentucky convents: "The Sacrifice of the Maidens," by Elizabeth Madox Roberts, which won the O. Henry Memorial Award in 1930, and James Lane Allen's "The White Cowl," which as late as 1923 appeared in a representative collection of American short stories. In Allen's story a young Trappist is seduced immediately upon hearing the voice of a woman. After his portrayal of a monk, the yarns of the *Arabian Nights* read like stark realism. Elizabeth Madox Roberts is satisfied to open very quietly the door of a Dominican chapel during a reception ceremony.

With the brother of one of the young brides we savor the full meaning
of young womanhood, and with the author, through an adroit use of
the Hail Mary as a symbol, we sense, with sudden illumination, the
meaning of birth, of life, of death. Here the author has invented
nothing. The facts themselves are incomparably more eloquent and
dramatic than the violent fabrications of the recent past.

Those inventions stopped at nothing short of a woman in
disguise taking vows in a monastery for men, which the reader may
investigate for himself, if he wishes to look at "Brother Sebastian's
Friendship," by Harold Frederic, which Stephen Graham included in
*Great American Short Stories* as late as 1931. Nor has this fantastic
fiction entirely disappeared with the coming of the "quality" story.
By substituting for romantic melancholy with its moonlight and roses
a kind of gross pseudo-realism, Aldous Huxley carried on the bad
tradition and bad art in "The Nuns at Luncheon," which Somerset
Maugham included in *Tellers of Tales*, 1939. But all of this is as
remote from the new realism as spectacular fireworks from the
evening star.

The sister, the priest, the brother, and the monk, as normal,
intelligent persons doing normal, intelligent work, began to emerge in
fiction just as the short story emancipated itself from the artificial
requirements of plot and the pyrotechnics of the O. Henry surprise
ending. It is difficult to set dates, but toward the end of the second
decade, the new tendencies in fiction were fairly well established.
Between 1930 and 1940, thanks largely to the pioneering efforts of
Martha Foley and Whit Burnett, along with the stubborn insistence on
originality and quality by countless "little" magazines, the short story
has continued to recognize the enormous importance in life of the
apparently unspectacular. The new short story is free to recognize
what Masefield so brilliantly stated in his poem "Biography," that the
unrecorded moments are often the most poignant and memorable.

> And long before this wandering flesh is rotten
>   The dates which made me will be all forgotten;
> And none will know the gleam there used to be
>   About the feast days freshly kept by me.
> But men will call the golden hour of bliss
>   "About this time" or "shortly after this."

Chekhov, whose practice in the liberated short story antedated the
new freedom in England and America by two decades, defended his

position with less poetry and more pungency when he pointed out that people do not go to the North Pole and fall off icebergs; they go to offices, quarrel with their wives, and eat cabbage soup. Similarly nuns, monks, and priests are not seduced; they teach rapid addition to children in parochial schools, drink the proverbially bad coffee brewed in monastery kitchens, and are occasionally jealous of each other. Thus they are depicted in the contemporary short story.

And the form of the short story seems admirably adapted to interpret the convent and the monastery—particularly when several stories stand side by side, forming, as it were, glimpses of individuals who are, after all, normally part of a community. It is the communal aspect of their lives which a group of short stories suggests. An individual may deserve the full-length treatment of a novel, as Kate O'Brien has recently demonstrated in the best book ever written about the convent, *Land of Spices*. But normally the events in the lives of religious which justify fiction are slight. A right total impression emerges upon examining a series of these, so right that one is reminded of the Gallup reporter who said: "Taken one by one, people may be complacent and at times abysmally ignorant; taken ten by ten, they reveal a fathomless, a reassuring forthrightness, a basic innocence."

The emergence of the new fiction is important in the history of the Catholic Literary Revival, which is following, it seems, the normal development of literary forms in any society; poetry first and the prose of exposition and apologetics, with fiction awaiting its fulfillment rather late in the sequence of modes of expression. Francis Thompson, Alice Meynell, and Gerard Manley Hopkins started English Catholic poetry off at a high pitch. Cardinal Newman's prose—in his *Apologia, The Idea of a University*, and his sermons—has not been surpassed for sheer beauty and precision; but he wrote some very mediocre novels. Mauriac, Bernanos, and Sigrid Undset have produced distinguished novels which have come to us in translation. But not until the present moment, in the novels of Graham Greene, Kate O'Brien, and Harry Sylvester have we had many notable Catholic novels in the English language. That these should appear simultaneously with the kind of short stories included in this volume would seem to indicate that the Catholic Literary Revival has developed to the point where we may expect competent fiction both of the long and the short variety.

But there is grave danger that the short stories may be lost to the average Catholic reader. They are scattered to the four winds in magazines least likely to be suspected of publishing them. For the most part, Catholic magazines are entirely innocent of this new distinguished fiction. They have sinned along with the "slicks" in catering to popular taste. The large circulation magazines, particularly the women's magazines, consistently print happy-ending stories that glorify romantic love. The Catholic magazines patronize the same mentality, with a subtle philosophy of life conspicuously more harmful. They seem to say: "If you say your prayers (especially if they are repeated nine successive days), if you are good and do the right things, then you shall have a job, succeed in your ambitions, be crowned with the good things of this world"—a kind of back-stairs entrance to materialism, particularly enticing because its easy steps are padded and comfortable with a righteous piety. Edification at the expense of truth is always a doubtful good. The stories collected in the present volume are true in the best sense of the word. They are collected here for the convenience and delight of Catholic readers who might otherwise miss them, and for discriminating readers everywhere.

Their variety should appeal to many tastes. For those who like the ultra-refinements of the new method, which dispenses entirely with plot in the traditional sense, there is the delicate sustaining of a mood and a moment's impression in "Momento" and "The Sacrifice of the Maidens." For those who like the suspense and excitement of a good story there are "The Salvation of Pisco Gabar," which is perhaps one of the best yarns in contemporary fiction, "The Surgeon and the Nun," "First Confession," "A Fight for Sister Joe," "A Bountiful Providence" and "Benediction." Between these two extremes lie all shades and varieties of types.

It is a curious fact that the stories in this volume have almost all been written by persons outside of convents, monasteries, and parishes. At the present time sisters, monks, and priests do not demonstrate great interest in the details of their own special surroundings. For the most part they expend their creative energy in writing lyric poetry, which seems to have been carefully inoculated against the taint of local color.

A delightful exception to this rule is the entirely realistic story by Jack English (Brother Cajetan), which gives the uninitiated a sudden glimpse into the rather chilly, matter-of-fact acceptance of death in a monastery. There is room for much more honest writing of this sort. Only those who live the life can give it. But it is in "A

Nun's Diary" by Sister Mary Frances that one sees clearly for the first time what the new range of fiction might be if persons consecrated to God in a quite special way chose to write of the things that matter most to them. We trust that "A Nun's Diary" stands like a sign-post pointing in the direction of the Catholic fiction of the future. Here the arena of conflict is the human soul in its determination to find God. Long ago James Joyce demonstrated that the highest kind of dramatic intensity could be attained by just such subject matter, when he described the terrifying struggle of young Stephen Dedalus to make a good confession in *The Portrait of an Artist*. "Reading in the Refectory," Peter Whiffin's sympathetic sketch, deals with the discovery that certain prescribed methods can be stumbling blocks in the pursuit of holiness.

Here, then, are the three exceptions, three feathers in the wind, to indicate in what direction lie rich stores of heretofore unexplored material.

For the most part, however, the accuracy of observation of those outside the cloister is almost uncanny. Perhaps one would have to be a member of the sisterhood to appreciate the full rightness of Sister Cecilia's expert knowledge of baseball and her ignorance of football in Ernest Hemingway's "The Gambler, The Nun, and the Radio." Morley Callaghan is unique in being able to write of priests apparently "from within." Except for Paul Horgan, who writes of things Catholic less frequently, Callaghan is the only writer of the first order on this continent who consistently weds the things of the Church to the new realistic technique. He is appropriately represented in the present volume by three selections. Perhaps John Conley's brilliant sketch of a Jesuit novitiate can scarcely be counted as a case in point, since he spent a year with the Jesuits. Not less accurately observed, however, is F. Scott Fitzgerald's "Benediction," which opens the door to a Jesuit seminary. The validity of the one and the other might well be compared.

Superficially, these carefully observed details by outsiders seem to present persons dedicated to religion only on a humanistic level. Yet the life of the spirit clearly sheds its light on the characters, and often it is this light which determines the course of the story. In Paul Horgan's "The Surgeon and the Nun," we find a sister placed in a very trying circumstance. In the midst of a burning desert, her train stops near a shack where a Mexican is dying of acute appendicitis. She has no choice but to spend the night assisting the physician who was also traveling in the train, and who performs a successful operation in spite of almost overwhelming difficulties. The calmness and self-control of the sister may indicate something of the discipline of her life. But it is at the crucial point in the story where a single remark comes like a revelation, not only of her character, but also of where she consistently puts emphasis—no matter how naively. The doctor realizes that she is the only one who understands fully the brilliance of his achievement. In saying farewell he desires some little word of praise. He needed the little lift she could give him. But she says, "I will pray for you, doctor."

"What?"

"That you may overcome your habit of profanity."

It is not often that a story reveals so much with such economy.

But the careful reader will find the same kind of revelation in all the stories. The life of the spirit consistently marks and determines the human individuality. Yet the things of the spirit are for the most part revealed only obliquely. The story of the future will present them directly.

There are, indeed, new worlds to conquer. Perhaps the fiction writers of the future can bring something of the delicate feeling for truth represented in the present volume to bear upon the dramatic inward life of sisters, priests, monks, and nuns. For the present there are these stories, for the most part by those outside convents and monasteries, who have observed with conscience and written with skill about those who are within. Their stories deserve respectful notice and will reward with pleasure those who read them.

## Notes

1. Mariella Gable, O.S.B., *Great Modern Catholic Short Stories* (New York: Sheed & Ward, 1942). Retitled *They Are People*, 1944.

MARIELLA GABLE, 1930S

# Chapter 3

---

# Personality and Catholic Fiction[1]

What is Catholic fiction?  There are two schools of thought on the subject, one taking a catholic view and the other a Catholic view. Or, in other words, a comprehensive view and a specific view.  The purpose of this essay is to present the case for the second of these interpretations, the Catholic and specific.  But before this analysis is given, it is well to glance at the catholic and comprehensive view and to see why it seems necessary to reject it.

The case for the catholic and comprehensive view has been best stated by Sister Madeleva.  Taking a broad view of the whole field of writing, drama and poetry as well as fiction, she has defined Catholic literature as any literature that is treated as a Catholic would treat it. Theoretically, I believe that that definition is beyond dispute, particularly since Sister Madeleva defines the Catholic as one who is perfectly disciplined, a saint.  It is only when one applies this definition as a test to specific pieces of literature that confusion arises. Measure obvious cases like *Tess of the D'Urbervilles* or *Paradise Lost* by this yardstick, and the answer is easy—they are not Catholic.  But ask the question, How would a Catholic have written *Kubla Khan*, *Rip Van Winkle*, or *Alice in Wonderland* and you are immediately confronted with a problem.  You would have to admit, I believe, that the Catholic artist would have written them just as they are.  By this standard, then, much of the world's great literature, though it is in no way concerned with supernatural values or with ethics, much less with the local color of Catholic life, would have to be called Catholic literature. Make a collection of such pieces, label it Catholic literature, hand it to average Catholics, and they will frown in disappointment. This is not what they expected. I believe that the instinctive expectation of the average Catholic is correct.

In no field of writing, however, is the problem of determining what is and what is not Catholic literature so difficult as it is in fiction. It is, perhaps, an act of supererogation to add to the dispute, but I do not believe that a definition of Catholic fiction can be discovered until one has clearly understood the Catholic philosophy of personality. In fact, the correct concept of personality is a smooth spool onto which can be deftly wound all the tangled threads of the problems concerning Catholic fiction. Without it I believe that confusion must persist. If readers accept this view, they have accepted a Catholic and specific view of the problem.

No subject has so fascinated the average person as the modern notion of personality. Everyone wants to believe that they can win friends and influence people—that charm and magnetism are to be had for the asking—if they read the right books and pamphlets. But personality in this popular sense is not our concern here.

St. Teresa was born with a great deal of natural charm and magnetism. She had "personality." But when she reached middle age, our Lord showed her the place in hell which she would occupy for all eternity if she did not change her ways. She became a great saint. She developed her personality in the sense we mean here. Which is not to say that charm and magnetism are matters for eternal damnation, but it is to say that to become a great personality is a very different thing from being a charming individual.

What is a person? A person is the highest thing in nature, according to St. Thomas, and that which distinguishes him from all other beings is his intellect, his reason. Because human beings can know things, they respond to them according to their goodness, and love the good they discover. Knowing and loving, because goodness can be loved only when it is known—these are the special activities of a person, as such. We are all persons. We are not all personalities. One develops personality when one habitually makes an appropriate response to value. Thus has personality been defined by Dietrich von Hildebrand in his excellent study *Liturgy and Personality*.

What does it mean to make an appropriate response to value? It means that all the things we can know are ranged in a hierarchy of being, some deserving less love, some more. It means that we strive to give each thing the love it deserves, and that we are done once and for all with the feverish desire merely to be different. It does away with the romantic emphasis upon the ego. It does not ask: how do I feel about clam chowder and Gothic architecture? do I worship baby pandas and regard moral restraint as silly? It molds the classic personality, essentially noble, admirable, and balanced. A classic personality is never absolutely achieved, but the person striving to attain its perfection habitually endeavors to make an appropriate response to value. Appropriate—that which in the hierarchy of being this particular thing deserves.

Obviously it would be absurd to attempt to explore the whole range of being in order to see what appropriate responses are. But something can be done by way of illustrating the point. What are appropriate responses to nature, to human beings, to God? The classic personality rejoices in the beauties of nature. Its spirit is the spirit of the *Benedicite*—praising God, whose excellence is felt in the clouds, the hills, the streams, the winds. But nature is not honored more than it deserves. The classic personality would certainly not maintain with Wordsworth that "One impulse from a vernal wood / Can teach you more of man, / Of moral evil and of good / Than all the sages can." Nor would the classic personality seek ultimate repose in nature with Thompson's sinner flying from the Hound. Nature betrays only those who ask more of her than she can give. "Nature, poor stepdame, cannot slake my drought." But only a warped personality would seek to drink the happiness all desire at her pools.

The classic personality regards human love and friendship as the highest gifts in the world. Each of us is unique in God's sight. A friend discovers our uniqueness, and there is something God-like in the honor and love bestowed upon the beloved. We are much more tempted to rest in friends or in those loved than in nature. But if we give more than an appropriate response to this value, the value itself betrays us. Our soul will cry out with something of the anguished discovery of Shelley that there is always "The desire of the moth for the star, / of the night before the morrow, / A devotion to something afar / From the sphere of our sorrow." That "something afar" is God. God is the complete satisfaction of our need to know and to love. God is all Truth, utterly lovable. If we stop at less than God, our mistakes can be summarized in Etienne Gilson's memorable words:

No Christian philosopher can ever forget that all human love is a love of God unaware of itself. . . . The question is not how to acquire the love of God, but rather how to make it fully aware of itself, of its object, and of the way it should bear itself toward this object. In this sense we might say that the only difficulty is education, or if you prefer it, re-education of love.

It is this re-education of love that is the main life work of the person struggling to become a great personality. If we cultivate the habit of making an appropriate response to all values along the way, we will aid and not hinder the total response to be made to God's transcendent value.

But God must be known for what God is, or an appropriate response cannot be made. Philosophy and theology tell us, but not so effectively as does Dante, who has made us see what the possession of God in heaven means. In God we shall know all that the universe has ever contained, and knowing it we shall love it. What a metaphor he invents to make us understand! Gazing at the point of light which is God Dante says: "Within its depths I saw ingathered, bound by love in one volume the scattered leaves of all the universe."

The scattered leaves of all the universe—at last all together in a single volume, love the binding—there we have it. Dante's whole *Paradiso* is conceived in terms of personality—knowing and loving. His definition for heaven is this: "Light intellectual full-charged with love, love of true good charged with gladness, gladness that transcendeth every sweetness."

The opportunity lies open to every person to taste that reality experimentally here and now through contemplation—if we are willing to make the effort. If we are not willing to do that, we can take on faith the assertion of those who know experimentally. We must, if we are a Catholic, accept the teaching of the Church that it is so. But to those who live the life of grace, all arguments and proofs cease to be important, for such persons know simply and directly. They have discovered, with Alfred Barrett, S.J., that "The life of grace and glory is the same, / The life of grace is, by another name, / Heaven on earth, and death is but a change / In range— / And nothing strange!"

Nothing strange indeed for the classic personality. That person has not given an inappropriate response to the values here and now, has recognized them for shadows of the Truth and Goodness beyond, and has made, with the mystic Jessica Powers, a discovery and a resolution: "No man can stay / In any golden moment; and no more / Will I let any trick of light betray / Me to a house that is nothing but a door." In fact the classic personality is simply one that never mistakes a door for a house. And the house is our Father's.

Fiction is about people—persons. Catholic fiction is about persons dedicated in a special way to the development of full personality. It will record the dramatic conflict, the success and failure of those who are aware of life as an unbroken obligation to make an appropriate response to value. It is about persons who have accepted the tools of the Catholic Church as the means by which the best possible response can be made. It includes, indeed, all ethical problems upon which the Church has no monopoly whatsoever; but these problems become Catholic when treated from a God-centered point of view.

Catholic fiction of the center will be about saints—about the "little" people in your parish and in mine who in almost every act of the day are making some choice between one value and another. Though failing often, sometimes ignominiously, they will recognize their failure for what it is, a tragic choice of hell for heaven. Almost none of this fiction has been written. *The Star of Satan* by Georges Bernanos is a notable exception. Father Donnisan, modeled somewhat upon the the Curé of Ars, strives to become a saint. But his striving is done in his own peculiar way. It takes a certain color, as it were, from his individuality—as will all the striving in great Catholic fiction. There will be no plaster saints. Even if all the persons in the world attempted to make appropriate responses to value, yet the struggle of each would be amazingly different. The lives of the canonized, only recently being written with fair regard for historical accuracy, might have proved to us long ago that this is so. Life gives us no Barclay Street models. Though Catholic fiction will record both success and failure, the great literature will be that of accomplishment. It is incomparably easier to write of failure than of achievement. In fact, the present problem for all writers is the rediscovery of heroes and how to write of them truly. The world is sick of the vulgar, the borderline cases, the guttersnipes, the derelicts, the fools, the mountebanks, the suckers, and the sinners. The greatest heroes are the saints. The greatest fiction will be about them. *The Song of Bernadette* illustrates this point.

Catholic fiction as thus described we might call fiction of the center. In the present collection it is represented by such stories as Tolstoy's "God Sees the Truth, But Waits" and Bjornson's "The

Father," both of which illustrate the power which suffering has to toss the soul toward God. "Our Lady's Tumbler" demonstrates the manner in which the lowliest endowments may be made a worship of God. Among contemporary writers J.F. Powers writes memorably of the things which really matter. Concerning him a Catholic critic and novelist has written: "He is really a major writer. I would think he is the white hope of the Catholic novel in this country. He has the purity and knowledge that neither myself nor any of the other Catholic writers, so-called, have. It is wonderful to find someone as genuinely and deeply religious as he, who can write so well. He is virtually unique, certainly in this country."

Round the bull's eye of the Catholic fiction of the center are concentric circles of fiction. Some of it deals with the various teachings of the Church—on birth control, for instance, or the teaching of the Church on the race problem. In the present collection three stories deal with the problem of blacks and whites: "The Little Black Boys," "Glory, Glory, Hallelujah," and "The Trouble." So far as the Church is concerned, color is an accident. Just that. Those Catholic theorists who wax eloquent over the "complexity of the problems" are the minimizers who cannot accept the simple teaching that a man is their brother in Christ no matter what his race or color.

Only one story about birth control has been included, "Night in August," by Richard Sullivan.

There is, besides all this, what we might call peripheral fiction, that which does not have a Catholic message but is strong in the local color of life. Albert Eisele's story, "The Brother Who Came," illustrates the type. Its theme is that those who have the least often give the most, as true for Protestants as for Catholics, and equally true for persons with no religion whatsoever. But Eisele uses a Catholic background for what he has to say. "That Heathen Alonzo" is another story of the same type. Every church has its persons who are both pious and mean. That Derleth portrays Aunt May as a strong member of the Rosary Society does not make the story a Catholic story. In fact, I do not see how any of this fiction with a strong background of Catholic atmosphere, and only that, can strictly be called Catholic fiction at all. But I believe that it is important that much of this peripheral fiction be written and that a place be accorded it in any study of Catholic writing. We ought to become adept in our own idiom, to recognize that the local color of Catholic life is a fresh and almost untouched field of writing, and to respect the opportunities it offers the Catholic writer for hitherto unexploited detail.

The place for short fiction is the magazine. That is its normal outlet. That is where it ought to be found wielding, as it might, a much more potent popular influence than do articles and essays. Catholic magazines have failed tragically in their opportunity to present Catholic fiction. There are, first of all, the Catholic magazines which cater to the "pulp" mentality. They pour out miracles, three for a cent, cheaper than dirt. If the Catholic pulps had the writing of Tolstoy's, "God Sees the Truth, But Waits," they would have had momma and the children make a novena for papa. He would never have been sent to Siberia, where suffering made a saint of him. He would have remained "happily" at home, a mediocre Christian. The pulp writers think of themselves as having more pity than God. With the turn of the pen they rescue all and sundry from the cross. I have been told, I do not know how true it is, that Brendan Gill wrote his brilliant story, "The Knife," as a satire upon the fiction of the Catholic pulps. In this story Gill describes a little boy who recently lost his mother, saying his night prayers at his father's knee. At the close of his petitions for blessings on all relatives, the child asks God for a knife. In the night his father goes out and purchases a shining blade for his little son, only to overhear him the next morning assure the slovenly housekeeper that his mother will soon be back. He's going to ask God, for he tried God out on something easy and it worked. There is, of course, nothing for the father to do but explain immediately. Like the father in Gill's story, who has been "kinder" to his son than God, one sees Catholic editors on some far day of reckoning having to make some dreadful explanations to the readers they have fooled.

Catholic philosophy is opposed root and branch to the popular magazine fiction which features only happy-ending stories. The Church has the recipe for the only real happy ending there is. It is contained in her teaching on the mystery of suffering. To make prayer a means to material satisfactions, as if they were the end of all things to be desired, is a terrible betrayal. Life proves its untruth at every turn. Here we have not only a choice of wrong values, but an inversion of values.

The Catholic "slicks" have done no better. Their stories ape the secular slicks. Shallow adventures, the "happy" ending, a rosary or a candle for garnishing and general craftsmanship far below that of the secular magazines is all they have to offer. Their only purpose seems to avoid the lust and sin occasionally exploited in the secular magazines. This is indeed a worthy purpose. But they are like cooks who have the opportunity to serve rich, stuffed peppers and instead offer stale, warmed-over mashed potatoes with a dash of pepper on the top. As if a rosary in a bureau drawer made a Catholic story!

Very few Catholic magazines print "quality" stories. And those that do are able to find very few that have Catholic substance. There are, of course, many reasons why the situation is as it is. Competent Catholic writers are not going to send their stories, rich in Catholic local color or substance, to a Catholic magazine when they can get a far larger check from secular magazines. The curious result of this condition is that the best Catholic stories of our time have appeared in secular magazines. Perhaps this volume may show the Catholic reader what competent Catholic fiction is like.

Very recently, in all justice let it be said, editors of certain Catholic magazines have exerted themselves to the utmost in order to get better stories, recognizing fiction as by far the weakest type of Catholic writing. One wants to cheer their efforts mightily, for they are hampered on two sides—on the one hand by their readers whose taste is abominably undeveloped, and on the other by writers who do not give them what they want.

It is a pity that those who write for Catholic magazines could not be persuaded to develop an art of their own—simple, strong, true—instead of copying the tawdry practice of the pulps and the slicks.

Count Tolstoy might teach us all a valuable lesson. Sometimes it happens that a person who sees only a part of the truth responds to that single ray more completely than the children of light who bask in the full floodlight of truth and have done so since childhood. Tolstoy is such a writer. Coming in middle age with astonishment upon the teaching of the New Testament, he succumbed with mind, heart, and all his strength to Christ's gospel of meekness. Chesterton pointed out that Tolstoy's St. George would never have slain the dragon; he would have given it a saucer of milk and tied a pink ribbon round its neck. Tolstoy never arrived at an orthodox view of the Trinity. It would hardly be possible to find a more curious hodgepodge of heresies than "Tolstoism" contains, ranging all the way from a denial of the immortality of the soul to the theory that all government is evil, yet to what he understood he gave himself entirely. Charity to one's neighbor, the necessity for forgiveness, poverty as the only condition for passing through the needle's eye to happiness—these truths he embraced entirely, living like a poor peasant and practicing the most amazing Christian charity to all those around him.

Moreover, he who had written two of the greatest novels the world has ever seen, *Anna Karenina* and *War and Peace*, turned all his genius to converting the masses. He decided that the tool par excellence for teaching them was the short story. And in his zeal to convert others he produced some of the greatest short stories of all time, written, as was *The Divine Comedy*, for the explicit purpose of propaganda. There is an incandescent glow of charity in them, like nothing else in the whole range of short fiction. Curiously, none of Tolstoy's heretical views contaminated their gospel of love and forgiveness. It is as if one virtue adequately described could flood the outer darkness with light, or at least keep itself safe from all suspicious shadows. Two of the greatest stories of Tolstoy, long recognized as world classics, are here included. Incidentally, there is nothing in these stories which would make them less acceptable to Protestants than to Catholics. They are essentially Christian. The same is true of all the stories by the great continental Europeans: Bjornson, Coppée, Lagerlöf. Furthermore, there is a power and simplicity in all these stories and a universality which contrasts sharply with stories by English, Irish, and American authors.

As has been pointed out, then, in this volume [*Our Father's House*] are stories of the Catholic center, those which are, in its narrowest and most indisputable sense, Catholic short stories. Along with them are stories which demonstrate how deeply founded in the natural law are the teachings of the Church on birth control and the race problem. There are, furthermore, a large number of stories which are of interest to Catholics only because of their strong Catholic local color. In perusing them readers will discover that large areas of Catholic life remain unexplored in these stories. This lacuna is not the fault of the compiler. Competent writers have barely scratched the surface of Catholic life as material for fiction. If *Our Father's House* calls attention to this great untouched reservoir of inspiration at the same time demonstrating the excellence that can be attained by tapping its reserves, then one objective of the compiler will be realized.

The stories have been arranged in what seems to be a simple order, beginning with stories of children, followed by those of youth and ignorance, and concluded by stories which have profound and mature implications. Some of the stories of children are, however, as profound as any in the book.  The artistic excellence of all these stories has already won for them an acclaim which transcends a Catholic audience.  Art speaks a universal language, and though these stories have been collected for the convenience of Catholic readers, their charm and perfection will continue to bring pleasure to all who read them.


## Notes

1. Mariella Gable, O.S.B., "Introduction," *Our Father's House* (New York: Sheed & Ward, 1945).  Reprinted in Mariella Gable, *This is Catholic Fiction* (New York: Sheed & Ward, 1948).

# Chapter 4

## Introduction to *Many-Colored Fleece*[1]

This book is the third series of anthologies in which I have collected short stories which ought, for one reason or another, to be of special interest to Catholics. For the sake of convenience they will be referred to hereafter as Catholic fiction.

Because art speaks a universal language the appeal of these stories is, however, not limited to Catholics. This fact is attested by their publication in secular magazines, ranging all the way from *Horizon*, the *Atlantic*, and *The New Yorker* to *The Woman's Home Companion*, and in books, not one of which was brought out by a Catholic publisher. Only two of the stories in this volume made a first appearance in Catholic magazines.

The role of an anthologist is important as both a salvager and a critic.

An anthologist is first and foremost one who salvages for countless readers what would otherwise be lost to them. Since our best Catholic fiction continues to appear in secular magazines, widely divergent in type and locale, most of it would be lost to the general reader unless it were collected and made easily accessible. And since the Catholic writers who have published single volumes of fine short stories often include many secular stories, there is need for selecting their Catholic stories and collecting them, along with the best from magazines, in a volume such as this.

Moreover, by the very act of selecting the best that has been written, and making it generally known, the anthologist brings strong influence to bear upon taste and upon the direction of new developments.

The second function of the anthologist is to be a critic, particularly a constructive one. Where the fiction writer hypnotizes, it is "the function of criticism to supply the sharp sound that awakens us." The critic sees beyond the achievement of the present, which in Catholic fiction is only a vigorous beginning, to the vast undeveloped potentialities of the future. The critic indicates what are the unsolved problems of Catholic fiction, and examines the literary temper of the present as well as the social milieu in order to see whether or not we have an appropriate climate in which to solve our problems.

To begin with the last. Never since the popular development of prose fiction, about two centuries ago, have we had a climate so favorable as we have now for the development of Catholic fiction. The western world has tried to live without God. The result is such chaos, bitterness, and despair that the world, both Catholic and Protestant, is experiencing a profound spiritual revival. Humanity stands terrified and starving, arms out begging, as it were, for great fiction of spiritual affirmation.

It asks and asks for the power of such an art. I use the word "power" advisedly. For this word calls our attention at once to the peculiar role of fiction as compared to non-fiction. DeQuincey in his essay, *The Literature of Knowledge and the Literature of Power*, named the distinction between the two: Non-fiction is like the rudder on a boat; without the knowledge of truth one cannot steer straight. But fiction is like the sail or the engine; without it there is not power to move. Our spiritual revival has produced a magnificent body of non-fiction, ranging all the way from the profound philosophical contributions of Jacques Maritain to Thomas Merton's popular odyssey of a soul. That is as it should be; nobody wants a boat without a rudder. But a rudder is not enough. If we had a comparable Catholic fiction, the power and might of a great spiritual wind would move the world to stunned astonishment.

Not only are people psychologically ready for a fiction of spiritual affirmation, but they are also due to be helped by the very science which has so long deceived them into thinking that technology could make them happy. Science and religion could never, of course, really be in conflict with each other, for truth is one; and if science goes far enough, it must support and confirm religion. We are, at the moment, on the threshold of such a development, as has been pointed out by the eminent scientist, Dr. Charles Steinmetz, in his forecast for the science of the next fifty years. Says Dr. Steinmetz:

> I think the greatest discoveries will be made along the spiritual lines. Some day people will learn that material things will not bring happiness and are of little use in making men and women creative and powerful. Then the scientists of the world will turn their laboratories over to the study of God and prayer and the spiritual forces which, as yet, have been hardly scratched. When that day comes the world will see more advancement in one generation than it has seen in the last four.

We have, of course, already turned our laboratories over to such study, though the drift of psychiatry has scarcely been recognized as yet for what it is: a powerful movement of science toward religion. For as soon as we begin to ask what makes people tick, what makes them happy, what makes life tolerable or intolerable to human beings, we are bound to end up with God. Regrettable as was the pan-sexualism of Freud, he was still asking the right questions. Psychiatry has steadily gone forward in its correction of his wrong answers. Science will ultimately reveal that the only sound psychology in the world must be built up on the rock-bottom truth expressed by St. Augustine: "Thou hast made our hearts for Thee, O God, and they are restless (psychotic, neurotic) until they rest in Thee." Science is moving faster than we realize toward a new synthesis with religion.

At the same time the development of secular fiction has arrived at the point where either it will die or become profoundly spiritual. The great Spanish philosopher, Ortega y Gasset, has stated this point by defining modern fiction as "mature." Avenues of experiment on the natural level have all been explored. For the future there can be only the cultivation of techniques accompanied by diminishing vitality.

The need for freshness in fiction has been a progressive movement downward toward an ever lower, sub-human, animal interpretation of humanity, culminating in naturalism. The smart young men who were its purveyors "thought they were being sophisticated when they were only unbuttoned." Mere exhibitionism won by shock what art earns by blood and tears.

But nastiness and perversion are not infinite in variety. In spite of contemporary interest in psychiatry, minute analyses of degenerates, homosexuals, introverts, pathological personalities, sadists, masochists, cretins, and idiots have become intolerably boring. Naturalism is dead.

But freshness is a necessity of art. Jean Cocteau, in writing to Jacques Maritain, gave us a profound statement concerning it:

> The need of change in art is nothing other than the need of finding a fresh place on the pillow. Put your head on the fresh spot, it soon ceases to be so; newness is freshness. The need for novelty is the need for freshness. God is the only freshness that never grows warm.

God is not only the only freshness that never grows warm; God is the only unexplored freshness left to the writer of fiction. Fiction has gone as far away from God as it can go. There is no unexplored nastiness, perversion, or animality. Either fiction will bring God in, or perish in stagnation.

Nor is this alternative like the others: today mysticism; yesterday romanticism, realism, humanism and all the rest. We are not here dealing with just another cool spot on the pillow—a new area of experience, a new angle of vision. We are here concerned with a new dimension.

And this brings us to the heart of the distinction between secular and Catholic fiction. Even Catholics have wrongly supposed that Catholic fiction is limited, narrower in its subject matter, curbed and curtailed in what it may do. The fact is: Secular fiction is limited. Catholic fiction is unlimited; it embraces all reality. Secular fiction is one-dimensional; Catholic fiction is three-dimensional.

Let me explain. Fiction is about people. Take any drawing-room full of people. The first reality with which we are confronted is the individuality of all present. God never repeats himself. God manifests something on the mystery of fecundity as a Creator in the infinite variety of human beings—no two on the face of the earth precisely alike. In our drawing-room are the witty, the depressed, the insecure, the amicable, the lonely, the garrulous, the silent. But one witty person differs from another witty person, one silent man from another inarticulate one as color differs from color. Yet they are all bound by the bond of coloredness—the mystery of the one and the many. Moreover, a psychological and social chemistry takes place whereby color fades into color or clashes with it. Traditional fiction has been sociological. It has dealt with the relationship of one human being to another. It has interpreted the many-coloredness of the human beings in society—whether transcending their environment or becoming victims of it. It has dealt with the reality of a material world, and in doing so has projected a fiction of one dimension.

But there is another reality in that drawing-room. Every person present is either in a state of grace or of damnation. In other words, hell and heaven are present in the room. A fiction which extends its boundaries to include this reality is eschatological, besides being sociological. It is three-dimensional. Three-dimensional fiction embraces all planes of reality. It extends boundaries.

Graham Greene's distinction is that he has done more than any other contemporary writer of fiction in English (the French have, of course, gone farther) to extend these boundaries. *The Heart of the Matter* is eschatological. People cared tremendously whether Scobie was damned or saved. His plight was argued by the literary elite and callow youth—at cocktail parties, in bars, in monastery parlors, and over Cokes in drugstores. Greene has only faintly indicated, however, the amazing complexity of human psychology in three-dimensional fiction. In further exploration of this psychology lies the one clear avenue for development of fiction.

The title of this collection of stories symbolizes the complexity of three-dimensional fiction. It suggests the many-colored individuality of human beings as they manifest themselves to each other, but it is many-colored *fleece*. Fleece, for we are all God's sheep, in reality either black sheep or white sheep, no matter what brilliant hues of red, or blue, or gold we exhibit to the world. If the title seems to put the emphasis on the color rather than the fleece, it is because our Catholic fiction is still largely in the mode of a one-dimensional art. Yet there is the clear indication of a strong development in the apprehension of spiritual values—as the stories in this volume indicate.

In the Middle Ages when human thinking was popularly and predominantly eschatological, fiction assumed the form of allegory. The spiritual reality was more important than human individuality. In medieval allegory the characters were only symbols—often dehumanized.

The question arises as to whether or not we can expect at the present time a return to allegory. Really, it raises a larger question which must be answered first: a question which involves the whole relationship of substance and form. We have witnessed, during the past three decades, the emergence of the New Critics, such men as Yvor Winters, I.A. Richards, William Empson, Robert Penn Warren, Kenneth Burke and others. One of their sound contributions to literary criticism, and one on which they are fairly unanimous, though they differ in so many other respects, is their conviction that substance and form are integral. Form is not something added. It is not a style, not a decorative metaphor, not a glove on the hand. Form and substance are one.

Furthermore, they have been preoccupied with an analysis of contemporary literature as communicating human loss of faith, human loss of God. Its form is chaotic, disturbed, often unintelligible, reflecting in its mode of expression the thing it expresses.

The way, therefore, to not be a great Catholic writer is to sit at the feet of contemporary artists and study their form. The craft of the God-less cannot be the craft of the God-filled. The substance expressed will always determine the form of expression.

Nor is it a matter of indifference, in so far as artistic excellence is concerned, what the substance is. T.S. Eliot has expressed this truth with memorable accuracy. It ought to be burned into the consciousness of every Catholic critic, for *mirable dictu*, we still have many of them who maintain that the whatness of the thing communicated is unimportant if the howness is artistically correct. Here is T.S. Eliot's statement: "The greatness of literature cannot be determined *solely* by literary standards; though we must remember whether it is literature or not can be determined only by literary standards."

I should like to go farther and state the same in positive terms: The greatness of literature can be determined by the degree to which a three-dimensional substance is integrated with perfect artistic expression. But the artistic expression of three-dimensional content can never be in the same mode of expression as one-dimensional content, for substance and form are one. A three-dimensional fiction lays greater demands on the artist *qua artist* than does one-dimensional fiction. Catholic writers must be greater artists than their secular confreres. And by the standards of pure art three-dimensional fiction must be a greater fiction.

Will it, then, return to allegory as an appropriate form? It has already done so. The new interest in allegory ranges all the way from the heretical existentialism of Jean Paul Sartre to the mildly inadequate excursion into the symbolism of Purgatory by Anthony West. But perhaps most illuminating for our purposes is the allegory of Franz Kafka (1883-1924). Kafka was a God-smitten man. Strongly influenced by Kierkegaard's minute study of the "razor-edge decision" of human free will which determines a personal relation to God, he has written allegories which explore the complex psychology of faith. A strong Kafka cult among the literary elite testifies to the contemporary human hunger for God. Though Kafka never arrived at an orthodox theology, his preoccupation with God and with the human need for submission to God found appropriate expression only in the form of allegory. Esoteric to a degree, his allegory seems scarcely fourth-cousin to the simple, and easily equatable medieval allegory.

But this is as it should be, for cycles of literary trends never repeat exactly. Yet there are cycles. According to Sorokin, there are three: First, an ideational art, highly spiritual in content, which normally expresses itself in allegory; second, an idealistic art which unites the best of the spiritual with a full and faithful portrayal of humanity in all its fascinating individuality; and third, a sensist art which gradually eliminates all spiritual values until it exhausts itself in decadence. We have just lived through the third; the first is again due.

But the first, allegory, is not three-dimensional. The third is not three-dimensional. Only the second is three-dimensional—and it is, by all odds, the greatest and the most to be desired. And by some strange accident of acceleration in our own day we seem to have moved very swiftly past allegory into the second. To return to *The Heart of the Matter*: Scobie is an individual, not an allegorical abstraction.

But perhaps in a very specific sense, we as Catholics have served a longer apprenticeship in allegory than we realize. The countless number of undistinguished, but "edifying" stories in the popular Catholic magazines are essentially allegories, for they sacrifice the truth of human nature to the purposes of pious teaching. Of course, allegory is a type which can be either good or bad, great or poor. Yet, on the whole, it is small praise of God to ignore our first-dimensional world in which the infinite variety and immeasurable complexity of human nature testify to God's creative fecundity.

Dante is our greatest Catholic writer and one of the few great poets in the world. His art, for all its intricate symbolism, is three-dimensional. He knew exactly how to unite an eschatological and a sociological emphasis. He knew how to communicate the Hell of sin and the Heaven of grace without ever sacrificing the human individuality of his characters.

He placed his beloved teacher, Brunetto Latini, in Hell for being a homosexual. But how does he depict Brunetto as he walks and talks with him under the rain of burning flakes? As cultivated, charming, intelligent, affectionately devoted to his most gifted student, noble, lovable and indescribably individual. He does more. When Brunetto explains that most of the homosexuals are highly cultivated, professional people, he has pin-pointed a nexus between individuality, the profession it chooses, and the moral failure stemming from that peculiar combination. Modern writers of three-dimensional fiction could well sit at Dante's feet. We need to see how the three dimensions touch and affect each other.

We not only need to see how the three dimensions interlock, but also, and this is perhaps our greatest unsolved problem, we need to interpret the dimension of goodness with artistic integrity. The psychology of goodness is very rarely explored with anything like the artistic success that commonly distinguishes the analysis of evil or of spiritual failure. Here the techniques are, for the most part, still undiscovered. Here lies the challenge to the artist of the future.

Consider the dichotomy as it now exists: Most of the people we know are orientated toward goodness; most of the people in fiction are orientated toward evil. St. Augustine remarked in the *City of God*, Book XI, Chapter 9: "Evil has no positive nature; but the loss of good has received the name evil." In the art of literature it would seem to be the other way round.

We know how difficult it is to write of goodness convincingly. The intention to present the side of the angels is never enough. Milton meant to argue God's cause, but his devils are magnificent, while God the Father and God the Son talk like two smug Presbyterian ministers sipping tea before a fire-place. Artistically they are a failure; artistically the evil in his poem comes off with stunning success.

In other words, as soon as human beings begin to write fiction, these souls have joined a nudist colony and strange revelations are made. Kenneth Burke puts it this way: "A writer may *profess* allegiance to a certain cause, for instance, but you find on going over his work that the *enemies* of his cause are portrayed with greater vividness than its advocates." Here is the truth about his profession of belief.

It is simply a fact that if we want our good characters to be as artistically successful as our villains, we must have holy writers. This fact is not news to the critics. Usually it is stated something like this: Artists cannot write what they thinks they ought to say but only what is dictated to them by their deepest subconscious and conscious natural allegiance.

If, then, we are to have a successful fiction which gives us an acceptable psychology of goodness—an art which moves the reader to accept the good as lovable—then we must have writers who have made some progress in the spiritual life.

Such a fiction will certainly not be dull. It will, in fact, be most exciting, for the sharpest conflict in the world begins to take place the moment a soul sets out to seek God in earnest. Self immediately kicks and screams for the center of attention. And if somewhat flouted in the struggle, self-seeking can disguise itself in a million ways to look like God-seeking. The fiction of the future which will present a sound psychological analysis of the struggle will be a new kind of who-done-it, a mystery thriller with all the suspense of an Erle Stanley Gardner, plus a substance and reality, which will make most contemporary fiction seem intolerably shallow and dull—which it is.

I had hoped, in this volume, to illustrate the kind of fiction about which I am writing by including the brilliant story, "Brother Ass," by the well-known South American writer Eduardo Barrios. Its length (it is a short novel) and some other considerations made it impossible to do so. But the reader is strongly encouraged to investigate this story, which may be found in the volume called *Fiesta in November*, edited by Flores and Poore, and published by Houghton Mifflin, 1942. In the first place, its method is exactly right. The center of interest is the soul of Brother Lazaro—what takes place between himself and God. The entire story is in the form of a diary, which Lazaro addressed to God. But Lazaro is, like so many of us, a romantic egoist, and he fools himself into thinking he is seeking God when he is seeking himself. Since this is the great, universal mistake made by those who fail in the spiritual struggle, and often made for many years by those who succeed, and since this story is artistically of the first order, it is unquestionably a classic which will become well-known as time goes on. Already accepted by the Latin

Americans, they have taken it to their hearts as one of the great stories of the world.

It points up, moreover, a distinction that needs to be made, the distinction between stories which deal with spiritual problems as different from ethical problems. In life there are many areas of experience. The most neglected area of experience in fiction is that which deals directly with the human search for God—the good person trying to unite self with God here and now by knowing and loving in contemplation and in doing God's will. What happens between the soul and God? Everyone wants to know. But the task of fiction is not only to give the information, but to impart on the level of pure art the vicarious experience.

It is true, of course, that spiritual experience is bound up closely with ethical problems. But the barrenness of much fiction in the past stems from the fact that ethical experiences are examined only on the natural level—are seen in terms of only the first dimension.

But in much bad Catholic fiction a different fault has predominated. Good characters are presented as being in a state of simon-pure goodness. A holy character is never even tempted to pride, envy, anger, sloth, avarice, gluttony, or lust. In other words, this Catholic fiction assumes that a certain amount of goodness transfers the character from the state of original sin to some Eden-like perfection never seen on land or sea. The presupposition is heretical. What we need in the new psychology of goodness is plain honesty—the kind of truthfulness which makes "The Devil in the Desert" a fine story. Here Father Louis is a hero, but we see that pride, anger, and wilfulness are the defects of his virtue.

Artists might long ago have taken a hint from the liturgy and from Scripture—especially from the psalms. There we see human beings rising and falling alternately. At one moment they are full of trust in God, at another they are despairing; at one moment yhey adore, in the next he has sinned and strike their breast. Their soul day after day makes contact with both the second and the third dimension. But how they tick when they move toward goodness, what their spiritual problems are as they make three steps forward and two back, this is the area of experience in which lies the development of future fiction. But if it is written for edification at the expense of truth, or if the writing springs from the desire to create what ought to be written rather than from deep compulsion, then it has already failed.

Though we look forward to a new fiction in which spiritual success will be communicated as effectively as failure, we must realize that negative fiction often carries a tremendously positive impact. In fact, the story of failure is often like the hole in the wall, without which we could not *see* the thickness, strength, and solidity of the masonry. For instance, the great story on birth control, "Missis Flinders." In it a husband and wife have freed themselves from the troubles, expense, and responsibility of parenthood by an abortion. Apparently unhampered by any religious scruples, they suffer frightfully in their subtle contempt of each other. They have broken a natural law, and nature punishes them. Since many Catholics feel that Mother Church is hard on them in holding immovably to her legislation against birth control, it is well to see from what horrors, even on the natural level, the apparently rigorous ruling saves her children. The strength and thickness of the protecting wall could scarcely have been seen unless a hole in it had been exposed by what we call negative fiction.

Let no one suppose, however, that I hold a personal preference for negative fiction. In making the selections for this book, as well as for the two preceding anthologies, I have always chosen the positive story, where the quality of writing has permitted such an alternative. Sometimes anthologists are blamed for not including stories which have not as yet been written. But perhaps they can cause them to be written by collecting the best which have appeared up to the present moment and appreciating their achievement, thus forming a strong beach-head for further conquest of unsolved problems.

Along with learning to portray the psychology of goodness on the spiritual level successfully, the Catholic fiction of the future must move its center of focus from nuns, monks, and priests to the layperson. If one judges by extant fiction one must arrive at the conclusion that religion is the nearly exclusive possession of the clergy. Here there is an almost incredible lag between reality and art. For the most important aspect of the great Catholic revival, in the midst of which we are living, is the discovery of the Catholic layperson.

For the first time in history all the techniques of the spiritual life which were formerly regarded as proper only to monks and nuns have been taken over generally by average people in the world. Spiritual reading, for instance. Our age will be remembered for its spate of brilliant and readable spiritual books which are read eagerly by layperson.   Laypeople are understanding and participating in the liturgy.   Forty years ago one could not have bought a Missal if one had wanted to.   Now the layperson commonly assists at Mass by following the service.   They meditate; they understand that contemplation is the normal fruit of Christian life, not an esoteric delicacy reserved for Trappists and Carmelites.   They savor in a new way the whole meaning of the Christian life and the sacraments.

They are becoming increasingly aware of the terrifying incompatibility between the pagan society in which they live and their Christian responsibility.   Many of them are developing a union with God, a charity, a spirit of abnegation which would put many religious to shame.   All around us we see beautiful Christian families where the deepest type of spiritual growth is manifest, where there has been a complete shedding of the whole deplorable shuck of externalism so common for generations.

Cardinal Suhard begged for "great daring, originality, and novelty" in making the treasures of the faith accessible to all. Catholic laypeople have manifested their charity in a stunning diversity of apostolates:  Friendship House, *The Catholic Worker*, the cell movement, the editing of *Commonweal, Integrity, Today*, the apostolate for the Negro, the poor, the neglected wherever they are. Laypeople have responded wholeheartedly to clerical leadership in such movements as Cana conferences and the Christophers.

But for the most part, this new Christian vitality in family life has been left unexplored by the writers of Catholic fiction.  A notable exception is Jill O'Nan, whose story "A Table Before Me," with its thoughtful consideration of the problems involved in rearing a Christian family within a worldly environment, stands alone in the present collection, as representative of a fresh development capable of a great yield in fiction about laypeople.

Meanwhile there is an alarming gap between reality and art. Father Reinhold complained recently that America is the most clerical of Catholic countries.   I do not know whether America is actually more clerical than Ireland, but the fact remains that in English writing the Catholic story is almost inevitably a story of the clergy.   When the *Cosmopolitan* recently advertised on its cover that it was serializing "the first great novel of Catholic life," it was a foregone conclusion that the story would be about the hierarchy.   One student recently asked, "*Must* Catholic fiction be about priests or nuns?"

It might well be that *They Are People* did something to crystallize that impression.  The publication of that anthology of short stories about nuns, monks, and priests in 1942 was the fruit of long searching for stories of quality which gave a fairly accurate portrayal of religious life. Now such stories can be had for a dime a dozen. In making this book it would have been a simple matter to collect a volume of them and turn them over to the public under the title, *More People.*

But such editing would have added impetus to a tendency which ought to be stemmed. In 1942 there was every reason to rejoice at the kind of story which appeared in *They Are People.* The stories in that book marked a great advance in Catholic fiction. In the past, fiction had depicted convents as cemeteries for broken hearts. If a monk so much as saw a maiden, he fell in love. It was a matter of significant progress that we began to get a realistic interpretation of conventual life, in spite of the fact that the stories dealt for the most part with surface appearances rather than with the depth of spiritual problems. I wrote in the "Introduction" to these stories: "The things of the spirit are for the most part revealed only obliquely. The story of the future will present them directly."

The story of the future will present the relationship of human beings to God directly, not only in so far as monks, nuns, and priests are concerned, but more especially in so far as the layperson is concerned. Laypeople themselves will have to break the bad tradition they have created. The very strange thing about all these stories of nuns, monks, and priests is that they are written by laypeople. We cannot accuse the clergy of lifting a single pen point to keep themselves in the limelight, except in the recent *Vessel of Clay* by Father Trese. The persistent preoccupation of laypeople with the clergy as the only subject for religious art may well testify to strong clerical influence in social consciousness.

Since one of the basic laws of art is that the writer must create out of personal experience, it would seem axiomatic that laypeople would write of their own spiritual problems. Of course, there is this to be said: human nature remains the same no matter how thickly covered by cassock, cowl, or habit. Out of the firm conviction that he could not go astray if he remembered that churchmen are human beings, Anthony Trollope created the memorable portraits of Anglican bishops and minor clergymen which have made the Barchester novels cherished classics. Yet they are only one-dimensional. Since the laypeople are fast achieving a spiritual adulthood and learning first-hand what are the conflicts, problems, costs, and rewards of the spiritual life, and since these are the same in "religion" or out of it, they can, of course, give us a more profound art—if they wish to continue their interest in the clergy.

But laypeople ought to write of themselves. Here is the unexplored area of experience. They ought to bridge the gap between their spiritual struggles and Catholic art. There are countless beautiful Christian families where matrimony is lived as a sacrament every day, all day. Where large families are accepted in a Christian spirit in spite of nearly insurmountable economic handicaps. Where in the bosom of the family an intelligent and loving spirituality is being developed through family worship, through a complete participation in the liturgical life of the Church, but most of all through a vital discovery of the Beatitudes. No longer do these people ask: what do I get out of this? They ask: what can I give? They practice an astonishing charity. Could those among them to whom God has given the gift to write be persuaded to communicate their experience? To close their eyes firmly upon the bad tradition in Catholic art which has not dared to explore the psychology of goodness realistically? To share on the level of artistic creation the violent conflicts they suffer in learning to build Christian homes in a pagan society?

Recently an average white-collar worker, the father of four children, wrote, after reading von Hildebrand's *Transformation in Christ*: "I actually wept over my own barren state. To be even a mediocre Christian this day and age calls for a superhuman effort of the will and intellect. Most Catholics, including myself, labor and live in a world completely given over to materialism, peopled with creatures whose only god is self . . . To live in this kind of world and associate with its people and at the same time *to try* to live a life in Christ calls for heroic fortitude."

Where are the Catholic writers who will communicate to us in a worthy art this heroic fortitude? All around us it exists. All around us are lay apostles embracing voluntary poverty. All around us lies the reality out of which a great and noble fiction might be made. Yet the laypeople will not look within themselves; they prefer to perpetuate the dress-parade of nuns, monks, and priests.

Perhaps we will have to wait for the next generation. Out of our new Christian homes must come a great Catholic fiction. By the very law of averages some of the children will be born with the gift to write. The depth and strength of their own spiritual life will be such that in merely expressing what they need to say, they will communicate the highest reality we know, the person's contemplative experience of God. The as-yet-unthought-of form will be born as part of the bright and burning splendor of the art which makes articulate this transcendent experience. Until that generation comes with its great Catholic art (and I firmly believe it is coming), those who have not the gift to write, create the fiction of the future by creating the homes from which it must come.

In the meantime there will be many books, each one moving a little closer to the goal. Among them is this anthology, *Many-Colored Fleece.* Whenever literary quality made it possible I gave preference to the stories of laypeople over stories about nuns, monks, and priests. Yet the clergy are in the majority. This clerical preponderance, however, interferes in no way with the entertainment value of these stories. Perhaps enjoyment is even increased, for there is the perennial curiosity of laypeople to peer behind the serge curtain and discover the secrets of parsonage and cloister.

Looking at this book from the viewpoint of contemporary secular standards, it seems to me that it exhibits a general high level of literary proficiency, a much higher-than-usual level of entertainment, and a humor so dominant that one is forced to consider the place of humor in Catholic fiction.

Is humor an element that must of necessity be part of Catholic art? Perhaps yes. The incongruous incites to laughter. In spite of people's high dedication as children of God, they still remain weak and human and full of vagaries. They are like kings and queens in royal robes who seven times a day slips on the banana peel of their weak human nature. Viewed from one angle their failure is uproariously funny. From another it is immeasurably serious and gives a resonance and spiritual significance to one's concept of human nature. Only a noble view of human nature can be humorous. There is nothing funny about an art which depicts human beings as falling off the floor.

Particularly representative of the humor which ranges from gay to wry and ironic are the stories, "Song Without Words," "Santa Lucia," "Unholy Living and Half Dying," "The Road to the Shore," "Trouble With the Union," and "Prefect of Discipline." Yet perhaps even more significant is the flavor of humor which pervades a solemn study of conscience like "The Reluctant Hangman," or the pure poetry of "Brother Boniface," or the fantasticalities of "Yung Mari Li."

Looking over the contents of this book from a different point of view (or is it the same?) one cannot but be struck by the predominance of Irish authors. Irish writers seem to find the form of the short story much more congenial than do authors of other nations. To begin with, there are the big five: Frank O'Connor, Sean O'Faolain, Michael McLaverty, Bryan MacMahon, and Mary Lavin. Though Mary Lavin was born in America, she returned with her parents at the age of ten to Ireland where she has lived since, and to all intents and purposes is regarded along with the other Irish-born authors, who have published, not just occasional fiction in magazines, but volumes of distinguished short stories.

In America only two Catholic authors have published comparable volumes and both of them are Irish: J.F. Powers, well known for *Prince of Darkness*, traces his lineage directly back to the auld sod, while W. B. Ready, whose volume of short stories, *Barring the Weight*, will be published in 1951, is a Cardiff Irishman.

In England both Graham Greene and Evelyn Waugh have published books of short stories, but there are two things to be noted of their volumes: both men are primarily novelists whose shorter fiction is secondary; Waugh's short stories are completely innocent of Catholic substance, while the Catholic interest in Greene's short stories is very infrequent. As Catholic short story writers they scarcely rank with the Irish.

To turn from the Irish writers, who have published volumes of short stories, to those who publish occasionally in magazines, we find that here again the Irish practically have a corner on short fiction with a special Catholic interest. To mention just a few: Paul Horgan, Richard Sullivan, Dennis Harrington, Joseph W. Carroll, Brendan Gill—and one can make a safe bet that if it's a new Catholic writer of promise, the odds are five to one that he is Irish.

Finally, there is the basic question: Are the stories in this volume three-dimensional? The degree to which a second and third dimension can be made manifest in fiction varies greatly. Elsewhere I have defined the categories of Catholic fiction by means of a symbol, that of a target, showing that Catholic fiction ranges all the way from peripheral, giving only the externals of Catholic local color, to that which is God-centered and hits the bull's eye. The critical essays in which I have described these categories have been published by Sheed and Ward under the title *This Is Catholic Fiction*. There seems no valid reason for redefining them here.

It does seem necessary, however, to repeat the fact that a story which is rich in the local color of Catholic life without any further spiritual significance is only one-dimensional, or at best suggests by indirection the existence of a second and third dimension. Some of the stories in this book, such as "The Road to the Shore," "Prefect of Discipline," and "Barring the Weight," utterly charming in their human insights, are of this peripheral variety. I think it important, however, to cherish this fiction which depends for its appeal on the local color of Catholic life, giving us on the natural level the precise flavor and atmosphere of daily life in the bosom of Mother Church. Catholic artists are only beginning to mine this heretofore unexplored rich vein of experience. The more we have of it in literature the sooner we will outgrow our feeling of inferiority and begin to feel at home in the cultural mores with which the Church surrounds the life of a Catholic.

But it is also important that we do not overestimate this one-dimensional fiction and place it in the same category with fiction of spiritual depth. *Many-Colored Fleece* opens and closes with two strong stories which come to grips directly with the basic problem of good and evil. "The Devil in the Desert" and "The Hint of an Explanation" are as different as two stories can be, yet both say something significant about the same problem which drew into being *Paradise Lost* and *Prometheus Unbound*. Between these two stories the whole range of human individuality as it is wedded to various ethical and spiritual experiences is fairly well covered. Yet there is no story which hits the bull's eye directly as would have "Brother Ass," if that story might have been included. The fiction which communicates humanity's experience in its serious effort to keep the first commandment has not as yet been written—except, in the highest ranges, by Bernanos in his novels.

But much that comes close to hitting the precise spiritual center has been written, and in order to assist the reader in discovering to what degree the second and third dimensions have been touched, critical notes have been prepared to stand at the head of each story. For those who resent preliminary critical judgment, there is the simple expedient of skipping.

Not all the stories lend themselves to groupings. But some of them do. For instance, there are the stories which interpret the commonest Christian experience: turning to God in prayer of petition under the pressure of suffering or acute need. Does God suspend the natural laws of the universe and answer such prayers by working a miracle? Four stories in this volume approach this same problem from different angles. They are "Santa Lucia," "The Miracle of Tepayac," "Baa-Baa, Black Sheep," and "The Knife." "The Miracle of Tepayac" is John Steinbeck's flawless retelling of the apparition of Our Lady of Guadalupe, based carefully on fact. Here the heavens open and, without any petition from poor Juan, the miraculous surrounds him as dazzlingly as it did the three apostles on the Mount of the Transfiguration. Fittingly, it stands as an indisputable affirmation in this group of stories, which are concerned entirely with characters who have a profound faith in God's miraculous intervention in their affairs. What happens to them presents appropriate variety: one miraculous answer to prayer, one chilling negation, and two doubtful cases. But because the stories are artistically right, they open depth upon depth of insight transcending any abstract statement of the spiritual problems they explore.

To turn to a different group, five stories throw some light on marriage: "Prothalamion," "Missis Flinders," "I Took Thee, Constance," "The Little Girls," and "A Table Before Me." "Missis Flinders," a remarkably strong story on the problem of birth control, and "I Took Thee, Constance," which underlines with striking originality the strength of the bonds of the sacrament of matrimony, are flanked on either side by "Prothalamion" and "The Little Girls" for reasons which readers are invited to discover for themselves.

Then there is the race problem. In this country it concentrates itself largely around the Negro, simply because Jim Crowism has taught us to suppose that pigmentation prevents people from being human beings like their white brothers and sisters. Exactly like. No less, no more. Two stories throw light upon this problem: "Saturday Nocturne" and "Home." In the first of these we see the problem as it is apprehended in the parsonage, where two priests find themselves in disagreement as to methods for ameliorating racial prejudice. In spite of the young priest's zeal for action, one cannot but feel that the full horror and criminal injustice suffered by his black brothers in Christ is only dimly realized. "Home," a stark story of lynching, shocks the reader into full awareness. It is the hope of the editor that no one will ask why a story like "Home" finds a place among Catholic stories. Both it and "Missis Flinders" communicate the reality of a natural law upon which the Church has built legislation.

A brief view of the personnel functioning in Catholic educational institutions is provided by "Barring the Weight," "Gingerbread," and "Prefect of Discipline."

"Trouble With the Union" is the only story which embodies the Christian attitude on labor problems, and "Yung Mari Li," the only one which deals with the problem of bringing a stray sheep back into the fold. Any zealous priest looking for practical pastoral hints will, however, have to look elsewhere for guidance—for only in a globe-time would such fantastic methods for winning the back-slider be invented or attempted by a pastor. Also among the single stories is "The Reluctant Hangman," a classic statement concerning the primacy of conscience.

Finally, three stories stand as a climax to this anthology, stories which probe the experiences of old age and death. Age and death are two of the least attractive words in the English language and might well frighten away the reader who is looking for entertainment. The fact of the matter is, however, that the fullness of life on its most meaningful level as well as on its most human and entertaining, has been distilled in these stories. There is the broad humor of "Unholy Living and Half Dying," the zest and vitality of "The Jilting of Granny Weatherall," and the pure poetry of "Brother Boniface." But over and above all that makes these stories lovable as interpretations of the natural world, there is the clear vision of a second and third dimension giving to life as well as to death appropriate significance.

The making of this book has been a communal project. Interested readers of *They Are People* and *Our Father's House* have sent short stories from England, Ireland, Australia, Canada and the United States. For all of these stories, both those which were not suitable for inclusion and those which were, I am deeply grateful. Out of an alert and constructive spirit of cooperation must come a climate in which a three-dimensional art will flourish. I thank the authors and publishers who have given their kind permission to reprint the stories in this volume, and the generous people who have assisted the editor with typing, proof-reading, and critical advice.

Before conquest there is always the laborious building of the beach-head. In literature I believe this initial establishing of a foot-hold is accomplished by appreciation for what has been accomplished, along with the firm refusal to regard a beach-head as a continent. In this spirit *Many-Colored Fleece* has been assembled. In this spirit may it be received.

## Notes

1. Mariella Gable, O.S.B., "Introduction," *Many-Colored Fleece* (New York: Sheed & Ward, 1950).

MARIELLA GABLE, REMBERTA WESTKAEMPER,
COLLEGE OF ST. BENEDICT, 1950S

# Chapter 5

## The Novel[1]

### ACHIEVEMENT

It is now approximately 140 years since Catholic fiction was born in the beautiful novel, *The Betrothed*, by Manzoni. Since that moment, the countries of the western world have produced scores of superb novels which have communicated something of the mystery of the spiritual and moral dignity of the human condition. They have been lauded by secular as well as by Catholic critics. And that is as it should be. For, unless a work is first a piece of art, it cannot qualify as a piece of Catholic art.

> Everyone is familiar with stories in which "good" ideas emerge as cruel parodies of themselves, brutally debased by insensitive style and crude characterization and arbitrary psychology, or else sentimentalized by defects in logic and mechanical plot management.[2]

Religious fiction marred by any such ineptitudes will be ignored in this discussion. For the output of competent Catholic novels is so impressive in quantity and quality that, at the present time, it is regarded by secular critics as a badge of distinction for an author to be designated as a Catholic novelist.[3]  Among those who are writing authentic Catholic fiction are those in the vanguard of bringing modern fiction to a new and higher level of excellence. It is common to hear critics lament that no novelists since James Joyce have been able to pick up the craft of fiction at the point where he made such remarkable innovations and to carry on to newer frontiers. The great German Catholic novelist, Elizabeth Langgaesser, however, who is regarded on the continent as one of the most gifted writers of the century has done just that.

> She is the only Catholic novelist of stature who has taken up the novel where James Joyce and Hermann Brach left it, as a form which in rehandling the real, moves into the realms of poetry, of drama, of myth, of the subconscious...[4]

With pioneers in form joining giants of Catholic fiction such as Manzoni, Dostoevski, Undset, Mauriac, Bernanos, Bergengruen, Waugh, Greene, Stolpe, Gironella, Musil, Ramuz, and Silone, and many others of stature, the position of Catholic fiction at the present time commands the respect of the whole literate western world.


## DEFINITION

Let us see why this is so. Immediately, we face the difficult problem of defining the Catholic novel. Those who are entitled to have an opinion have been in great disagreement. This disagreement, however, is easily understood when one realizes that it takes its rise, as do most disputes, from an overemphasis on one part of a complex truth. To bring into focus the whole of the truth about Catholic fiction, it is necessary to keep in mind three facts.

These facts seem to be contradictory. Now, most of us have learned to entertain an apparent contradiction and tag a paradox. There is no reason why one may not entertain a three-prong paradox and discover it to be the humble garden tool with which honest critical judgment can be cultivated. Each one of the following statements is true; without a grasp of their coexistence, no satisfactory definition of Catholic fiction can be formulated.

1. Strictly speaking, Catholic fiction does not exist.
2. All the great literature in the world is Catholic fiction.

3. Fiction which artistically communicates through the use of Catholic symbols something of the spiritual and moral mystery of the human condition may properly be designated Catholic fiction.

These three statements will now be elucidated.

1. *Strictly speaking, Catholic fiction does not exist.* Fiction explores the mystery of the human condition for the purpose of giving pleasure. It is a story. There has always been the story; there always will be. In the beginning, it was the epic, the saga, the tale, the metrical romance. In our own day, the novel takes the place of the epic. Its great glory is, as Aristotle discovered long ago, that fiction is truer than history.[5]

One can understand why fiction is truer than history only by discovering what constitutes the pleasure which is the purpose of fiction. The highest human pleasure comes from knowing—specifically, from knowing *through vision*—something of the mystery of life. The artist's vision fixes in the concrete what no abstraction, no recounting of history, no nonfiction writing of any sort can communicate. Fiction does not tell something; it shows something. It is the incarnation of reality. It is the Word (the mystery of reality) made flesh.

And that incarnation in its very basic concept includes the whole of the human condition. By very definition, the idea of fiction embraces the entire gamut of human experiences. And of these, of course, the most constant, the most ubiquitous, the most germane to the human heart, is the religious experience. Why should the expression of that experience in fiction be regarded as something special? It is not. It is only one of the experiences for which fiction, by its very definition, has provided.

Let us put it this way. The human condition is like sunlight which by the prism of fiction can be broken up into the spectrum of life: the red of emotions, the orange of all that is animal in human beings, the yellow of perversions, the green of the essentially human, the blue of morality, the indigo of the intellectual life, and the violet of spiritual experiences. Great artists mix these colors with infinite variety. They need not even use all the colors on the pallette; they choose. Incidentally, this matter of choice has particularly interested the convert-critic, Allen Tate. He declared that, since in any given work an author must be limited to one segment of experience, by that very fact the author becomes a heretic.[6] For heresy is precisely the giving of excessive emphasis to any one truth to the neglect of counterbalancing truths.

The greatest writers of fiction have been comprehensive enough to suggest the highest as well as the lowest range of human experience. They use violet as well as scarlet. Comparative religion shows how constant in the world has been human beings' need for God, for someone other than themselves upon whom they might feel dependent and to whom they might render worship. They may have imagined many gods or wicked gods. But their literature has portrayed human beings as religious and spiritual. "The religious dimension is something intrinsic to and constitutive of the nature of literature as such."[7] The spiritual and the religious can be conveyed in literature through many kinds of symbols—Buddhist, Mohammedan, Mormon, Jansenist, Jewish, Protestant, Catholic, and many others. No matter what the symbolism, the work of art which uses that symbolism is still simply fiction in its most basic provision for all types of human experience. It is true, therefore, that Catholic fiction is simply fiction. And those who insist that there is no such thing as Catholic fiction certainly have grounds for their position.

And with equal justice do those have a right to their opinion who maintain that:

2. *All the great fiction in the world is Catholic fiction.* There are two types of visions open to writers of fiction. Subconsciously, they know (feel, believe, understand) that life is either of two things: either the material world as it can be observed and nothing more, or, on the other hand, a sense-observed world permeated by God's presence in such a way that human beings are intuitively conscious of being creatures of God. Artists who possess this second world view write Catholic fiction. If they subscribe to the first, what they write is materialistic or rationalistic and lacks the spiritual dimension.

All great literature has a spiritual dimension and therefore may be regarded as Catholic literature. No one was more convinced of this than the non-Catholic critic, Arthur Machen. In formulating a new definition of the old, old question as to what makes literature the art that it is, he defined it as "the expression through the aesthetic medium of words of the dogmas of the Catholic Church," adding that "anything which is out of harmony with these dogmas is not literature." Later on in the same lecture, noting the amazement of his audience, he clarified this startling generalization. He said:

> Think of it, and you will see that from the literary standpoint, Catholic dogma is merely the witness, under a special symbolism, of the underlying facts of human nature and the universe; it is merely the voice that tells us distinctly that man is *not* the creature of the drawing room and the stock exchange, but a lonely, awful soul confronted by the Source of all souls, and you will realize that to make literature it is necessary to be at all events subconsciously Catholic.[8]

Obviously, Machen is simply pointing out that artists must be sensitive to spiritual realities, or what they write will not be literature.

Thus, it is that secular fiction is circumscribed, incomplete; Catholic fiction is all-inclusive. May no one assume that Catholic fiction is geared to a ghetto mentality. Indeed, it is secular fiction which is limited, and Catholic fiction which is comprehensive. Secular fiction is two-dimensional; Catholic fiction is three-dimensional. Or, to return to the symbolism of color—secular fiction uses some of the colors of life's spectrum; Catholic fiction includes all the colors. Secular fiction composes with the red of human emotions, the orange of all that is animal in humans, the yellow of human perversions, and even the pale green of natural humanism. But when one passes from natural humanism to Christian humanism and all the colors of the spectrum in which blue appears up to the highest types of the contemplative life, these ranges are closed to secular apprehension. These cannot be communicated by secular fiction.

Because Machen was so sensitive to spiritual communication wherever he found it, he could include as great literature and therefore as Catholic literature "the Greeks, celebrating the festivals of Dionysius, Cervantes recounting the fooleries of Don Quixote, Dickens measuring Pickwick's glasses of cold punch, Rabelais with his thirsty Pantagruel."[9]

It is very important to realize that Catholic literature need not treat of Catholic matters at all. On this subject Cardinal Newman made the classical pronouncement:

> By Catholic literature is not to be understood a literature which treats exclusively or primarily of Catholic matters, of Catholic doctrine, controversy, history, persons, or politics, but it includes all subjects of literature whatever, treated as a Catholic would treat them, and as he only can treat them.[10]

In other words, it is not the subject-matter, not the *particular symbolism* used by artists which make the difference, but the depth and insight of their spiritual vision.

This brings us to a consideration of the third statement:

3. *Fiction which communicates artistically through the use of Catholic symbols something of the spiritual and moral mystery of the human condition may properly be designated Catholic fiction.* Of the two elements in this definition one is essential, the other accidental. Essential is the communication of spiritual and moral insight. Accidental is the use of Catholic symbols. The strong bond between the spiritual apprehension of God and the moral law is clearly suggested in St. John's Gospel 14:23: "If anyone loves Me, they will keep my word, and my Father will love them, and We will come to them and will make our abode with them: they that loveth Me not keepeth not my words."

### Catholic Symbols

Since it is well to dispose of the inessential before interpreting the essential, let us first examine some important distinctions to be made about Catholic symbolism. Ordinarily, Catholic symbols are twofold: the appearance of Catholic characters in fiction and secondly the use of Catholic local color, that is, the practices, beliefs, problems, and observances peculiar to Catholics. It is very important to remember that Catholic local color cannot make a Catholic novel. Unwary readers may easily think that a book which is materialistic in its philosophy or filled with only natural goodness is a Catholic novel just because the book has used Catholic symbols, especially if the main character wears a Roman collar. We have an example of the first error in that grossly materialistic "best seller about a clerical Organizational Man called *The Cardinal*."[11] If Catholics—whether they are laypersons, priests, bishops, or cardinals—concentrate on worldly advancement (even if it is ecclesiastical preferment), they thereby marks themselves as dedicated to the honors of the world, no matter how honest or cultivated their behavior. If a novel presents goodness as entirely springing from natural virtues without reference to supernatural grace, even if this goodness is incarnated in a priest-character, such natural goodness cannot make the book qualify as a

Catholic novel. Horton Davis has made some helpful observations in this connection. He thinks that the term "hero" is applicable only in a humanistic novel and that the terms "saint" or "martyr" are the appropriate designations for characters in a great religious novel. On the basis of this judgment, he makes the following discrimination concerning the priest in *The Keys of the Kingdom:*

> For this reason it was felt that Cronin's Father Francis Chisholm in *The Keys of the Kingdom*, admirable as were his charity, his honesty, and his courage, was a hero, not a saint—that is, the character was explicable on humanistic presuppositions.[12]

A purely humanistic interpretation of life can never satisfy as a Catholic novel.

Another warning concerning Catholic symbols is in order. In the wake of the promising ecumenical movement alive in the world, one wonders sometimes if one ought not be talking of Christian fiction rather than of Catholic fiction. The incisiveness of the problem can well be seen by considering a beautiful book like Alan Paton's *Cry the Beloved Country*[13] which, through Protestant symbols, presents a deeply moving insight into Christian humility, faith, and charity. In the person of the peasant Protestant Negro minister, Stephen Kumalo, Christian simplicity and hard-tried faith shine out, and the concluding chapter, where Stephen climbs a mountain to pray on the tragic night of his son's execution, comes close to biblical eloquence and grandeur. Then there is a formal heretic like Tolstoy, who, staking his all on only one tenet of the Gospel, formulates a religion of nonresistance and love, though he does not formally believe in the divinity of Christ. Yet his short stories come as close as anything that we have in fiction to making manifest the real meaning of Christian love. The short novel, *The Death of Ivan Ilyich*, is so piercing a protest against worldly living and so urgent a plea for the bonds of Christian charity in a family that no one can afford to miss reading it. Its adoption among the Great Books for study may impress all with its sheer excellence. The Anglican, C.S. Lewis, and the Russian Orthodox, Dostoevsky, present Catholic novels with exceptionally radiant spiritual insights. They prove that the essence of the definition lies in the quality of the spiritual communication, no matter what symbols have been used. In the spirit of the ecumenical movement, in which the Holy Spirit manifests the human need for Christian unity, critics ought, I believe, to keep their boundaries of Catholic fiction open to all great Christian books, not by any patronizing sufferance, but by the urgencies of truth, which cannot be gainsaid.

### Spiritual Communication

Turning now to that essential element in Catholic fiction, the communication of something of the spiritual and moral mystery of the human condition, Catholic fiction has been positively apocalyptic. It is a vision of love. What in the whole range of human experience can compare with humanity's contact with God? This contact is, of course, not possible if people go through merely mechanical, conventional religious practices prescribed by no matter what church. Catholic fiction is a piercing trumpet call to a living and true love for God. If people, recognizing the *ersatz* quality of most religious observance, take a smug, superior attitude toward such formalities, they are farther away from God than if they stupidly conformed. There is only one way: to accept the magnificence of the continually present Incarnation of God in the liturgy of Mother Church, in her guidance, and to live that acceptance with a new love, a new faith, and with such hope in the joys of heaven as will make the material comforts of this life seem the extremely unimportant things they are. The vision as to what human contact with God can actually mean has been much more brilliantly communicated through Catholic symbols than through other symbols.

The Catholic fiction of the last 140 years heralds a new age of love. In the view of the hatred rife in the world at the moment, such a statement may sound irresponsible. But it is not; it is a most heartening truth. Let me link this generalization with what Pierre Teilhard de Chardin, S.J., has said in his epoch-making book, *The Phenomenon of Man*.[14] Those who have read this most remarkable history of evolution will remember that de Chardin, as a trained and responsible scientist, not only traces the stages of evolution in the past, but also, on the purely scientific evidence of what the past promises, looks forward into the future. He knows that human beings will finally enter a stage of love—a love which will dominate just as now we are anchored in a period of knowing. He calls this present moment in the history of humankind, the time during which we have arrived at knowing, "the noosphere." Actually the noosphere at present is going through the necessary crisis to arrive at an age of love. He begs us not to be discouraged at the spectacle of the hate-ridden Communists. They are working out part of the new evolutionary urgency to move on to an age of universal love. But de Chardin knows, as a scientist, that when nature makes a wrong thrust toward the solution of its problem in evolution, it will back up and try another thrust.

That other thrust is the perfect love of God and human beings which is being expressed so prophetically in Catholic fiction. As we know, ages in culture do not actually follow one another—they overlap. For the past four centuries, the western world has gone through a crisis of skepticism, moving farther and farther away from God. This has been our Great Defection, our experiment in trying to find out whether or not we can be sufficient unto ourselves. Chewing now in disgust the dry ashes of this experiment, we are spitting out the gagging mouthful. We are already making the Great Return. Dom Bede Griffiths has wise words to say on the Great Defection and the Great Return. He simplified the history of skepticism this way: The Protestant revolt rejected the Catholic Church, the rationalists rejected Christ, and the Russian communists rejected God. He thinks the Great Return will be made in reverse order: first to God (we see this in the world-wide renewal of interest in religion), then to Christ, and finally to the Church.[15] The ecumenical movement in the Christian world is moving faster than we realize toward this triple Great Return.

Human beings are proverbially blind to what is closest to them. Catholic fiction, which was born and matured just as the age of skepticism began to go soft in decadence, trumpets a new wholeness of society. But even those who hear the trumpets and love the golden tone scarcely realize that the trumpets are heralds of a new age of love. They are like Shakespeare and his contemporaries who did not regard the plays of Shakespeare as literature, and, therefore, took no formal measures to have his dramas properly published during his lifetime. Ultimately, of course, these priceless plays which so charmed Elizabethan audiences were suitably honored as literature. So will Catholic fiction in time be seen for what it is, the prophetic voice announcing a new age of love. But a full awareness now of its significance, of the revelation in its pages, might well serve to hasten the new day. The dawn is now. A glimpse of the rose and gold in the East is given in the chronological survey of the most important writers. Since no generalization is worth anything without the concrete proof, it is hoped that the reader who has read thus far will examine the contributions of the most important writers to see how they illustrate this prophetic attitude.

## INEPT CATHOLIC CRITICAL JUDGMENT

Before this survey is made, some remarks are in order about the hindrances Catholic fiction has suffered through the ineptitude of a critical sense. The Catholic Puritans have done their best to hinder Catholic fiction. The Catholic Puritans are still with us, though their viciousness seems to be waning and a slow battle is being won against their Philistinism. To the Jesuits[16] goes much of the credit for waging this difficult war against the Puritanism among Catholics. Catholic Puritans can be recognized by three characteristics:

1. They want edification at the expense of truth. They do not understand art or recognize its absence.
2. They are determined to make their narrow views prevail—even if they have to abuse their neighbor and break all the laws of Christian charity. They do not know what dialogue is. They are positive, even in the definition of Ambrose Bierce, meaning to be mistaken at the top of one's voice.
3. They are so literal-minded that they can never see the positive values in a negative treatment.

### The Negative and Positive

A word is in order here on the positive and negative in fiction. Fiction, like life, has only one theme: The conflict between good and evil. A negative treatment communicates evil (the absence of good), and a positive treatment communicates good directly. But often the good can be truly appreciated only through a negative treatment. For instance, take a great, sturdy stone wall. Its thickness and durability can scarcely be appreciated by staring at it directly. But if a hole is cut into the wall, the thickness of the masonry can be seen at once. So it is with negative in fiction. It is there only to make the good more manifest.

All fiction of quality demonstrates the values of the negative in many different ways. Perhaps one of the finest such examples appears in Mauriac's *The Woman of the Pharisees*.  Here, the female Pharisee, Brigitte Pian, does good works, gives good advice, thinks she is admirably religious, but loves no one.  Because she does not love, she poisons the lives of all around her and becomes a frightfully destructive influence.  No more eloquent argument for the primacy of love can be imagined.  Another remarkable example of a negative study appears in Sven Stolpe's *The Sound of a Distant Horn*.  The gifted Dominican, Don Perezcaballero, popular as a preacher and confessor, is yet happy to persecute a brother Dominican whose intellectual achievements surpass his own.  He is rotten with self-love and nearly dies of humiliation when he discovers his nearly total lack of faith and love.  Nothing is easier than to mistake self-adulation for religious zeal.  A portrait of such self-deception is a particularly potent way to communicate the positive value of personal integrity.

## Satire

The use of the negative for a positive effect shows up especially in satire.  The satirist kills evil with the bullet of ridicule and with amused laughter uncovers sham and abuse.  In the twentieth century, we have had much telling satire[17] on our society and its abuses, both by Catholics and by those outside the Church who are yet interested in preserving the values of a Christian and humanistic culture.

The Catholics first.  Nothing can match the artistic excellence of the seven early burlesque satires of Evelyn Waugh in which he pokes fun at twentieth-century society.  Here are "these dreadful bright young things who imagined that they had invented alcohol, agnosticism, free verse, zipper fasteners, and sin."[18]  Waugh's detachment in portraying modern stupidity for precisely what it is—without argument, comment, or indignation—results in hilarity.  In *The Loved One*, he treats modern mortuary practices with atrocious levity.  Some of his technique as a stylist was picked up from another Catholic writer, Ronald Firbank.  Aubrey Menen is another satirist whose viewpoint is of special interest in a world in need of amalgamating the Orient and the Occident.  Born of an Indian father and an Irish mother, through whom he inherited the faith, Menen has explored in lighthearted satire many facets of our society.  He pokes fun at everything from the absurdity of the Anglo-Saxon attitude toward the Orient to the professional do-gooders who think they can help unfortunate sufferers without a Christian love.

A more astute stylist than Menen is Muriel Spark who, in *Memento Mori*, has been able to make the reader see life from the viewpoint of death. She uses a very simple technique: Someone calls up various elderly people and without another word simply announces, "Remember you shall die." The reactions to this message are varied. Some characters are furious—as if merely speaking of death could in any way alter its imminence, or as if one ought not at every moment to be prepared to depart this life. Inevitably, this novel suggests comparison with the brilliant study made of the same subject by Tolstoy, *The Death of Ivan Ilyich*.

Among the Catholic fiction writers in America, the three best are satirists: Randall Jarrell with his acidulous view of "progressive" education; J.F. Powers who, in his superb short stories, is manifestly an idealist having fun in presenting from various angles the priests who have permitted the materialism of our society to make them seem rather foolish as professional followers of the unworldly Christ; the extraordinarily gifted southern writer, Flannery O'Connor, uses with brilliant effectiveness the grotesque to communicate her fierce opposition to a decadent society. She says:

> The novelist with Christian concerns will find in modern life distortions which are repugnant to him and his problem will be to make these appear as distortions to an audience which is used to seeing them as natural; and he may well be forced to take ever more violent means to get a vision across to this hostile audience.[19]

O'Connor gets her vision across with brilliant effectiveness to Catholics and non-Catholics alike.

Among the non-Catholics whose works aim to preserve the values of a Christian humanism are two of the most potent satirists of our century: Aldous Huxley in *Brave New World*, warning us of the dangers to society in a culture dedicated to making human beings entirely comfortable, and George Orwell in *Nineteen Eighty-Four*, demonstrating the absolute horror of the loss of personal freedom in a totalitarian society. No Roman Catholic could have written a more effective satire against the modern disbelief in the devil than did the Anglican, C.S. Lewis. What becomes clear through his clever invention, *The Screwtape Letters*, is that the devil's most potent weapon is to persuade people that the devil does not exist. This point is made through the letters which pass between a senior devil, Screwtape, and his nephew, Wormwood.  A cultivated humanism pervades the book, as does a profoundly Christian conception of human beings in his books devoted to space fiction.

## SURVEY OF CATHOLIC FICTION

Like Athena, who stepped full grown from the brain of Jove, Catholic fiction of the modern world was born in matured excellence. There was no period of slow growth and development.  The first Catholic novel, Manzoni's *The Betrothed*, is a classic.  It was followed by the works of Dostoevsky and Tolstoy, among the finest in the world, while the tradition of Catholic fiction was further carried forward by the works of Leon Bloy, Joris-Karl Huysmans, Paul Bourget, Rene Bazin, Emile Baumann, Henry Bordeaux, and Gertrude von LeFort.  These writers bring us to the end of the first century of the Catholic novel, up to the year 1928, when a new period of fulfillment begins with *Kristin Lavransdatter* winning the Nobel Prize.  This new period is one of great richness, variety, and daring, culminating in the superb achievement of *The Cypresses Believe in God* by Gironella.

Let us turn back now to that first Catholic novel, *The Betrothed*. It is a beautiful book, recognized from the beginning as marking a new strength in Italian literature.  Published in Italian between 1825 and 1827, it was followed almost immediately by an abridged English translation in 1828.  And though it passes through several English translations thereafter, it has to wait for the English version by Archibald Colquhoun in 1951 to capture the poetic pathos and the colloquial raciness of Manzoni's style.  Here we are confronted with the first instance of a delayed translation meeting the English-speaking world only in the twentieth century.  Over and over again, this same phenomenon presents itself, with the effect of a great richness of Catholic fiction after 1928 partly accounted for by delayed translations of nineteenth-century Catholic novels.

*The Betrothed* was inspired by the success of Scott's historical novels.  Broadly, in the manner of Scott, it recreates the times of the robber barons in seventeenth-century Italy with an unforgettable evocation of the horrors of the plague suffered in Milan at that time. Manzoni was a much more careful and accurate historian than Scott, a

greater poet, and having studied Shakespeare closely with a most
sensitive awareness of Shakespeare's method in developing character,
he created in his own novel wonderfully living, vivid, psychologically
satisfying people.  Particularly successful are his religious
characters—the extraordinarily holy ones, like Cardinal Federigo
Borromeo and Padre Cristoforo, and also the poor, fearful, weak Don
Abbondio.  The radiance of a profound spiritual experience pervades
the book.

## The Historical Novel

It is important to notice that Catholic fiction not only began with
the historical novel, but also that historical novels seem to dominate
right up to the present moment.  In fact, the three greatest Catholic
novels are all historical novels:  Manzoni's *The Betrothed*, Sigrid
Undset's *Kristin Lavransdatter*, and Jose Marie Gironella's *The
Cypresses Believe in God*.  Moreover, these three novels are
landmarks in Catholic fiction.

As has already been noted, we have two periods with which to
deal:  the first century from *The Betrothed* to *Kristin Lavransdatter*
(1828-1928), a period beginning with novelists of the first rank and
followed by others of great promise; and the second beginning with
*Kristin Lavransdatter* (1928) and coming down to our own time.  *The
Cypresses Believe in God* (1955) does not put a period to this age of
great fulfillment.  It stands as a symbol of the general excellence.

A slight indication of the degree to which the historical novel
has prevailed up to our own time may be indicated by glancing at
representative novels.  Some of them have not been written by
Catholics.  It would seem that a conscientious historian in recreating
the ages of faith or in developing a novel around the character of a
saint is compelled by a respect for truth to capture the essence of the
spiritual life which gives significance to this subject matter.  Some of
the very fine novels by non-Catholic authors include that remarkable
study of Harold of England and William the Conqueror by Hope
Muntz, which she titled *The Golden Warrior*, and H.F.M. Prescott's
*The Man on the Donkey*, which so memorably declared the faith
during the time of Henry VIII.  It is a bit difficult to see why Willa
Cather never came to the Church, since her sympathies were so
markedly with it, and certainly her classics, *Death Comes for the
Archbishop* and *Shadows on the Rock*, belong on any list of Catholic
novels.  So, too, does *The Song of Bernadette* by the Jew, Franz

Werfel. Lew Wallace's *Ben Hur*, interpreting the influence of the living Christ on a young Jew, must also be included in such a list.

Among the Catholic writers of historical novels must be included Sienkiewicz, the author of *Quo Vadis*, Robert Hugh Benson, who wrote many historical novels of the recusants in England, and Gertrude von LeFort, with her distinguished *Song of the Scaffold* and *The Pope from the Ghetto*, the knowledgable Helen C. White and her sister Olive White, Helen Waddell, author of *Peter Abelard*, Charles Brady with *The Stage of Fools*, Evelyn Waugh with *Helena*, and the two popular writers of historical novels, Alfred Duggan and Louis de Wohl.

But to return now to the first century of the Catholic novel, 1828 to 1928. We have already glanced at Manzoni; Dostoevsky and Tolstoy must also be noticed. Dostoevsky (1821-1881) is a towering figure among novelists of the world. Born with the Russian aptitude for the most profound spiritual awareness, he was a member of the Russian Orthodox Church, which is separated from Rome, but has valid sacraments and orders. In his personality are united two tremendous opportunities: a deeply religious disposition and a gnawing skepticism. All his life he was torn by the conflict between faith and doubt, and by that very fact becomes a symbol of the age in which he lived. In fact, *Crime and Punishment* may be taken as a magnificent commentary on the crisis of skepticism through which the world was passing in the nineteenth century.

This great novel appeared in 1866, just seven years after Darwin's *The Origin of Species*. This juxtaposition of the two books is important. The growing skepticism of the people fastened upon Darwin's book with almost hysterical belief that the idea of evolution made it reasonable for them to discard belief in the creation and therefore in the Creator. *Origin of Species* made it seem rational to doubt the existence of God.

In *Crime and Punishment*, the main character is a skeptic, Raskolnikov. In him, the whole problem of the age of skepticism is made concrete. Dostoevsky saw one thing clearly: If human beings reject their faith in Christ, that is, in the God-human, then they will try to make themselves human-Gods. Raskolnikov tries to be a human-God. In demonstrating to himself that he is sufficient unto himself, without any obligations to a higher law, he commits without cause a heinous murder. But the psychology of the guilt is a terrible thing. Through anguish comes the miracle of redemption—brought about for him through the intense spiritual realizations of the prostitute, Sonia. Her faith supports the broken murderer in his climb back to God. She follows him to Siberia where, in the closing chapter, we see them in a dreamlike setting at Eastertide confronted in the pale sunlight of the North with the symbols of resurrection and redemption. The end of this book symbolizes the fullness of the Great Return.

In *The Idiot*, Dostoevsky succeeds in that most difficult of all problems faced by the fiction writer, the creation of a good character, Prince Myshkin, who is entirely credible and also winning. In the monumental *Brothers Karamazov*, he illustrates with absolute greatness the epigraph he has placed on the title page: "Unless the seed falling into the ground die, it shall not have life everlasting." In fact, there is no truer commentary on the works of Dostoevsky than the words of Maurice Baring:

> If one were asked to sum up briefly what was Dostoevski's message to his generation and to the world in general, one would do so in two words: love and pity. The love which is in Dostoevski's works is so great, so beautiful, so overflowing, that it is impossible to find a parallel to it, whether in ancient or in modern literature. Supposing the Gospel of Saint John were to be annihilated and lost to us forever, although nothing could replace it, Dostoevski's work would go nearer to replacing it than any other book written by any other man.[20]

The works of Tolstoy naturally divide themselves into two groups, those before his conversion, which began about 1876, and those which came after. In spite of the heretical denial of certain aspects of the faith dear to all Catholics, Tolstoy grasped with intense awareness the place of love for God and for neighbor in the pattern of life. Since the art of fiction normally restricts the artist to presenting only one segment of human experience effectively, and since Tolstoy has chosen over and over again in his short stories and longer works after 1876 to communicate most movingly the mystery of love, they rank with the greatest of Christian literature. The shorter works, *The Death of Ivan Ilyich, Master and Man,* and *Memories of a Madman,* are "on a level with the greatest religious writings of the world." It is hoped in judging Tolstoy that the basic tenet for competent appraisal will be accepted: that one must always judge the work, not the writer. Though Tolstoy, as a person, gave himself with the dedication of a saint to Christianity as he saw it—a dedication to love and service and to the humble doctrine of nonresistance to evil—the things of faith which his doctrine denied did not find a place in his fiction. He is one of the very few modern writers whose work is helped by a didactic purpose.

## Twentieth-Century Catholic Fiction

Space does not permit a comment on the other important writers of Catholic fiction who were born before Sigrid Undset in 1882. We move quickly, therefore, to that brilliant period of wealth and variety in Catholic fiction which began with the bestowal of the Nobel prize on Sigrid Undset for *Kristin Lavransdatter* in 1928 and continues up to the present moment. As has already been observed, some of the effect of great wealth in Catholic fiction in the English-speaking world came from the fact that books which had appeared in the nineteenth century in Europe did not appear in English translations until the twentieth century. For instance, Gertrude von LeFort's *The Song of the Scaffold* did not appear until 1933, *The Pope from the Ghetto* not until 1934, and Bloy's *The Woman Who Was Poor,* which had been published in France in 1897, did not appear in America until 1939 and was republished in English in 1947. A translation of Bergengruen did not appear in English until 1952, of Langgaesser until 1953, of Stolpe until 1957. Hence, the 1950's, topped in 1955 by an English translation of *The Cypresses Believe in God,* seem to be a particularly rich period in Catholic fiction.

The distribution of the writers of Catholic fiction includes most of the countries of the western world. From France, we have the towering and apocalyptic novels of Bernanos and the soul-searching of Mauriac's psychological studies, with the folk simplicity and urgent faith in the novels of Henri Queffelec; from Germany the novels of Gertrude von LeFort, with the superb achievements of Werner Bergengruen and Elizabeth Langgaesser; from Switzerland, the artist of peasant life, F.C.F. Ramuz; from Austria, the astounding Robert Musil; from Sweden, the nervous and intensely spiritual novels of Sven Stolpe; from Norway, the monumental achievements of Sigrid Undset; from England, the novels of Evelyn Waugh, Graham Greene, and Muriel Spark; from Australia, Morris L. West's best seller, *The Devil's Advocate*; from Italy, the powerful novels of Ignazio Silone, a

Communist returned to Catholicism and the serious novels of
Coccioli, both of which are in contrast to the delightful fooling of
Guareschi in the *Don Camillo* stories; from Ireland, the urbane stories
of Kate O'Brien and a cluster of brilliant writers of the short story,
Frank O'Connor, Sean O'Faolain, Mary Lavin, Liam O'Flaherty,
Bryan MacMahon, Michael McLaverty, Seamus MacManus; from
Spain, Gironella's magnificent *The Cypresses Believe in God* and
Descalzo's *God's Frontier*; from Scotland, the broad humor of Bruce
Marshall; and from America, besides the excellent satirists already
noted, there are many novelists of such distinction as to command the
respect of cultivated readers—Paul Horgan, better in his short stories
than in his novels, Richard Sullivan, Margaret Culkin Banning,
Richard Coleman, William Barrett, and Carolyn Gordon. Space does
not permit the mention of many other writers of competent Catholic
fiction whose achievement ranks with some of those who have been
named.

Nor does space permit a comment of many of the writers of the
first rank. Only a brief sampling here and there must serve as an
indication of the variety and spiritual intensity of the contributions.

*Kristin Lavransdatter* is the full-length portrait of a great
Christian woman who, though she lives in medieval Norway,
encompasses the whole sweep of human experience. She falls,
conceals her guilt, rises, stumbles, continues to stumble, repents,
aspires, fumbles through the handicap of a personality committed to
ideals but unable to achieve those ideals, and finally in old age arrives
at a high degree of holiness. The book might be called *Everywoman*.

The fiction of Mauriac has always been marked by psychological
insights and the capacity to anatomize the human heart. There is a
marked difference, however, between the novels which appeared
before 1931 and those which appeared after that date. Before 1931,
Mauriac had been accused by his Catholic readers of being an
immoral novelist.[21] They claimed that he not only made perceptible
and tangible the world of evil, but that he also made it appear
seductive. The charge was not so much against his subject matter as
against its tone. Mauriac took these reproaches much to heart and
thereafter produced some of his finest novels, especially *The Viper's
Tangle*, *Woman of the Pharisees*, and *The Lamb*.

Brigitte Pian, the female Pharisee in *The Woman of the
Pharisees*, has already been described as an example of a negative
treatment. But Mauriac was equally adroit in portraying a positive

character.  As a foil to Brigitte in the same novel, he painted the portrait of the ideal Christian priest in Abbé Calou.  Brigitte reports him to his cardinal, who deprives him of even the insignificant curacy he had held and also deprives him of the privilege of saying Mass. He becomes the symbol of Christ—despised, rejected, humbled, but always helping others and always forgiving those who have harmed him.  Nothing ever shocks him.  Nothing deflects his love for the wayward, evil Brigitte.  It is through his holiness that Brigitte finally discovers that "our Father does not ask us to give scrupulous account of what merits we can claim.  She understood at last that it is not deserts that matter but our love. "[22]

No one has gone farther than Georges Bernanos in communicating the highest mystical experience.  Destined by his mother to become a priest, Bernanos decided to remain a layman and use his pen to reach those who would never be touched in any other way with the mystery of God's love.  First, here is a view of life as he saw it.  He realized with acute grief that most Christians do not, for all their profession of faith, believe in God and a hereafter.  He saw how one part of Christianity is suppressed while another is greatly overemphasized.  The suppressed part is belief in God and the life of the world to come.  Because people do not really believe in the supernatural, they try to find their happiness in this world.  How much harder they work to be comfortable than to save their souls. Yet, they are not happy.  A sense of guilt depresses them.  To salve their sense of guilt they strongly overemphasize the ethical aspects of Christianity, the corporal works of mercy, the equal importance of every individual.

In eight memorable novels, Bernanos has delivered himself of what he wants to say about this revolting society.  To him, there are only three classes of people:  the saint, the mediocre Christian, and the possessed.

Let us first take a look at one of the possessed, then at one of the saints, and finally at the average mediocre Christian.  Usually, the satanic influence in Bernanos is felt in the extremely intellectual characters.  They are without faith, but permit a rank curiosity to develop into diabolism.

In *Joy*, such a diabolical character is the Abbé Cenabre, a Canon, an authority on the mystics, a very learned man.  He no longer believes in God, but pride prevents him from becoming a defrocked priest.  His external behavior is impeccably priestly, while his inner personality is utterly divested of love. He has a mortally disruptive influence on souls, depriving them of their shams but offering them nothing by way of compensation. He slides downward in degradation until the final catastrophe.

In that catastrophe, we discover the opposite of unfaith; it is the highest type of holiness dramatized in the person of a young girl, Chantal. Chantal is a mystic who has reached a very advanced stage of the contemplative life. In a moment of illumination, she sees the frightful condition of Abbé Cenabre. She offers up her life for his salvation. Almost immediately she is raped and murdered by the pervert, Fiodor.

The cook speaks memorable words over the murdered body of Chantal—words which throw some light on the degree of self-denial practiced by those who are as holy as was Chantal. The cook says:

> You will never get it out of my head, Abbé, that it is the death she wanted—no other—just this one! You couldn't ever humiliate her enough, she wanted nothing but scorn, she would have lived in the dust. That Russian was surely the wickedest of us all. So she would have wanted her end to come from him. . . She never thought like you or me, the poor angel. . .And now people will be shaking their heads and gossiping; they'll say she was crazy or worse. . .She will have renounced everything, Abbé, everything I tell you, even her death.[23]

To renounce one's death—it is a tremendous concept. Bernanos alone of all the great fiction writers has the experience, the insight, and the power to explore this kind of reality in the spiritual life.

But what of the Abbé? In one fierce flash of memory, he sees his life as it really is, his sterile pride in all its ugliness. The vision of himself drives him irrevocably insane, but not before he has turned to God and uttered only two words: "Our Father." Then he falls on his face before the dead girl who offered her life to save him.

Thus does Bernanos bring together the two extremes—the saint and the possessed. But what of the great middle class of the spiritually mediocre? As John W. Simons has pointed out, "The saints are rare and so are the possessed. This in itself is not alarming. What is alarming is Bernanos' belief that both the possessed and the mediocre have severed ties with God and live outside him.[24]

In effect, Bernanos is telling the millions of mediocre Christians that they are as evil and as dangerous as the possessed. He summarizes his horror of mediocre Christianity thus in *Plea for Liberty*:

> The most dangerous shortsightedness consists in under-estimating the mediocre; mediocrity is a colorless and odorless gas; allow it to accumulate undisturbed, and suddenly it explodes with a force beyond all belief. . . .The dire omen for all of us is. . .not that Christians should be less numerous but that the number of mediocre Christians should increase.[25]

Bernanos is a disturbingly effective writer. His plots are wretchedly constructed, yet one has to listen, for he is like an angry prophet of the Old Testament foretelling the fall of Jerusalem. His novels are like storms at midnight during which one can make out the landscape only by intermittent flashes of fierce lightning. Great as are his books, he creates a disturbing question in the minds of his readers—What are our hopes of salvation? Chantal by her death saved the wretched Abbé. Who shall save us all? In Bernanos, there is great pessimism, perhaps even a sort of despair. He seems to feel that evil is historically cumulative, while good is static.[26]

In sharp contrast to his pessimism is the sweet balance in the works of Werner Bergengruen, a German novelist who deserves to be much better known than he is. He has faith in an eternal rightness of things. Great evils there are, but also a counterbalancing good. It is the privilege of human beings to find the good and to trust it. Weakness conquers where strength fails. "The softest outreaches the hardest in the world, the water defeats the rock, the female defeats the male, the weak defeats the strong."[27]

This world view dominates Bergengruen's masterpiece, *A Matter of Conscience*, which appeared in English in 1952. Its form is that of a detective novel. In the Renaissance town of Cassano, Italy, a murder has been committed on the grounds of the Grand Prince. His Magnificence orders his chief of police to discover the murderer in three days. In violent fear of being accused, the people pile intrigue upon intrigue, in order to throw suspicion on someone other than themselves. In the pool of life an evil stone has been dropped, and the reader is filled with horror to see how the concentric ripples spread wider and wider. Finally, dismayed by the lies and intrigues engulfing the town, a poor dyer, Sperone, gets an idea. He is a very holy man, but his decision is not easy. He will accuse himself of the

murder so that the people may be free from the evil in which they are
caught. He does so. He becomes another Christ to save the people.
But the Grand Prince, a detestable despot who has played fast and
loose with everyone's conscience, is shattered by the avowal. He
calls all the people together and explains that he himself is the
murderer. He has just been experimenting with human nature. The
humility and charity of one man, like oil poured out upon water, has
calmed the spreading circular waves of evil.

Evil manifests itself in many ways when religion is less than
sincere. Graham Greene's novels are dedicated to demonstrating the
way God's grace is manifested in situations which seem shockingly
indecorous. He has no time at all for the sentimentalized lives of the
saints. In *The Power and the Glory*, he presents a sanctimonious
mother reading the traditional saccharine lives of the saints to her
little son, while near at hand the poor whiskey priest is going to his
martyrdom in circumstances the conventional-minded reader finds
repulsive. Many Catholic readers hold their noses when this wretched
priest is mentioned. The father of an illegitimate child, so weak that
his mortal sins arouse only the contempt of those who know him, how
can he be anything but a source of embarrassment to Catholics? In
the Mexican persecution, though, he goes on doggedly risking his life
to visit the poor people who, except for him, would not have Mass
nor the opportunity for confession. The priest is not the hero of the
book. The priesthood is the hero. For one sees how, even in so weak
a vessel, the mark of the priesthood is eternal and bears its own most
special fruit. He dies a martyr to the faith.

Many Catholic readers have objected to the picture of so sorry a
character having the grace to die for his faith. They cannot stomach
the idea of so weak a wineskin being filled with the wine of grace.
To these objectors, the English Dominican, Father Vann, has given a
wonderful answer. In *The Water and the Fire*, he has pointed out that
we can be grateful to Graham Greene and other contemporary
Catholic novelists for having increased our understanding of "what
might be called the theology of weakness." He proposes a basic
question: "Can holiness be compatible with weakness?" In answering
the question, Father Vann makes clear that while the weak sinner
cannot reach up to God to be united with Him, "God can reach down
and does reach down, to unite Himself with the humble of heart
despite their sins and squalors." He goes on to say, "Perhaps the
deepest mystery of redemption and divine love is precisely that we

can be redeemed not only *from* our squalors but in a sense *in* our squalors. "[28]

Greene has been accused of Jansenism, Lutheranism, and an unhealthy preoccupation with pus-green revolting details. It might be better to appreciate his eschatalogical value. An author who can set the western world arguing heatedly over whether Scobie was damned or saved has done much to restore to human beings' caring consciousness the reality of another life, the reality of heaven and hell. And pity—he has extended the boundaries of pity until the average heart cannot endure the sense of stretch.

Stolpe is a master in marshalling the unconventional, even in letting his form reflect his courage to break with "accepted" standards. Unafraid to shift his point of view as often as he needs to, his novels give the impression, on a superficial reading, of being disjointed. But all the sharp shiftings bear only one message: the need for love to dominate the world. A literal-minded reader may think *Night Music* is a novel on the threat of Communism. It is, rather, a study in rash judgment. "The thing that is causing harm. . . is not so much the actual deeds (of others) but the image that each constructs in his own mind of the deeds and characters of his antagonists. "[29]

By choosing an extraordinarily shocking situation, the French novelist Henri Queffelec, in *Island Priest*,[30] is able to underline most effectively "the invisible things that distinguish a church from a praying club. "[31] On a barren, wind-swept island, no priest is willing to remain to serve the Breton fishermen. In their hunger for God, they persuade Thomas, the sacristan, to move into the parsonage and act as their priest. His prayerful dedication to serving them as Christ would serve brings the fisherfolk spontaneously to confess to him. In compassion for their anguished need he, though unordained, says Mass. Nothing can equal his joy when he is actually ordained. But literal-minded readers find themselves called upon to frown upon the mere idea of an unordained man assuming priestly duties. Yet this aspect of the story is only a scaffolding upon which is skillfully constructed a wonderful statement about the human need for God, for the formalities of worship, and the response human beings will make to a sincere religious spirit about which they cannot be fooled.

Gironella's *The Cypresses Believe in God* is a monumental achievement—a great book among many great ones published in the 1950's. One of the three greatest Catholic novels, it is historical in being a wide-canvas painting of the Spanish civil war of the 1930's. It is symbolic, too, in suggesting that the chaos in Spain is somehow the chaos of the world in the twentieth century. Perhaps the recognition of the global implications of this novel accounted for its being hailed upon publication as the great Catholic novel of contemporary society for which all had been waiting.[32]

Gironella boasted that his novel demonstrates how far implacability can go. In it, he realizes in the concrete not only the amazing variety of political attachments in Spain but also the many types of Catholics whose allegiances spread from the cynical atheism of the fallen-away Catholic to the very narrow conformism of his pious wife and the unusual holiness of their young son. Of his method Gironella says: "My chief occupation has been objectivity, conceding to all those involved both their best and their worst motives."[33]

Because Gironella's work is so deeply rooted in detached honesty, it is particularly interesting to see what he does with young Cesar Alvear, the boy whose holiness is exceptional. We follow him from his tenth to his sixteenth year, seeing how gauche, awkward, and socially unprepossessing is this young fellow in whom grace blossoms into holiness. Perhaps we are a little revolted at his charity in setting up a shaving service for the very poor. Suddenly Spain goes wild in the revolution. Gerona is emptying its ciboriums onto church floors and burning churches. Cesar sees the suffering of his country as caused by sin. He offers his life in reparation. Though he could have remained at home fully protected, he goes to a despoiled church and, kneeling, reverently consumes from the floor as many desecrated hosts as he can. Then carefully concealing one in his pocket to receive just before he is shot, he submits to arrest and is lined up with dozens of others to be mowed down by the bullets of the insurgents. Next to him stands Corbera, exploding with rage against his executioners. Cesar shows him the host. He offers it to him—depriving himself of his own viaticum. Corbera blinks in amazement, understands, receives it. Cesar feels something pierce his skin. Then his heart closes.

Perhaps in a book as comprehensive as *The Cypresses Believe in God* it is unfair to select any scene as representative. If exquisite tenderness marks the interpretation of the death of Cesar, a comparable excellence interprets the amazing variety of other types of religious experience.

Morris L. West's best seller, *The Devil's Advocate*, unites many elements the reader of Catholic fiction does not expect to find coexisting in the same book: a gripping plot manipulated with economy and precision, the profoundest theological truths,[34] an extension of theological problems into areas not as yet investigated by professional theologians, living characters conceived with suitable respect for the autonomy of each, a pervading awareness of the primacy of love, and, finally, that which integrates the whole book, the place of the cross, of human suffering in uniting human beings to God. Actually, Blaise Meredith, the priest designated as "the devil's advocate" in the investigation of the alleged saintliness of Nerone, is the most important character rather than the putative saint, Nerone. He is dying of cancer and has spent his life as a dry and pedantic servant of God. But we find him learning to love, discovering compassion and pity, learning to see that under most unconventional exteriors God's grace is burning with dazzling beauty. Indeed, it is the love he discovers which brings him to heights of holiness long closed to him. He could, indeed, have saved his soul as a mechanically conforming member of the Church. But this novel, like all the other great Catholic novels, shouts of the need to love greatly, to love at the price of great suffering, to love so much that, as the Church prays in the hymn at Tierce, "other hearts will be kindled by the spectacle of each one's love."

The love so forcefully communicated in great Catholic fiction has kindled many hearts discouraged by empty conformism. The fountains of love springing up in the heart united to the pleasure which it is the purpose of art to communicate give serious readers of Catholic fiction refreshment of spirit which more than justifies their trust that Catholic fiction will continue to be written in which truth and beauty and goodness will shine out.

## Notes

1. Mariella Gable, O.S.B., "The Novel," *The Catholic Bookman's Guide*, ed. S.M. Regis Reynolds (New York: Hawthorn, 1962), 409-51.

2. Cleanth Brooks and Robert Penn Warren, *Understanding Fiction* (New York: F.S. Crofts, 1948), 15.

3. Studies in Modern Fiction, *Critique* (Fall 1958): 11.

4. J.C. Reid, "The Novels of Elizabeth Langgaesser," *Downside Review* (Spring 1960): 118.

5. Aristotle, *On the Art of Poetry*, an amplified version with supplementary illustrations for students of English, by Lane Cooper (New York: Harcourt, 1913), 10.

6. Allen Tate, "Orthodoxy and the Standard of Literature," *New Republic*, 5 January 1953, 24-5.

7. Nathan A. Scott, Jr., *Modern Literature and the Religious Frontier* (New York: Harper, 1958), 47.

8. Arthur Machen, *Hieroglyphics* 1923, *Literature, the Channel of Culture*, ed. Francis X. Connolly (New York: Harcourt, 1953), 143.

9. Ibid., 143-4.

10. John Henry Newman, "English Catholic Literature," *Idea of a University* (New York: Longmans, 1921), 296.

11. Henry Morton Robinson, *The Cardinal*, 1950. Quotation from "Corn-Squeeze Artist," *Time*, 20 June 1960, 84.

12. Horton Davis, *A Mirror of the Ministry in Modern Novels* (New York: Oxford University Press, 1959), 176.

13. Alan Paton, *Cry the Beloved Country* (New York: Scribner's, 1951).

14. Pierre Teilhard de Chardin, S.J., *The Phenomenon of Man*, introduction by Sir Julian Huxley (New York: Harper, 1959), 264 *ff.*

15. Bede Griffiths, O.S.B., *The Golden String* (New York: Kenedy, 1954), 13.

16. Harold C. Gardiner, S.J., *Norms for the Novel* (Hanover House, 1960). If all Catholics would master the norms laid down in this book, the foundations for valid criticism would be laid. Also indispensable is the chapter, "Obscenity," in Harold C. Gardiner, S.J., *Catholic Viewpoint on Censorship* (Hanover House, 1958). Other Jesuits who have fought effectively by suitable critical standards are Robert Boyle, S.J., and Maurice B. McNamee, S.J.

17. See especially "Prose Satire and the Modern Christian Temper," Sister Mariella Gable, O.S.B., *American Benedictine Review*, (March-June, 1960): 21-34.

18. Bruce Marshall, "Graham Greene and Evelyn Waugh," *Commonweal*, 3 March 1950, 551.

19. Flannery O'Connor, "The Fiction Writer and His Country," *The Living Novel*: A Symposium, ed. Granville Hicks (New York: Macmillan, 1957). In this remarkable chapter Flannery O'Connor pays high tribute to Catholicism as an aid to the artist.

20. Maurice Baring, *Landmarks in Russian Literature* (London: Methuen, 1960), 252.

21. Wallace Fowlie, "Catholic Orientation in Contemporary French Literature" in *Spiritual Problems in Contemporary Literature*, ed. Stanley

Romaine Hopper (London and New York: Harper, 1952), 298.

22. Francois Mauriac, *Woman of the Pharisees*, trans. from the French by Gerard Hopkins (London: Eyre and Spottiswoode, 1946), 203.

23. Georges Bernanos, *Joy* (New York: Pantheon, 1946), 296.

24. John W. Simons, "Salvation in the Novels." *Commonweal*, 25 April 1952, 75.

25. Georges Bernanos, *Plea for Liberty*, Letters to the English, the Americans, the Europeans, trans. Harry Lorin Binsse (New York: Pantheon, 1944), 165-6.

26. Donat O'Donnell, *Maria Cross*, Imaginative Patterns in a Group of Modern Catholic Writers (New York: Oxford University Press, 1952), 53.

27. Quotations from Lao-tse stated to have been accepted by Bergengruen in "Werner Bergengruen-Aspects of His Life and Work" by Ida Bentz and W.A. Willibrand, published in *Books Abroad* (University of Oklahoma Press, Winter 1958), 9.

28. Gerald Vann, *The Water and the Fire* (New York: Sheed, 1954), 39-40. In connection with the views expressed by Father Vann, the reader may like to investigate a detailed study of the sinner as saint in *The Picaresque Saint*, by R.W.B. Lewis (New York: Lippincott, 1959).

29. Sven Stolpe, *Night Music*, trans. John Devlin (New York: Sheed, 1960), 169-170.

30. Henri Queffelec's *Island Priest* has been made into the movie, "God Needs Men."

31. Donald Barr review of *Island Priest*, *The New York Times*, 28 September 1952, 4.

32. W.P. Clancy's review of *The Cypresses Believe in God*, *Commonweal*, 15 April 1955. "The search for the Great Catholic Novel of contemporary life can end. It was published in Spain in 1953 and now appears in English. *The Cypresses Believe in God* is a work of such power, compassion, and significance for our century that its publication in the United States is a major literary event."

33. Stanley I. Kunitz and Vineta Colby, *Twentieth Century Authors*, a biographical dictionary of modern literature, First Supplement (New York: Wilson, 1955), 368.

34. James M. Connolly, "Theology and *The Devil's Advocate*," *America*, 28 May 1960, 312.

## Recommended Novels

**Banning, Margaret Culkin. 1891-  .**

Born in Buffalo, Minnesota; B.A., Vassar, 1912; research fellow, Russell Sage Foundation; active civic leader, traveled widely; frequent contributor of stories, serials to women's magazines; articles, reviews for *The Saturday Review*; four children, two deceased; member of advisory committee of Writer's War Board during World War II; in 1942, at invitation of British Ministry of Information, studied England's industrial, home conditions; lecturer and radio speaker.

*The Convert.* Harper, 1957 o.p.                                    **P1**

*The Dowry.* Harper, 1955 o.p.; W. H. Allen, 1956.        **P2**

*Echo Answers.* Harper, 1960.                                      **P3**

*Fallen Away.* Harper, 1951 o.p.                                  **P4**

**Barrett, William E. 1900-  .**

After completing education in New York, moved to Denver as advertising manager with Westinghouse. Since 1929, he has been a free-lance writer.

*The Edge of Things.* Doubleday, 1960.                          **P5**

*The Empty Shrine.* Doubleday, 1958; PB.                        **P6**

*The Left Hand of God.* Doubleday, 1951; PB.                  **P7**

*The Sudden Strangers.* PB, 1959.                                **P8**

*Woman on Horseback:* The Story of Francisco Lopez and Elisa
        Lynch. Doubleday, 1952.                                    **P9**

**Benson, Robert Hugh. 1871-1914.**

Son of Anglican Archbishop of Canterbury; educated at Eton and Cambridge; Anglican Orders; convert 1903; priest, Rome 1904; Domestic Prelate, Rt. Rev. Msgr.; Lenten preacher in Rome and the United States alternate years, 1909-1914.

*An Average Man.* Burns, O., 1945. **P10**

*By What Authority.* Ed. by Riley Hughes. Kenedy, 1957; Burns, Oates, 1952. **P11**

*Come Rack! Come Rope!* Ed. by Philip Caraman, S.J. Kenedy, 1957. **P12**

*The King's Achievement.* Ed. by Francis X. Connolly. Kenedy; Burns, O., 1957. **P13**

*Lord of the World.* Dodd, 1907. **P14**

*Oddsfish!* Ed. by Ann Fremantle. Kenedy, 1957. **P15**

*Richard Raynal Solitary.* Intro by Evelyn Waugh. Regnery, 1956 o.p. **P16**

**Bergengruen, Werner. 1892-  .**

Born in Riga, Latvia; an anti-Nazi poet and short story writer in Germany; convert.

*The Last Captain of Horse:* A Portrait of Chivalry. Trans. by Eric Peters. Thames & Hudson, 1953; Vanguard, 1954. **P17**

*A Matter of Conscience.* Trans. by Norman Cameron. Thames & Hudson; Vanguard, 1954. **P18**

**Bernanos, Georges. 1888-1948.**

Born in Paris, devout Catholic and Royalist; spent many years in Palma; political writer; after fall of France in 1940, took up residence in Brazil with wife and six children; returned to France in 1945; later moved to Tunisia; at time of death was writing the life of Christ.

> *Diary of a Country Priest.* Awarded the Grand Prix by the Academie Francaise in 1936. Trans. by Pamela Morris, Lane, 1937; Macmillan; Im., 1948; Collins, 1956.    **P19**

> *Joy.* Trans. by Louise Varese. Pantheon, 1946 o.p.; Lane, 1948.                                                              **P20**

> *Night is Darkest.* Trans. by Strachan. Lane, 1953.         **P21**

> *Under the Sun of Satan.* Trans. by Harry L. Binsse. Macmillan, 1940 o.p.; American edition, *The Star of Satan,* Pantheon, 1949.                                                            **P22**

## Bloy, Leon. 1846-1917.

Born in Periguex, France; after agnostic and unhappy youth, worked as railway official after attempts at artistic career in Paris; was secretary to Barbey d'Aurevilly through whom he took up literature; came into prominence, 1884, with publication of *Les propos d'un enterpreteur de demolitions;* convert; *Pilgrim of the Absolute* (Pantheon, 1947 o.p.) selected, introduced by the Maritains, whom he led to Catholicism, contains selections from his journals.

> *The Woman Who Was Poor.* Trans. by I.J. Collins. Sheed, 1939.                                                                **P23**

## Bordeaux, Henri. 1870-   .

Born in Thonon, France, where his father was chief magistrate; forsook law studies for letters; elected to French Academy, 1919; poet, critic, biographer, novelist.

> *Lost Sheep.* Trans. by Frances Frenaye. Macmillan, 1955.  **P24**

*Pathway to Heaven.* Trans. by Antonia White. Farrar, 1952. **P25**

**Brady, Charles Andrew. 1912-  .**

Born in Buffalo, New York; second generation Irish; educated Harvard University; married, four daughters; chairman department of English, Canisius College; highly regarded lecturer.

*This Land Fulfilled.* Dutton, 1958. **P26**

*Stage of Fools.* Dutton, 1953 o.p. **P27**

*Viking Summer.* Bruce, 1956. **P28**

**Cather, Willa. 1875-1947.**

Born in Virginia, spent early life among Bohemian and Scandanavian families; graduated from Univ. of Nebraska; newspaper work; editor, *McClure's* Magazine after publishing first book, a collection of short stories in 1905; non-Catholic; sympathetic and intelligent handling of Catholic characters and themes.

*Complete Works.* Autographed ed. designed by Bruce Rogers. 13 vols. Houghton, 1938. **P29**

*April Twilights.* Knopf, 1923. **P30**

*Death Comes for the Archbishop.* Knopf, 1927. **P31**

*Five Stories.* Vint., 1956. **P32**

*Lost Lady.* Knopf, 1923. **P33**

*Lucy Gayheart.* Knopf, 1935. **P34**

*My Antonia.* Houghton, 1926. **P35**

*O Pioneers.* Houghton, 1933.                                    **P36**

*Obscure Destinies.* Knopf, 1932.                                **P37**

*Old Beauty, and Others.* Knopf, 1948; Cassell, 1956.            **P38**

*One of Ours.* Knopf, 1922.                                      **P39**

*Professor's House.* Knopf, 1925.                                **P40**

*Sapphira and the Slave Girl.* Knopf, 1940.                      **P41**

*Shadows on the Rock.* Knopf; Cassell, 1931.                     **P42**

*Song of the Lark.* Houghton, 1915.                              **P43**

*Young and the Bright Medusa:* Short Stories. Knopf, 1920. **P44**

**Chesterton, Gilbert Keith. 1847-1936.**

Born in Kensington, near London; educated Kings College; founder, 1925, and editor till death, *G.K.'s Weekly,* now *The Weekly Review;* left Anglicanism for socialism, and in 1922 socialism for Catholicism; Knight Commander of St. Gregory by Pius XI, 1934; honorary LL.D., University of Edinburgh; Litt.D., University of Dublin; poet, novelist, historian, essayist, artist, illustrator, controversialist, lecturer.

> *Father Brown.* World's Classics. Oxford University Press, 1955; *Father Brown Stories.* Cassell, 1952; *Father Brown's Omnibus,* rev. ed. Dodd, 1945; *Innocence of Father Brown.* Penguin, 1956.                                **P45**

> *The Man Who Was Thursday: A Nightmare.* Dodd, 1958; Dent, 1949.                                                  **P46**

> *Tales of the Long Bow.* Sheed, 1956.                          **P47**

**Coccioli, Carlo. 1920-  .**

A veteran of the Resistance movement; later assigned to Allies' Psychological Warfare work in Tuscany; first novel appeared in 1946; ten others by 1952 when living in Florence; short-story writer; a Catholic, but he does not consider himself a Catholic writer; travels widely; reads Arabic; composes easily in both Italian and French; received degree of Doctor of Colonial Administation from a Naples University before the war; lecturer.

*Heaven and Earth.* Trans. by Frances Frenaye. Prentice, 1952 o.p.                                                                **P48**

*The Little Valley of God.* Trans. by Campbell Nairne. Simon, 1957 o.p.; Heinemann, 1956.                                        **P49**

*Manuel the Mexican.* Trans. by Hans Konigsberger. Simon, 1958.                                                                    **P50**

*White Stone.* Trans. by Campbell Nairne. Simon, 1960.      **P51**

**Coleman, Richard. 1907- .**

Born in Washington, D.C.; educated in Catholic schools through college; resident of Charleston, South Carolina since 1932; magazine writer. "Fight for Sister Joe," a short story first published in *Story Magazine*, was made into the movie, "Bells of St. Mary's." Most recently, "The Fury of Sister Borromeo" was published in *Story* (February 1961).

*Don't You Weep, Don't You Moan.* Macmillan, 1935 o.p.      **P52**

**Conrad, Joseph. 1857-1924.**

Born Teodore Konrad Korzeniowski in South Poland; parents exiled by Russian government after Polish rebellion, 1862; reared by his uncle; educated Cracow, 1868-1873; joined French Merchant Marine, 1844; naturalized Englishman, and Master in English Merchant Service, 1884; left the sea in 1894; wed an English woman and settled in England; unable to speak a word of English till 1878; his Catholicism rarely a factor in his stories.

*Almayer's Folly:* A Story of an Eastern River. Macmillan, 1895 o.p.; E. Benn, 1951.                                  **P53**

*Arrow of Gold.* Doubleday, 1919 o.p.; E. Benn, 1951; Dent, 1947                                                   **P54**

*Lord Jim.* Doubleday, 1915; W. Blackwood, 1948; Dent, 1946; Evman; Ban.                                         **P55**

*Nigger of the Narcissus.* Blackie, 1949; Doubleday, 1914; Heinemann, 1949; Dent, 1951; Dell.          **P56**

*Nostromo:* A Tale of the Seaboard. Doubleday; Dent, 1947; NAL.                                                    **P57**

*Portable Conrad.* Ed. by Morton D. Zabel. Viking, 1947.  **P58**

*Tales of East and West.* Ed. by Morton D. Zabel. Hanover, 1958.                                                   **P59**

*Tales of Land and Sea.* Intro. by William McFee. Hanover, 1953.                                                   **P60**

*Typhoon and Other Stories.* Doubleday, 1921.          **P61**

**Cronin, Archibald Joseph. 1896- .**

Educated St. Aloysius College, Glasgow; M.B., Glasgow University; practiced medicine in South Wales and London; took M.D., Diploma in Public Health, member Royal College of Physicians; gave up medicine for writing, 1930; member of council of Author's Society; married, 3 sons; resident of Storrington, Sussex.

*Beyond This Place.* Little; Gollancz, 1953.          **P62**

*The Citadel.* Little, 1937; Gollancz, 1939; Ban.; Grosset.   **P63**

*Green Years.* Little, 1944; Bd. with *Shannon's Way,* Little, 1960; Gollancz, 1945. **P64**

*Hatter's Castle.* Little, 1931; Gollancz, 1932. **P65**

*The Keys of the Kingdom.* Little, 1941; Gollancz, 1943; Ban.; Grosset. **P66**

*Northern Light.* Little, 1958. **P67**

*Shannon's Way.* Grosset; Little, 1948; Gollancz. **P68**

*Spanish Gardener.* Little, 1950; Gollancz, 1952. **P69**

*Stars Look Down.* Little, 1955; Gollancz, 1935. **P70**

*Thing of Beauty.* Little, 1956. **P71**

*Three Loves.* Little, 1957; Gollancz, 1932. **P72**

## De Wohl, Louis. 1903-

Born in Berlin of Hungarian father and Austrian mother; educated at Prinz Heinrichs Gymnasium, Berlin; now a British citizen; first book, *The Great Flight,* published when he was 21; seventeen of his books have been filmed; captain in psychological warfare, British Army, World War II; world traveler; resident of London.

*Citadel of God:* A Novel of St. Benedict. Lippincott, 1959. **P73**

*The Glorious Folly:* A Novel of the Time of St. Paul. Lippincott, 1957. **P74**

*The Golden Thread:* A Novel of St. Ignatius Loyola. Lippincott, 1952. **P75**

*The Joyful Beggar:* A Novel of St. Francis of Assisi. Lippincott, 1958. **P76**

*The Last Crusader:* Story of Juan de Austria. Lippincott,
1956.                                                      **P77**

*Living Wood:* A Novel. Lippincott, 1947.                  **P78**

*The Quiet Light:* A Novel of St. Thomas Aquinas. Lippincott,
1950; Im., 1958.                                           **P79**

*The Restless Flame:* A Novel of St. Augustine. Lippincott,
1951; Im.                                                  **P80**

*The Second Conquest:* A Novel. Lippincott, 1954.          **P81**

*Set All Afire:* A Novel of St. Francis Xavier. Lippincott,
1953.                                                      **P82**

*The Spear.* Lippincott, 1955.                             **P83**


**Dostoevsky, Fedor Mikhailovich. 1821-1881.**

Born in Moscow; sad and tragic life; exiled to Siberia for
association with liberal groups, from which *House of the Dead* was
drawn; tendency to epilepsy; traveled in Europe with his wife; settled
in St. Petersburg in 1871.

*The Brothers Karamazov.* Trans. by Constance Garnett,
Macmillan, 1912; Trans. by David Magarshack, Penguin,
1958; ML; Dell; Evman, 2 vols., 1957; Grove, 1956;
Harper, 1960.                                          **P84**

*Crime and Punishment.* Dutton, 1911; Trans. by Jessie Coulson,
Oxford Univ. Press, 1953; Trans. by David Magarshack,
Penguin; Trans. by Constance Garnett, Macmillan, 1955;
Evman, 1948; Harper; ML, 1950; Ban.; Dell; Penguin,
1954.                                                  **P85**

*Devils (The Possessed).* Trans. by David Magarshack, Penguin,
1954.                                                  **P86**

*Eternal Husband and Other Stories.* Trans. by Constance Garnett, Macmillan; Heinemann, 1950. **P87**

*Gambler and Other Stories.* Trans. by Constance Garnett, Macmillan; Heinemann, 1949. **P88**

*Grand Inquisitor.* Ed. by Anne Fremantle, Ungar, 1956; trans. S.D. Kaliansky, Secker, 1935. **P89**

*Honest Thief.* Trans. by Constance Garnett, Macmillan; Heinemann, 1950; Trans. by N.A. Berdiaev, Merid.; Mayfair, 1957. **P90**

*House of the Dead.* Trans. by Constance Garnett, Macmillan, 1950; Heinemann, 1950; Grove, 1957; Dell. **P91**

*Idiot.* Trans. by Constance Garnett, Macmillan, 1935; Trans. by David Magarshack, Penguin, 1955; Evman, 1953; ML; Ban. **P92**

*Insulted and Injured.* Trans. by Constance Garnett, Macmillan; Heinemann, 1950; Evgreen, 1955. **P93**

*Letters from the Underworld and the Grand Inquisition.* Trans. by Ralph Motlow. Evman, 1953; Trans. by Hogarth, Dent. **P94**

*Memoirs from the House of the Dead.* Trans. by Jessie Coulson, Oxford University Press, 1956. **P95**

*Poor Folk* and *The Gambler.* Trans. by Hogarth. Dent; Evman, 1956. **P96**

*Possessed.* Trans. by Constance Garnett, Macmillan; Heinemann, 1950; ML, 1936. **P97**

*Raw Youth.* Trans. by Constance Garnett, Macmillan; Heinemann, 1950. **P98**

*Short Novels of Dostoevsky.* Intro. by Thomas Mann, Dial,
1950.                                                    **P99**

*The Short Stories of Dostoevsky.* Trans. by Constance Garnett,
Dial, 1946.                                             **P100**

*White Nights and Other Stories.* Trans. by Constance Garnett,
Macmillan, 1923; Heinemann.                             **P101**

*Winter Notes on Summer Impressions.* Criterion; English title,
*Summer Impressions.* Trans. by FitzLyon; J. Calder,
1955.                                                   **P102**

**Duggan, Alfred Leo. 1903-  .**

Born in Buenos Aires; lived in England since 1905; attended
Eton, Balliol College, Oxford; served in London Irish Rifles;
collector for British National History Museum.

*Children of the Wolf:* The Foundation of Rome. Coward, 1959;
English title, *Founding Fathers,* Faber, 1959.         **P103**

*Devil's Brood.* Illus. by George Hartmann. Coward; Faber,
1957.                                                   **P104**

*King of Pontus:* Life of Mithradates Eupator. Coward, 1959;
English title, *He Died Old: The Story of Mithradates
Eupator, King of Pontus*, Faber, 1951.                  **P105**

*The Lady for Ransom.* Coward o.p.; Faber, 1953.        **P106**

*Leopards and Lilies:* King John of England. Coward; Faber,
1954.                                                   **P107**

*Little Emperors:* Fifteenth-Century Britain. Coward, 1953 o.p.;
Faber, 1951.                                            **P108**

*Knight With Armour.* Coward; Faber, 1950.              **P109**

*My Life for My Sheep:* Story of St. Thomas a Becket. Coward, 1955; English title: *Thomas Becket of Canterbury*, Faber, 1952.                                                              **P110**

*Three's Company.* Coward, 1958.                                **P111**

*Winter Quarters:* Imperial Rome. Coward, 1956; Faber; Ace.                                                                        **P112**

**Firbank, Ronald. 1886-1926.**

Born in London; attended Cambridge; traveled extensively; novelist; dramatist; essayist.

*Five Novels: Valmouth, Artificial Princess, Flower Beneath the Foot, Prancing Nigger, Eccentricities of Cardinal Pirelli.* New Directions; Duckworth, 1948.                                **P113**

*Santal.* Grove, 1955 o.p.                                         **P114**

*Three More Novels: Caprice, Inclinations, Vainglory.* New Directions; Duckworth, 1950.                             **P115**

*Valmouth.* New Directions; Duckworth, 1956.        **P116**

**Gironella, Jose Maria. 1917-  .**

Born in Spain; married; lives in Barcelona; his *Un Hombre* (P118) won the Nadal Prize.

*The Cypresses Believe in God.* Trans. by Harriet de Onís. Knopf, 1956.                                                          **P117**

*Where the Soil Was Shallow:* A Translation of *Un Hombre.* Trans. by Anthony Kerrigan. Regnery, 1957 o.p.        **P118**

**Gordon, Caroline. 1895-  .**

Born in Kentucky; B.A. Bethany College, West Virginia, 1916; honorary LL.D., 1946; Guggenheim Fellowship, 1932; convert, 1950; novelist; critic; short-story writer; former wife of Allen Tate; they have one child.

*Green Centuries.* Scribner's, 1941 o.p.                          **P119**

*Malefactors.* Harcourt, 1956.                                    **P120**

*None Shall Look Back.* Scribner's, 1937 o.p.                     **P121**

**Greene, Graham.  1904-**

Educated Birkhamsted College, Oxford; editorial staff, *The Times,* 1935-1937; film critic, *The Spectator,* 1937; literary editor, *Night and Day;* married, 2 children.

*Brighton Rock.* Viking, 1938; Compass, 1956; Penguin.    **P122**

*Confidential Agent.* Chatto, 1956; Heinemann, 1939.      **P123**

*The End of the Affair.* Viking, 1951; Heinemann.         **P124**

*England Made Me.* Heinemann, 1935; American title:
    *Shipwrecked,* Viking, 1953.                         **P125**

*The Heart of the Matter.* Viking, 1948; Heinemann; Compass,
    1960.                                                **P126**

*Loser Takes All.* Viking, 1957; Compass; Heinemann,
    1955.                                                **P127**

*The Man Within.* Viking, 1929; Heinemann.               **P128**

*The Ministry of Fear.* Heinemann, 1943.                 **P129**

*Nineteen Stories.* Viking, 1949 o.p.; Ban.; English title, *Twenty-
    One Stories,* Heinemann, 1955.                       **P130**

*The Power and the Glory.* Compass, 1946; Heinemann, 1940; Chatto. **P131**

*The Quiet American.* Ban.; Compass, 1957; Heinemann, 1955. **P132**

*The Third Man* and *The Fallen Idol.* Heinemann, 1950. **P133**

*Three by Graham Greene: This Gun for Hire; The Confidential Agent; The Ministry of Fear.* Viking, 1952. **P134**

**Guareschi, Giovanni. 1908-  .**

Born in Parma; edited *Bertoldo*, humor magazine, Milan; in German concentration camps, 1943-1945; now editor of *Candido*, magazine, Milan; married, 2 children.

*Don Camillo and His Flock.* Trans. by Frances Frenaye. Farrar, 1952. **P135**

*Don Camillo and Prodigal Son.* Trans. by Frances Frenaye. Gollancz, 1952. **P136**

*Don Camillo's Dilemma.* Trans. by Frances Frenaye. Dell; Grosset, 1957; Gollancz, 1954. **P137**

*Don Camillo's Omnibus: His Little World,* and, *His Dilemma.* Farrar, 1954. **P138**

*Don Camillo Takes the Devil by the Tail.* Trans. by Frances Frenaye. Farrar, 1957. **P139**

*House that Nino Built.* Trans. by Frances Frenaye. Farrar, 1953; Gollancz. **P140**

*Little World of Don Camillo.* Trans. by Uno V. Troubridge. Farrar, 1951; Grosset; Gollancz. **P141**

**Hemon, Louis. 1880-1913.**

Born in Brest, France; son of a university professor; wrote his masterpiece while visiting Canada, where he was killed in a railroad accident.

> *Maria Chapdelaine:* A Tale of the Lake St. John Country. Trans. by W.H. Blake, Macmillan, 1921; Im., 1956; Ed. by E.A. Phillips, Cambridge University Press, 1927. **P142**

**Horgan, Paul. 1903-  .**

Living many years in New Mexico as librarian and writer, he wrote the history of the southwest; his *Great River: The Rio Grande in the North American History* (2 vols., Rinehart, 1954) received both the Pulitzer Prize and the Bancroft Prize.

| | |
|---|---|
| *The Centuries of Santa Fe.* Dutton, 1956. | **P143** |
| *Distant Trumpet.* Farrar, 1960. | **P144** |
| *Figures in a Landscape,* 2nd ed. Harper, 1940 o.p. | **P145** |
| *Give Me Possession.* Farrar, 1956; PB. | **P146** |
| *Humble Powers.* Im., 1954. | **P147** |
| *The Saintmaker's Christmas Eve.* Farrar, 1955. | **P148** |

**Hulme, Kathryn Covarly. 1900-**

Born in San Francisco; traveled extensively; during World War II served as Major of the community of 15,000 persons in Wildflecken, Germany, displaced persons' camp, this story told in her *The Wild Place* (Little, 1953, PB); latest story is based on life of her grandfather.

*The Nun's Story.* Little, 1956; PB. **P149**

**Huysmans, Joris Karl. 1848-1907.**

Born of Dutch parents in Paris; served in Franco-Prussian War, with Ministry of the Interior, 1868-1897; founder of Goncourt Academy; awarded Cross of Legion of Honor; his early novels were immoral, became Catholic after visiting Trappist monastery, 1895; due to eye affliction, had to have eyelids sewn shut.

*Against the Grain.* Trans. by Robert Baldick. Fortune, 1951. **P150**

*Against Nature:* A new translation of *A rebours.* Trans. by Robert Baldick. Penguin, 1959. **P151**

*Down There (La Bas):* A study of satanism. Trans. by Keene Wallis. Intro. by Robert Baldick. University Books, 1958. **P152**

*Downstream.* Trans. by Robert Baldick. Fortune, 1954. **P153**

*Marthe.* Trans. and with Intro. by Robert Baldick. Fortune, 1956. **P154**

**Jarrell, Randall. 1914-  .**

Born in Nashville, Tennessee; B.A., M.A. Vanderbilt University; English staff, Kenyon College, 1937-1939, University of Texas, 1939-1942; 1942 saw publication of first volume of poetry; served as control tower operator at B-29 training center during World War II; won Guggenheim Fellowship, 1946; permanent position as associate professor, Women's College of University of North Carolina, 1947; visiting professor; lecturer; poet—several magazine prizes; critic-contributor to many literary reviews.

*Pictures From an Institution: A Comedy.* Knopf, 1954; Mer. **P155**

## Kaye-Smith, Sheila. 1887-1956.

Born in England; educated privately; published first novel at 20; married Anglican clergyman 1924; in 1929, both converted to Catholicism.

| | |
|---|---|
| *Happy Tree.* Harper, 1949 o.p. | **P156** |
| *Joanna Godden.* Dutton, 1922 o.p. | **P157** |
| *Mrs. Gailey.* Harper, 1951 o.p. | **P158** |

*Superstition Corner.* Preface by G. B. Stern. Regnery, 1955;
    Im., 1958.                                                      **P159**

*Views from the Parsonage.* Harper, 1954 o.p.; Cassell o.p. **P160**


## Langgaesser, Elizabeth. 1899-1950.

Born in Alzey, Rhineland; wife of philosopher Wilhelm Hoffman; four daughers; won the Literature Prize for German women, 1932; Jewish, expelled from the Literaturkammer in 1936; publication forbidden by Nazis; four novels; five volumes of poetry; four volumes of short stories; elected to Academy of Science and Literature of Mainz; awarded Georg Buechner Prize of Darmstadt, 1950; died in Rheinzabern.; *Quest* is the only one of her works translated into English.

*Quest.* Trans. by Jane B. Greene. Knopf, 1953.              **P161**


## LeFort, Gertrude von. 1876-   .

Born of French Protestant titled family in Germany who fled there for religious reasons; convert, 1925; resident of Bavaria; received Swiss literary award, the Gottfried Keller Medal, 1952; educated at University of Heidelberg and Berlin; worked under the

Protestant philosopher, Ernst Troeltsh, whose works she edited in 1925, the year of her conversion.

> *The Pope from the Ghetto:* The Legend of the Family of Pier Leone. Trans. by Conrad M.R. Bonacino. Sheed, 1935 o.p. **P162**

> *Song at the Scaffold.* Trans. by Olga Marx. Sheed, 1953 o.p. **P163**

> *The Wife of Pilate.* Trans. by Marie C. Buehrle. Bruce, 1957 o.p. **P164**

## Lewis, Clive Staples. 1898-

Born in Ulster; Fellow of Magdelen College, Oxford; Anglican.

> *The Great Divorce:* A Dream. Macmillan, 1946; Bles, 1945. **P165**

> *Out of the Silent Planet.* Macmillan, 1943; Avon; Lane, 1945. **P166**

> *Perelandra.* Macmillan, 1944; Lane, 1943. **P167**

> *Screwtape Letters.* Macmillan, 1943; Bles, 1942; Collins. **P168**

> *That Hideous Strength:* A Modern Fairy-Tale for Grown-Ups. Macmillan, 1946; Lane, 1945. **P169**

> *Till We Have Faces:* A Myth Retold. Harcourt; Bles, 1957. **P170**

## McLaverty, Michael. 1907- .

Irish schoolmaster living in Belfast; writer for the *Irish Monthly, Catholic World,* etc.; represented in O'Brien's *Best Short Stories* of 1933.

*The Choice*. Macmillan, 1958.                          **P171**

*The Game Cock, and Other Stories*. Devin, 1947.        **P172**

*In This Thy Day*. Macmillan, 1947 o.p.                 **P173**

*School for Hope*. Macmillan; Cape, 1954.               **P174**

*Three Brothers*. Macmillan, 1948.                      **P175**

*Truth in the Night*. Macmillan, 1952.                  **P176**


**MacMahon, Bryan. 1909-  .**


Born in Listowel, County Kerry; educated St. Patrick's College, Drumcondra, Dublin; teaches in National School in Listowel; one play recently accepted by Abbey Theatre; reviewer, radio scriptwriter, poet, now writing a novel.

*Children of the Rainbow*. Dutton, 1952 o.p.            **P177**

*Jack O'Moora and the King of Ireland's Son*. Dutton, 1950
    o.p.                                                **P178**

*The Lion-Tamer and Other Stories*. Dutton, 1949; Evman,
    1958.                                               **P179**

*The Red Petticoat and Other Stories*. Dutton, 1955;
    Macmillan.                                          **P180**


**MacManus, Seamus. 1869-  .**

Born in County Donegal; educated Glen Cuach School; appointed pupil-teacher in Iniskillen Model School, County Fermanagh at 16 where he taught for ten years; later appointed master of Glen Cuach School; *The Shamrock, Harper's, Century* and *McClure's* accepted his short stories, launching him as a full-time

writer in this country; author of over twenty-five books, poetry, more
than a dozen plays.

*Heavy Hangs the Golden Grain.* Macmillan, 1950; Talbot,
1953.                                                    **P181**

*The Well o' the World's End, and Other Folk Tales.* Devin,
1949.                                                    **P182**

**Manzoni, Alessandro. 1785-1873.**

Born in Milan; educated University of Pavia; at his wife's
conversion, 1810, he returned to the Church; poet, novelist,
dramatist, patriot.

*The Betrothed* (I Promessi Sposi): A Tale of Seventeeth-Century
Milan. Trans. by Archibald Colquhoun. Evman, 1956;
Dent.                                                    **P183**

**Marshall, Bruce. 1890-  .**

Born in Edinburgh, Scotland; accountant by profession; lost a
leg on the Western Front five days before Armistice; convert, 1918;
won the Harrap Prize Novel competition in 1924; resident of Paris.

*The Accounting.* Houghton, 1958; English title, *The Bank
Audit*, Constable.                                       **P184**

*Divided Lady.* Houghton; Constable, 1960.               **P185**

*Fair Bride.* Houghton; Constable, 1953.                 **P186**

*Father Malachy's Miracle:* A Heavenly Story with an Earthly
Meaning. Im., 1955; Constable, 1947.                     **P187**

*Girl in May.* Houghton; Constable, 1956.                **P188**

*Satan and Cardinal Campbell.* Houghton, 1959.           **P189**

*Vespers in Vienna.* Houghton, 1947; Penguin, 1956.     **P190**

*White Rabbit.* Houghton; Evans, 1952.                  **P191**

*The World, the Flesh and Father Smith.* Houghton, 1945; Ban.;
    Im., 1957; English title, *All Glorious Within*, Constable,
    1944.                                               **P192**

*Yellow Tapers for Paris.* Houghton; Constable, 1946.   **P193**


**Martin-Descalzo, Jose Luis, S.J. 1930-  .**

Spanish Jesuit; won Nadal Prize for first novel.

*God's Frontier.* Trans. by Harriet de Onis. Knopf, 1959. **P194**


**Mauriac, Francois. 1885-  .**

Born in Bordeaux; began as critic, *Le revue du temps present*,
1910; in French Army, World War I; elected to French Academy,
1933; about 1930 rediscovered the Faith; has also written several
books of verse.

*Desert of Love*, and *The Enemy*. Trans. by Gerard Hopkins.
    Farrar, 1951; Eyre, 1949.                           **P195**

*Flesh and Blood.* Trans. by Gerard Hopkins. Farrar, 1955;
    Eyre, 1954.                                         **P196**

*The Frontenac Mystery.* Trans. by Gerard Hopkins. Eyre,
    1952.                                               **P197**

*Kiss for Leper*, and *Genetrix*. Trans. by Gerard Hopkins. Eyre,
    1950.                                               **P198**

*The Lamb.* Trans. by Gerard Hopkins. Farrar, 1956,; Eyre,
    1955.                                               **P199**

*Lines of Life.* Trans. by Gerard Hopkins. Farrar, 1957; Eyre, 1951. **P200**

*The Loved and the Unloved.* Trans. by Gerard Hopkins. Farrar, 1959; Eyre, 1958. **P201**

*Questions of Precedence.* Trans. by Gerard Hopkins. Farrar, 1959; Eyre, 1958. **P202**

*River of Fire.* Trans. by Gerard Hopkins. Eyre, 1954. **P203**

*Therese.* Trans. by Gerard Hopkins. Farrar, 1951; Eyre, 1948; Anch., 1956. **P204**

*Viper's Tangle.* Trans. by Warre B. Wells. Im., 1957; Sheed; English title, *Knot of Vipers,* Eyre, 1951. **P205**

*Woman of the Pharisees.* Trans. by Gerard Hopkins. Farrar, 1951; Im., 1959; Eyre, 1946. **P206**

**Menen, Aubrey. 1912-   .**

Educated at University of London; with the British Government in India, 1940-1947; convert.

*Abode of Love.* Scribner's, 1956; PB. **P207**

*Backward Bride.* Scribner's, 1950; Chatto, 1955. **P208**

*Dead Man in the Silver Market.* Scribner's, 1953; Chatto, 1954. **P209**

*Duke of Gallodoro.* Scribner's, 1952; Chatto, 1955. **P210**

*The Fig Tree.* Scribner's, 1959. **P211**

*Prevalence of Witches.* Scribner's, 1953. **P212**

*Ramayana.* Scribner's, 1954; English title, *Rama Retold*, Chatto, 1954.                                                    **P213**

*The Stumbling Stone.* Scribner's, 1949; Chatto.          **P214**

**Musil, Robert. 1880-1942.**

Born in Klagenfurt, Carinthia, Austria; educated at cadet school; at 26, first novel well received; variety of education and experience—military, engineering, philosophy, editor, civil servant, drama critic, librarian; published two collections of short stories in German, 1911, 1923; an expressionistic drama in 1921; a comedy in 1923. Spent twenty years on *Man Without Qualities,* of which a future definitive edition will contain twenty unrevised chapters; his death in Geneva, as a voluntary exile, interrupted this work.

*Man Without Qualities.* 2 vols. Trans. by E. Wilkins and E. Kaiser. Secker, 1953-1954.                                 **P215**

*Young Torless.* Trans. by E. Wilkins and E. Kaiser. Noonday, 1958; Secker, 1955.                                      **P216**

**O'Brien, Kate. 1898-   .**

Born in Limerick; educated Dublin University; began in journalism, *The Manchester Guardian;* with success of her first play became a free-lance writer.

*As Music and Splendour.* Harper, 1958.               **P217**

*For One Sweet Grape.* Doubleday, 1946 o.p.; English title, *That Lady,* Heinemann, 1946.                                  **P218**

*The Flower of May.* Harper, 1953 o.p.; Heinemann, 1953. **P219**

*Last of Summer.* Doubleday, 1943 o.p.                **P220a**

*Without My Cloak.* Heinemann, 1931.                  **P220b**

**O'Connor, Edwin. 1918- .**

Born in Providence, Rhode Island, educated at Notre Dame, radio broadcaster, 1940-42, radio writer-producer and free-lance writer. First novel, *The Oracle*, 1951. His second novel, *The Last Hurrah*, was awarded *Atlantic Monthly* Prize Novel award in 1956.

*The Last Hurrah*. Little, Brown & Company, 1955.     **P221**

**O'Connor, Flannery. 1925- .**

Born in Savannah, Georgia; B.A., Georgia State College for Women, 1945; M.F.A. State University of Iowa 1948; Kenyon Review Fellow in Fiction, 1953-1954; O. Henry First Prize 1957; magazine writer; received Ford Foundation scholarship in 1959; home in Milledgeville, Georgia.

*A Good Man is Hard to Find, and Other Stories*. Harcourt, 1955; English title, *The Artificial Nigger, and Other Tales*, Spearman, 1957 o.p.     **P222**

*The Violent Bear It Away*. Farrar, 1960.     **P223**

*Wise Blood*. Harcourt, 1952 o.p.; Spearman, 1955.     **P224**

**O'Connor, Frank. 1903- .**

Pseudonym of Michael O'Donovan; born in Cork, taught at Harvard and Northwestern Universities; librarian in Cork.

*Domestic Relations:* Fifteen Short Stories. Knopf, 1958.     **P225**

*Stories of Frank O'Connor*. Knopf, 1952; *More Stories by Frank O'Connor*. Knopf, 1954.     **P226**

*Stories.* Knopf, 1956; Hamilton, 1953.                    **P227**


**O'Faolain, Sean. 1900-  .**

Active in Ireland's fight for freedom before he took a degree at National University, Dublin; taught Gaelic at Harvard, 1926-1929; married, one daughter; resides in Dublin; biographer; numerous travel articles; historical studies; novelist; short-story writer, "Without faith himself he fails to do justice to Catholic Ireland. . ."—*Catholic World.*

> *The Man Who Invented Sin and Other Stories.* Devin, 1948.                    **P228**

> *The Finest Stories of Sean O'Faolain.* Little, 1957; Ban.    **P229**


**O'Flaherty, Liam. 1897-  .**

Born in Aran Islands; educated Rockwell College, Black Rock College, National University, Dublin; joined Irish Guards in 1915, saw service in Belgium; shell-shocked, discharged in 1917; Irish freedom fighter, he held the Rotunda in Dublin for a week with a small army; traveled to London; for three years worked as seaman, trimmer, stoker, and covered the globe, living for some time in Bowery; short-story writer; author of some twenty books.

> *The Informer.* Cape, 1949.                    **P230**

> *Two Lovely Beasts, and Other Stories.* Devin, 1950.    **P231**

> *Stories,* Devin, 1956; *Short Stories,* Cape, 1948; *Selected Stories,* NAL.                    **P232**


**Pasternak, Boris L. 1890-1960.**

Studied philosophy in German during World War I; worked for more than twenty years as translator of poetry into Russian; little of his original work known to world until *Dr. Zhivago* published, for which he was awarded the Nobel Prize 1958; known as Russia's greatest poet.

> *Doctor Zhivago.* Trans. by Max Hayward and Manya Harari. Pantheon, 1958; NAL. **P233**

**Paton, Alan. 1903- .**

Born in Natal, South Africa; principal of reformatory in Johannesburg; traveled widely.

> *Cry the Beloved Country.* Scribner's, 1948; Cape; Longmans. **P234**
>
> *Too Late the Phalarope.* Scribner's 1953; NAL; Cape. **P235**

**Pezeril, Daniel. 1911- .**

Born of French parents in Chile; studied at the Sorbonne; ordained, 1937; teacher, Superior, Order of St. Severin; former French Army chaplain; awarded Medal of Resistance.

> *Rue Notre Dame.* Intro. by Bruce Marshall, trans. by A. Gordon Smith. Sheed, 1953 o.p.; Burns, O. **P236**

**Powers, James F. 1917- .**

Born in Jacksonville, Illinois; educated Northwestern University; married, four children; faculty, Marquette University, 1949-1951; Guggenheim Fellow, 1948 and same year received grant from National Institute-American Academy of Arts and Letters; *Lions, Harts, Leaping Does* selected for O. Henry prize stories of 1944; taught creative writing, St. John's University, Collegeville, Minnesota; his work has been reprinted in numerous anthologies (P301, P303) and *The Commonweal Reader, The Best of the Best American Short Stories 1915-1950,* and others.

*The Presence of Grace.* Doubleday; Gollancz, 1956.      **P237**

*The Prince of Darkness, and Other Stories.* Im., 1947.      **P238**


**Prescott, Hilda F.M. 1896-  .**

Born in Latchford, Cheshire; B.A., M.A., Oxford; special lecturer, Oxford 1923-1943.

> *The Man on the Donkey: A Chronicle.* Macmillan, 1952; Eyre, 1953                                                    **P239**


**Queffelec, Henri. 1910-  .**

Born in Brest, Brittany; graduated Normale Superieure; married, three children; author of seven novels, short stories, essays; resident of Paris.

> *Island Priest.* Trans. by James Whitall. Dutton, 1952 o.p.  **P240**

> *The Kingdom Under the Sea.* Trans. by Len Ortzen. Pantheon, 1959.                                                   **P241**


**Ramuz, Charles F. 1878-1947.**

Born in Cully, Switzerland of French-Swiss parentage; studied at University of Lausanne; moved to Paris in 1902, lived in obscurity during which time he wrote four volumes of poetry, eight novels, two collections of short stories, none of which attracted attention; returned to Cully to begin long and successful writing career, publishing over twenty volumes of fiction; considered for Nobel Prize in 1945.

> *What is Man?* Pantheon, 1948.  Contains selections from the author's many works.                                    **P242**

> *When the Mountain Fell.* Trans. by Sarah Fisher Scott. Pantheon, 1947 o.p.                                          **P243**

**Sienkiewicz, Henryk. 1848-1916.**

Born in Lithuania of aristocratic Polish ancestry; educated University of Warsaw; traveled widely; founded a Polish colony in California, 1877; returned to Poland in 1880; $45,000 Nobel Prize in 1905 for "distinguished literary work"; imprisoned by Austrians during World War I at his Carpathian Mts. estate, a gift to him from the grateful Poles; died in Veray, Switzerland, while directing Polish relief.

> *Quo Vadis:* A Narrative of the Time of Nero. Trans. by Jeremiah Curtin. Little, 1943; Grosset; Dodd; Dutton Evman; Trans. by Hogarth, Dent; Ban. **P244**

> *Tales.* Evman; Dent. **P245**

**Silone, Ignazio. 1900- .**

Born in Pescina, Italy; educated in local schools as candidate for clergy until disastrous earthquake of 1915; from boyhood a champion of peasants, though not of that class by birth; became active leader in several extreme left, anti-war, militant Communist groups; spent brief periods in prison in Italy and Spain; left Communist Party in 1930, took up residence in Switzerland where major works were written; retired from active politics; member of International Congress for Freedom of Culture; correspondent for American Academy of Arts and Sciences.

> *Bread and Wine.* Trans. by G. David and E. Mosbacher, NAL. **P246**

> *Fontamara.*Trans. by Harvey Fergusson, II. Atheneum, 1960. Trans. by G. David and E. Mosbacher, Cape, 1948. **P247**

> *Handful of Blackberries.* Trans. by Darina Silone, Cape, 1954. **P248**

*Secret of Luca.* Trans. by Darina Silone. Harper, 1958.    **P249**

*The Seed Beneath the Snow:* Sequel to *Bread and Wine.* Trans. by Frances Frenaye. Harper, 1942 o.p.    **P250**

## Spark Muriel. 1918-  .

Born and educated in Edinburgh; spent some years in Central Africa; during World War II worked in Political Intelligence Dept. of Foreign Office; subsequently edited two poetry magazines; published works include critical biographies of nineteenth-century figures, editions of nineteenth-century letters, a volume of poems; stories in English and American magazines, in 1951 won first prize in the *Observer* short story competition.

*Comforters.* Lippincott, 1957.    **P251**

*The Go-Away Bird,* with other Stories. Lippincott, 1960.    **P252**

*Memento Mori.* Lippincott, 1959.    **P253**

*Robinson.* Lippincott, 1958.    **P254a**

*Ballad of Pickham Rye.* Macmillan, London, 1960.    **P245b**

## Stolpe, Sven. 1905-  .

Born in Stockholm, studied at Universities of Stockholm, Heidelberg, and Paris; much attracted by Swedish Oxford Movement for spiritual revival started by Frank Buchman; was one of founders of now famous "Stockholms Studenttheater" and the "Filmsstudio"; learned to understand Catholic outlook on life in France with authors such as Mauriac, Bernanos; his early works—such as *Burning Souls,* 1938, *Francois Mauriac, and Other Essays,* 1947, and *Spirit and Poetry,* 1950—kindled Swedish interest in Catholic literature; convert in 1947, preceded by wife; ranks as Sweden's first outstanding Roman Catholic publicist and essay writer; literary critic; novelist; *Jeanne d'Arc,* 1949, considered his best work.

*Night Music.* Trans. by John Devlin. Sheed, 1960.          **P255**

*The Sound of a Distant Horn.* Trans. by George Lamb. Sheed, 1957.                                                        **P256**

**Sullivan, Richard T. 1908-   .**

Born in Kenosha, Wisconsin, of Irish-German family; B.A. from Notre Dame, 1930; studied at Art Institute of Chicago and Goodman School of Drama before determining on literary career; stories, stage plays, radio plays, boys' adventure stories published before 1936 when he began teaching playwriting and poetry at Notre Dame; married, two daughters; book critic for New York *Times* and Chicago *Tribune.*

*First Citizen.* Holt, 1948 o.p.                           **P257**

*The Fresh and Open Sky, and Other Stories.* Holt, 1950 o.p.                                                       **P258**

*The Three Kings.* Harcourt, 1956.                         **P259**

*The World of Idella May.* Doubleday, 1946 o.p.            **P260**

**Tolstoy, Count Leo. 1828-1910.**

Born in Tula, 1828; studied at University of Kazan; in 1851 entered army, served in Causasus and at Sebastopol; after Crimean War left army to take up literary career; for many years interested in education and in later years devoted himself to religion; religious views set forth in *My Confession;* social reformer.

*Works.* 18 vols., World's Classics, Trans. by Louise and Ayler Maude. Oxford University Press; Dutton; Evman, 7 vols.                                                      **P261**

*Anna Karenina.* Trans. by Rochelle S. Townsend. 2 vols. Dutton; Evman; Dent; Heinemann; Trans. by Constance Garnett, ML.                                                        **P262**

*Short Novels.* Ed. by Philip Rahv. Dial, 1946.              **P263**

*Selections.* Ed. by Natalie Duddington and Nadejda Gorodetzky. Oxford University Press, 1959.                                   **P264**

*Tolstoy's Tales of Courage and Conflict.* Ed. by Charles Nieder. Doubleday, 1958.                                                **P265**

*War and Peace.* Ed. by Manual Komroff, Ban.; abridged ed. by Edmund Fuller, Dell, 1955; 3 vols., Evman; Grosset. **P266**

**Undset, Sigrid. 1882-1949.**

Born in Kallundborg, Denmark; educated in Oslo, Norway, where her father was professor of archaeology in the University; graduated from commercial college; became legal secretary; convert in 1928; awarded Nobel Prize in Literature in 1928.

*Four Stories.* Trans. by Naomi Walford. Knopf, 1959.      **P267**

*Images in a Mirror.* Trans. by Arthur G. Chater. Knopf, 1938 o.p.                                                              **P268**

*Kristin Lavransdatter.* Trans. by Charles Archer and J.S. Scott. Contains three novels originally published separately as *The Bridal Wreath*, 1923; *The Mistress of Husaby*, 1925; *The Cross*, 1927. Knopf, 1935; Cassell, 1954.              **P269**

*Madame Dorothea.* Trans. by Arthur G. Chater. Knopf, 1940 o.p.                                                              **P270**

*Master of Hestviken.* Trans. by Arthur G. Chater. Contains four novels originally published separately as *The Axe*, 1928; *Snake Pit*, 1929; *In the Wilderness*, 1929; *Son Avenger*, 1930. Knopf, 1952.                                            **P271**

*Return to the Future.* Trans. by Henriette C.K. Naeseth. Knopf, 1942 o.p.     **P272**

*Winding Road.* Comprises *Wild Orchid* and *Burning Bush.* 2 vols. Knopf, 1936 o.p.     **P273**

**Wallace, Lewis. 1827-1905.**

Born in Indiana; soldier, politician; novelist; served in Mexican War and Civil War; wrote *Ben Hur* while governor of New Mexico Territory.

*Ben Hur:* A Tale of the Christ. Harper, 1880; Grosset; Blackie, 1956; Norton; Random; abridged ed., Ban. and Dell; Collins, 1954; NAL; PB.     **P274**

**Waugh, Evelyn. 1903- .**

Born in London of literary family; educated at Lancing and Oxford; successively a student of painting, a schoolmaster, a journalist before beginning literary career; convert in 1930, since which time he has done most of his writing; served as 2nd Lt. in Royal Marines, and as a Commando during war; married, four children; considers *Brideshead Revisited* his best book.

*Black Mischief.* Little, 1946; Penguin, 1956.     **P275**

*Brideshead Revisited.* Dell, 1956; Grosset; Chap. & H., 1945.     **P276**

*Decline and Fall.* Grosset, 1958; Penguin, 1956; Chap. & H., 1928.     **P277**

*Handful of Dust.* (Bd. with *Decline and Fall*) Dell; New Directions; Penguin, 1956; Chap. & H., 1934.     **P278**

*Helena.* Little, 1950; Im., 1957; Chap & H.     **P279**

*The Loved One: An Anglo-American Tragedy.* Little, 1948;
    Chap. & H.; Penguin, 1956; Dell; ML.                    **P280**

*Men at Arms.* Little, 1952; Chap. & H.                     **P281**

*Officers and Gentlemen.* Little, 1955; Chap. & H.          **P282**

*Ordeal of Gilbert Pinfold.* Little, 1957.                  **P283**

*Put Out More Flags.* Little, 1942; Chap. & H.; Penguin,
    1956.                                                   **P284**

*Tactical Exercise.* Little, 1954.                          **P285**

*Vile Bodies.* (Bd. with *Black Mischief*), Dell; Little, 1944;
    Chap. & H., 1930; Penguin, 1956.                        **P286**


**West, Morris Langlo. 1915-   .**

Born and educated in Melborne; taught school ten years; with
R.A.F. in Pacific; founded recording company for syndicated radio
programs for which he wrote, directed, produced; sold out in 1952;
writes under pseudonym Michael East for paperbacks; with financial
success of one "East" paperback, moved family to Europe; worked for
couple of years on *Children of the Shadows;* visited Rome in 1958 as
special correspondent for the *London Daily Mail.*

*Backlash.* Morrow, 1958; PB.                               **P287**

*Children of the Shadows:* The True Story of the Street Urchins
    of Naples. Doubleday, 1957; English title, *Children of the
    Sun,* Heinemann, 1957.                                 **P288**

*The Crooked Road.* Morrow, 1957; English title, *The Big Story,*
    Heinemann, 1957.                                        **P289**

*The Devil's Advocate.* Morrow, 1959; Dell.                 **P290**

*The Second Victory.* Heinemann, 1958.                          **P291**

**White, Helen Constance. 1896-   .**

Born in New Haven, Conn.; B.A., Radcliffe College, 1916;
M.A., 1917; Ph.D., University of Wisconsin, 1924; Guggenheim
Fellowship; professor of English, University of Wisconsin.  Her
sister, Olive Bernardine White, has written two historical novels
which are out of print.

> *Bird of Fire:* A Tale of St. Francis of Assisi. Macmillan,
> 1959.                                                        **P292**

> *Dust on the King's Highway.* Macmillan, 1947 o.p.           **P293**

> *Four Rivers of Paradise.* Macmillan, 1955.                  **P294**

> *Not Built with Hands.* Macmillan, 1935 o.p.                 **P295**

> *To the End of the World.* Macmillan, 1939 o.p.              **P296**

> *A Watch in the Night.* Macmillan, 1933; Im., 1955.          **P297**

## SHORT STORY ANTHOLOGIES

> Brunini, John Gilland, and Francis X. Connolly, eds. *Stories of
> Our Century by Catholic Authors.* Im., 1955.                 **P298**

> Curtin, Mary Alice, comp. *Pilgrims All:* Short Stories by
> Contemporary Catholic Writers. Bruce, 1943 o.p.             **P299**

> Gable, Sister Mariella, ed. *Many Colored Fleece.* Sheed, 1954
> o.p.                                                        **P300**

> *Our Father's House.* Sheed, 1945 o.p.                       **P301**

> *Great Modern Catholic Short Stories.* Sheed, 1942 o.p.      **P302**

Garrity, Devin A., ed. *44 Irish Short Stories:* An Anthology of
    Irish Short Fiction from Yeats to Frank O'Connor. Devin-
    Adair, 1955.                                              **P303**

Gordon, Caroline, and Allen Tate, eds. *The House of Fiction:*
    An Anthology of the Short Story, with Commentary. 2nd
    ed. Scribner's, 1950.                                     **P304**

Grayson, Charles, ed. *The Golden Argosy:* A Collection of the
    Most Celebrated Short Stories in the English Language.
    Ed. by Van H. Cartmell and Charles Grayson. Dial,
    1955.                                                     **P305**

Jarrell, Randall, ed. *Anchor Book of Stories:* An Anthology.
    Anch, 1958.                                               **P306**

# Part Two: Individual Authors

# Chapter 6

## Arrows at the Center[1]

Recently it has been our good fortune in this country to be given in English translation Catholic novels by two French writers, Mauriac and Bernanos, and one by the South American writing in Spanish, Eduardo Barrios. Simultaneously in our own country appeared the work of Mr. J.F. Powers, the first American writer of Catholic fiction whose literary stature entitles him to stand with his foreign peers. To the fastidious critic of Catholic fiction the work of these men is a matter for rejoicing, a flock of golden arrows flying straight to the bull's eye at the center of Catholic fiction.

It is, of course, only the arrows shot by Georges Bernanos which hit the punctual center of the bull's eye. But the others come so close to hitting it, all piercing the small area of the bull's eye, that it is well to see how these expert marksmen took their aim. It is well to celebrate their success with understanding and enthusiasm. To Bernanos both of these have been quite generally denied. Many readers see in his work only a forbidding somberness. In fact, there are not many Catholics who realize that he is our master marksman.

But before his amazing achievement can be appreciated, and that of the others, we must stand back and get an appropriate perspective. We must see the target as a whole. At the center, of course, is the bull's eye, and around it lie three concentric circles (or as many as any individual wishes to designate). Beginning at the periphery, with the circle farthest removed from the center, we have Catholic fiction which gives us only the local color of Catholic life— descriptions of people attending Mass, keeping the feasts, receiving the sacraments, living in convents or monasteries. The purpose of this fiction may be no more than to answer the question, "Who done it?" as does *Murder in a Nunnery*. But we do ask that whatever the substance, it at least be harmless. Lower than this standard it is not possible to go.

Perhaps this absolute minimum needs to be insisted upon—in view of the fact that a vulgar, dangerous, blasphemous book like *Miracle of the Bells* was selected for Catholic readers by a Catholic book club, was recommended by Catholic libraries, was given an A rating in diocesan newspapers, and was first place among Catholic best sellers for several months. Let us insist that, though Catholic local color may entitle a book to be regarded as peripheral fiction, we also require that the book's message be at least harmless, no matter how shallow or frivolous.

In the second circle of the target fall all the novels concerned primarily with ethical problems. The Church, of course, has no corner on ethics, and it is possible to have a sound treatment of an ethical problem on the human level, as for instance in *Anna Karenina*. I am not inclined, however, to regard such books as Catholic novels. The great curse of our time has been the heresy that one can have right relations with human beings without right relations with God. It seems to me, therefore, that the ethical problem must be firmly anchored in conscience before the book can be called Catholic. That is, the problem must be explored not only from the viewpoint of the human but also from the viewpoint of the nexus between conduct and God. The classic example of this type of book is, of course, *Kristin Lavransdatter*. Among the recent books Kate O'Brien's *For One Sweet Grape* makes a wise and sensitive study in just this way. The peculiar value of this book lies in its careful study of the degree to which complicated psychological processes interfere with the tenets of a right conscience. The novel says, in effect, that one of the most stupid things about sin is our ignorance of our own motives.

We are sometimes taught to think of conscience as constituting simple decisions in black and white. The adult discovers large areas of gray; in fact, it may be said that maturity is indicated by the awareness of the grays. Kate O'Brien explores the grays. "Even in repentance one cannot afford to be self indulgent." Such are the subtleties of the novel.

Since seven of the ten commandments regulate the relationship of human beings to human beings, it is understandable that the greater number of novels fall in the second circle of Catholic fiction.

In the third circle, that lying nearest to the bull's eye, we find novels concerned with truth. Here are the stories on birth-control and race problems. Here are the stories which say in one way or another that in Mother Church is the truth.

But often these latter are deeply disappointing. We may, for convenience, call these unsatisfactory books the novels of entrance and exit. In them, for instance, we follow souls outside the Church in all their anguished seeking for truth coming into the fold in the last chapter. When the waters of baptism flow over the happy converts' heads, we hope that they live happily ever after. In the search of the hero for the light, some valuable dogmatic truth is ordinarily discovered, or some beauty or goodness in the Church is explained. But at the moment when the novelist might give us a picture of what life is like in the bosom of Mother Church, exit the author, the hero, and the story. In fallen-away Catholics who behave like fools and beasts through twenty-four chapters and stumble back into the fold on their deathbed, we have another type of the novel of entrance and exit, as in the enormously over-estimated *Brideshead Revisited.* Though in all justice let it be noted that Evelyn Waugh is the only British novelist besides Graham Greene who is giving us Catholic fiction of quality.

In spite of all their excellent teaching, these novels of entrance and exit remind one of the early secular romances. In these stories one followed the vicissitudes of boy pursuing girl until the last chapter closed on the ringing of the wedding bells. But people began to ask, what happened then? Life begins when the bride is carried over the threshold. How did the man and woman make out? What were their problems? What were their rewards? Similarly, the Catholic readers are not satisfied with fiction of mere entrance into the Church, and deathbed conversions. They have a right to ask: How does being in the Church affect life? What are the specific problems of those who have the light? There is no mistaking the meaning of that light: the terrible and overwhelming obligation, which does not cease by day or night, to love God with one's whole heart, one's whole soul, one's whole strength.

The white center of the target of Catholic fiction is devoted to a study of the human and spiritual problems involved in keeping the

first commandment—the forgotten commandment. The one great
fiction writer in the Church who has been able to hit the precise center
of the bull's eye is the French writer, Georges Bernanos. His arrow
went straight to the mark in *Diary of a Country Priest* and in *Star of
Satan*. In the recently translated *Joy* his aim is even more keen and
direct. And *Joy* is, from one point of view, a much more exciting
contribution than the other two novels in which the heroes were
priests, for it is a study of a layperson pursuing sanctity. Our age will
go down in the history of the Church, I believe, as the age in which
laypeople were rediscovered—as thinkers, leaders, and saints.
Bernanos, like all great writers, is ahead of his age; he is a prophet
and a seer.

   He sees with terrible clarity the curse of mediocrity among
Christians. All that he says is of a piece. Like Jeremiah and the
prophets of old he cries out in anger and exasperation to all of us to
convert before it is too late. He is more angry than Swift and Carlyle,
as urgent as St. Paul, as incisive and vivid in his prose as only
Bernanos can be. His avowed enemy is the bourgeois spirit in society
and in the Church. He summarizes his horror of mediocre
Christianity thus in *Plea for Liberty*:

> The most dangerous shortsightedness consists in underestimating
> the mediocre; mediocrity is a colorless and odorless gas; allow it
> to accumulate undisturbed, and suddenly it explodes with a force
> beyond all belief. . . . The dire omen for all of us, whether
> believers or unbelievers is not that Christians should be less
> numerous, but that the number of mediocre Christians should
> increase. (165)

What is the condition opposed to Christian mediocrity? It is holiness.
It is sanctity. It is the earnest pursuit of the spiritual life. It is the
perpetual consciousness that we are bound by the first commandment.
It is the practice of—let us not shy away from the word as if it does
not concern us—it is the practice of contemplation.

   The most amazing and unique gift of Bernanos is his ability to
present the experiences of the contemplative life. Ninety-nine
novelists out of a hundred can dramatize powerfully and artistically
the fiction of failure, sin, and human weakness. Bernanos is the only
novelist who can portray, with equal power, the step-by-step progress
of persons devoted to the spiritual life.

*Joy* is an amazing clarification of the final steps toward sanctity of a seventeen-year-old girl, Chantal. There are many types of sanctity in the Church. Chantal follows a very special pattern. It is the pattern made classic for us in the counsels of St. Francis de Sales—those counsels delivered so lovingly to laypeople, advising perfect submission to the will of God, moment by moment. To desire nothing, to refuse nothing, sounds very simple, and is in reality, even simpler than it sounds. When the idea is grasped, one sees that heaven, which is an eternal here and an eternal now, can be begun on this earth if past and future are ignored, and if the present alone concerns us as an opportunity to do what God wills for us in any given moment. Chantal has learned the secret. When the book opens, we see her in perfect peace and radiance of spirit having achieved the joy that comes with being a simple child in the hand of God. The reasons Bernanos gives for Chantal's refusal to enter a convent deserve the reader's special attention.

With such a saint as a heroine the book ought to present no difficulties. "It is what we have been praying for," say pious Catholics, and settle themselves comfortably to be edified in the Hollywood manner, with the ringing of bells for four days and the mass movement of thousands of excited spectators to view a heroine a hundred times better than Olga Treskovna. But the reader is bitterly disappointed. The book closes with one suicide, one murder, and one character having gone irrevocably insane. And the reader says, "No, thank you. If that is the effect of sanctity, I will have none of it. It is not only more comfortable but more decent to remain safely mediocre."

The difficulties presented by the book are twofold. When they are understood, it will be seen that Bernanos is not perversely somber and pessimistic, but that he is profoundly true.

In the first place, he undertakes to interpret Chantal at a very advanced stage in her spiritual development. She has for some time before the opening of the story experienced the joy of spirit which comes from having given herself entirely to God. The story proper is a description of Chantal's final spiritual purification—her passage through the dark night of the soul. That is a phrase, the dark night of the soul, used loosely and ridiculously by many persons who have not the slightest understanding of its meaning. The average pious person, feeling some spiritual depression, some aridity, or constitutional ineptitude, sighs and labels his doldrums the dark night of the soul.

Absurd!  The dark night of the soul is the final purification of perfect souls wherein God withdraws all sense of joy in service, all sense of support and liveliness of faith, in order that the perfect soul may detach itself entirely from the pleasure of the spiritual life, the last smallest shred of self-satisfaction, and embrace God entirely for God's own sake.

The dark night marks a very advanced stage in spiritual development, and in the average neglect of the spiritual life among Christians it is simply not known, much less understood.  Chantal, was, for some time under the guidance of a very holy confessor, the Abbé Chevance.  He died so hard a death as to try, if possible, the faith of Chantal.  The pious reader is disedified.  If the Abbé had only seen a statue come alive in his room and extend loving arms to him at the last!  If there had only been some sign of sweetness and light at the end!

Such readers must find the total dereliction of Christ on Calvary entirely disedifying.  They cannot remember that on the Cross He cried out in terrible anguish of spirit, "My God, my God, why hast thou forsaken me?"  Having read only such lives of the saints as have aimed at edification at the expense of truth, readers are shocked and horrified at reality.  They have seen sweet statues of Bernadette at our Lady's feet; they have failed to note her desolate little cry on her death bed, "I am afraid."

Perhaps a passage from *Joy* spoken by the cook at the scene of Chantal's bloody death which the girl received at the hands of the horrible Fiodore, will help clarify the whole notion of perfect abnegation:

> You will never get it out of my head, Abbé, that it is the death
> she wanted—no other—just this one!  You coudn't ever humiliate
> her enough, she wanted nothing but scorn, she would have lived
> in the dust.  That Russian was surely the wickedest of us all.  So
> she would have wanted her end to come from him. . . . And now
> people will be shaking their heads and gossiping; they'll say she
> was crazy and worse. . . . She will have renounced everything,
> Abbé, everything I tell you, even her death. (296)

To renounce even one's death—it is a tremendous concept.  Bernanos alone of all the great fiction writers has the experience, the insight, and the power to explore this kind of reality in the spiritual

life. We ought to come to him with humility and amazement—and
not complain of his temperamental somberness.

Besides exploring Chantal's spiritual development at the highest
point, the book undertakes one other major task, to record the effect
of Chantal on the persons of her household. And therein lies the
second great difficulty of the book—which, like the first, is no longer
a difficulty when properly understood.

The persons directly influenced by the motherless Chantal are:
her father, Monsieur de Clergerie, a desiccated little fossil of a man,
who was "born to have a career and not a life," and who has devoted
that career to sterile research and neurotic interest in his own
ailments; a psychiatrist, La Perouse, who probes cynically into the
cesspools of other people's minds and who takes on Chantal as his
patient at the request of her father; the Abbé Cenabre, who has lost
his faith but has never ceased to go through the motions of his priestly
life; and the suave white Russian chauffeur, totally evil and perverted.
Collectively these persons constitute the colorless and ordorless gas of
mediocrity, which Bernanos thinks so terrifyingly dangerous. When
the flame of sanctity is brought into contact with this seemingly
inocuous gas there must be a fearful explosion, says Bernanos. And
so there is. The Russian murders Chantal and then kills himself. The
priest goes irrevocably insane. And the pious reader is scandalized.

Why did Chantal not bring sweetness and light to her household?
the reader asks sulkily and not a little hurt. Because, shouts
Bernanos, mediocrity is a horror that cannot endure sanctity. We
might have remembered Joan of Arc burned at the stake by "good
people". We might have remembered Judas selling Christ and then
killing himself. The Russian who murders Chantal is a symbol of
Judas.

And the priest who goes irrevocably insane—there is a
tremendous poetic justice in his end. He saves his soul. Shaken to
the very depths of his being by his contact with Chantal, he does
recover his faith, but with the straining and rocking of all the powers
of his brilliant mind. Near Chantal's dead body he kneels and says
two words: "Our Father". He has returned to the arms of God's
mercy. But in the same breath he falls forward on his face exhausted
and never again gains his use of reason. There is a terrible justice in
his insanity. He who prostituted his reason, performing his priestly
duties without faith and refusing to leave the priesthood because it is
inexpedient, lives on without the use of reason. He might be a

character from Dante's *Purgatorio* where sinners pay their debt with uncanny appropriateness. The unwary reader may think the priest by no means an example of mediocrity; rather a symbol of unusual failure. But that is to misunderstand Bernanos. To him mediocrity is just that: going through the appropriate motions without a living faith.

Never has Bernanos written more savagely than he has in describing the persons of Chantal's household. Perhaps he is most savage of all in his treatment of the girl's father. Nothing happens to him—as if the worst possible curse were to remain in a state of spiritual mediocrity.

I have said that Bernanos has hit the precise center of the bull's eye of Catholic fiction. There are, however, the other arrows striking the white disk above and below and to the side of the center. These arrows are extremely important. They represent a Catholic fiction which deals with the problems of the spiritual life just as certainly as does the fiction of Bernanos. But with this difference: Bernanos writes of success, of the saint; the others write of failure. But they write, not of ethical failure, but of the mistakes of those who have given themselves in a most special way to the keeping of the first commandment. And the heroes of these books are all persons who have made the fundamental failures: They have supposed they were seeking God when they were seeking themselves. Here is the ABC of the whole problem.

And let it be understood that in the conflict between self and God lies the greatest conflict in their art. Well, as artists, Catholic writers have here the most rewarding grist that could conceivably come to any artist's mill. The new Catholic fiction which explores the subtle deception to which pious persons are exposed is a fiction of great wisdom. And it is a wisdom foundational for any building of a spiritual life. One cannot recommend too strongly the fiction which makes crystal clear the fact that the bowl which is full of the water of self cannot be filled with the wine of God.

There are three stories in this class of fiction which ought not to be missed: *Woman of the Pharisees* by F. Mauriac; "Lions, Harts, Leaping Does," by J.F. Powers in his *Prince of Darkness*; and *Brother Ass* by E. Barrios.

*Woman of the Pharisees* by Mauriac is a classic exposing the degree to which good works can become an incense burned to a cruel self rather than a sacrifice made for the love of God and neighbor. It is a book one wishes all Catholics could study. "Lions, Harts, Leaping Does" by Powers is a brilliant picture of an aged Franciscan who refuses to make a trip in order to see his very old brother. The reasons for his decision are extremely subtle and indicate a peculiar confusion of self-seeking and God-seeking, though the friar tells himself that it is a more perfect thing to mortify human attachments. *Brother Ass* by Barrios has long been a favorite with South Americans, and it is to be feared that the appearance in an English translation of this quite wonderful Spanish novella is nearly lost to Catholic readers in this country, since it is buried in a collection of other South American stories under the title *Fiesta in November*. But it ought to be read and known by everyone. For it makes an illuminating study of the romantic temperament in the pursuit of holiness. Perhaps there are more souls who have been led astray by the wolf of self in the soft, sweet fleece of romantic clothing than by any other lure.

Though Bernanos holds first place for portraying the white light of sanctity achieved, the writers of negative fiction deserve great credit for showing the subtle dangers of the blanket extinguisher—the self-seeking that masquerades as God seeking. And all of them have included minor characters who represent the saint's successful throwing off this blanket. All of the fiction of the center, positive and negative, is concerned directly with the problems of keeping the first commandment.

I believe that the Catholic fiction of the center which we have at present heralds the dawn on a new period—a period of great spiritual renascence, the rediscovery of the contemplative life, no less. All around us there are amazing indications of a renewal of interest in religion, not in the spirit of contention—orthodoxy, that's my doxy; heterodoxy, that's your doxy—but in the spirit of the lover seeking union with God. Mr. E.I. Watkin in *Catholic Art and Culture* has taken upon himself the role of a new John the Baptist announcing the coming reign of the Holy Spirit. He argues that since there are three Persons in the Trinity it is inevitable that the third Person will have a special epiphany and reign—signified by the common practice of the contemplative life—the union of souls with God. There is every indication that this age will be remembered for the discovery of the Catholic layperson as the vessel of holiness and leadership.

From so strange a witness as Aldous Huxley comes further evidence of the new emphasis. Outside the pale of organized religion he has been seeking with harrowing anxiety for a solution to the grave problems of the world. And he comes up with the gospel of the importance of contemplation in the social order if society is to be saved at all. He has long been telling us that saints are the necessary nexus between heaven and earth without which society dies. In *The Perennial Philosophy* he examined oriental and occidental contemplation to see just what all of them have in common—that which saves a sick world.

Coming from a very different quarter is the evidence from an exiled Russian, Pitirim Sorokin. Pointing out in *The Crisis of Our Age* the extreme decadence of our sensist culture, he shows that there is no place for the pendulum to swing now but back to a God-centered culture. It is a rosy hope.

We can hasten its consummation. We can read the great books of the center that we have. And loving these books, making them more, will help disperse our shameful mediocrity. Furthermore, once rid of our lukewarmness we shall cease to lose the loyalty of some of the artists who were born to the faith, but who have since fallen away. They represent the terrible leakage in the church—men of great power and high gifts who might have been on the side of the angels. As to their reasons for leaving the Church, James Farrell, perhaps, best epitomizes these. In all his books he complains about the spiritual sterility of Catholics—the making of motions rather than the living of the life of grace. Farrell's message amounts to an indictment of that same spiritual mediocrity against which the Catholic fiction of the center joins its blast.

But with this difference: Farrell sees a solution of the problem in a leap into outer darkness where there is only weeping and gnashing of teeth. The fiction writers of the center know that the light, the glory, the truth, the peace, and the love are all within—obscured though they may be by individual failure. Among them the negative writers point with helpful precision to the failure and beg us not to fail; the great positive writers see the light and flash its alluring splendor in our eyes.

Readers have tremendous obligations. They should remember that without a great Catholic audience a great Catholic literature is not possible. They should read the good books which we have and make them known. But more important than their duty to art and the artist is their Christian duty to themselves. They should note that they, too, must hit the bull's eye God has commanded them to hit: to love God with their whole heart, their whole soul, their whole strength. Suddenly they will be dazzled by the discovery that they as human beings and the Catholic artist as artist are aiming at the same target. No longer is there a divisive spirit.

## Notes

1. Mariella Gable, O.S.B., "Arrows at the Center," *The Catholic Library World* (April 1947): 219-24. Reprinted in Mariella Gable, *This is Catholic Fiction* (New York: Sheed & Ward, 1948).

# Chapter 7

## Catholic Fiction Arrives in America[1]

In order to have a great Catholic literature we must have a great Catholic audience. We must have readers, and a great many of them, capable of receiving pleasure from great Catholic writing.

In this country, sensing only vaguely something of this truth, we have mobilized the ballyhoo of advertising in support of the Catholic press—mistaking zeal for discrimination, best sellers for good books, numbers of names for great names. We have supposed that anything Catholic, no matter how cheap, sentimental, or shallow, deserved our Best in Modern Advertising. Perhaps it has deserved just that.

But promoting bad taste in Catholic literature is a terrible evil. In an atmosphere heavy with the stale perfume of sentimentality and the carbon dioxide of triteness a great book cannot breathe. It struggles and dies. In view of this fact, the publication of *Prince of Darkness* by J. F. Powers presents a test and a challenge to Catholic readers.

This book marks a milestone in American Catholic letters. In it for the first time in this country we have an indication that we can produce a Catholic fiction comparable to the great European Catholic fiction. *Prince of Darkness* will be received enthusiastically, of course, by the few fastidious readers who have rejoiced in the Europeans like Bernanos, Mauriac, Undset, Greene, Waugh, and O'Brien.

But the question is: can a current of air be circulated between the elite and the benighted so that the oxygen and fresh ozone from the small area of a sympathetic climate will ventilate the large stuffiness of Catholic taste?   Or will we permit this book to be stifled by neglect, or killed by the fear of fresh air and the strong light of the sun?   Upon our reception of this book depends to a large extent, I think, the course that Catholic creative art will take in America for some time to come.

*Prince of Darkness* contains eleven stories, of which several have been published before.  Let the reader begin anywhere he will with this book, he will know after reading four or five pages that Powers' gift is of the first order.

Take the few opening pages of the title story, "Prince of Darkness."  They present Father Burner accosted at the breakfast table by a B.C.L., a Big Catholic Layman, who is selling the priest insurance.  Here is needlesharp insight into human nature wedded to an uncanny ability to describe.  The reader is continually confronted with the sensation of having been exposed to nakedness—human nature in total undress.  So exciting and pleasant is the revelation that the story does not matter at all.

This insight, says the reader, is joy enough.  And so is it with all of the stories.  But their charm does not end there.  They have a power of invention equal to their insight and are sometimes crowded with violent action as in "The Trouble" and "The Eye."

The varieties of human experience which are probed indicate, moreover, the wide scope of the author's ability: in "Jamesie," the exquisitely sympathetic portrayal of a child's disillusionment; in "The Old Bird, A Love Story," a tender understanding of the old; in three stories, "The Trouble," "The Eye," and "He Don't Plant Cotton," insight into the very texture and temper of the Negro's personality.

The amazing versatility of Powers is as much at home with the deepest spiritual problems of an aged Franciscan as with the subtle psychological experiences of a refugee in a bar.  Here then, there is no mistaking a young writer whose gift of style, power of invention, and breadth of experience command the respect of the serious critic.

But, *mirabile dictu*, Powers is first and foremost a creator of Catholic fiction.  Out of his eleven stories eight are of very special interest to Catholics.  Five of these are about priests, and they pierce in a most searching way to the very heart of spiritual problems.

These five stories—"The Lord's Day," "Lions, Harts, Leaping Does," "The Forks," "The Valiant Woman," and "Prince of Darknesss"—include the best things Powers has written.

Furthermore, they leave the reader in no doubt whatsoever that the special area of life which fascinates Powers most is the rectory. In fact, some of Powers' readers have insisted that he must either be a wearer of the Roman collar or have had a prolonged experience in a seminary, else he could not write with his intimate understanding of details.

Powers has never been a seminarian. But he has been known to attend retreats for priests. His most intimate friends are priests—a flock of young men like Father Eudex in "The Forks." In fact, Father Eudex may be taken as a symbol of Powers' focal point of view. It is through the eyes of this zealous young man, allergic to the encroachments of materialism and commercialism upon the parsonage, that we are asked to look at the well-fed, well-groomed, golf-playing, car-driving priests in his pages.

He has given two full-length portraits of these priests. In "Prince of Darkness" Father Burner is a clerical Babbitt. In "The Forks" the Monsignor is a vulture for culture, who attempts to educate Father Eudex in the use of forks. Here is strong satire which is at the same time incomparably more than satire. One does not feel for a single moment that it is the purpose of Powers to convert, to point a lesson, to castigate.

He is fascinated, rather, by the human spectacle of the tension between the leaven and the loaf. Here are all the ironies of the universal struggles between the flesh and the spirit heightened to the point of roaring comedy. Behind the deft comment, the sharp phrase, there is the rumble of a Rabellaisan belly laugh. And because the laugh is so warm and human the shouting can be loud. This is how the Monsignor enters the rectory: "He held the screen door open momentarily, as if remembering something or reluctant to enter before himself—such was his humility." (129)

There are certain objections that have been brought against these stories. For instance, it has been said that no priest ever anointed with the holy oils was so completely Babbitt as is Father Burner. To raise the question is to miss entirely something significant about the technique of Powers. His method is that of the classicists. He isolates, as does Ben Jonson, a single trait or characteristic. It is a literary method extraordinarily effective in the hands of a writer like J.F. Powers, who individualizes every person whom his pen touches.

It has further been objected that it is not advisable to air dirty clerical linens in public. But there are no soiled pieces brought to light here which have not been waving for years before our faces in every average parish in the United States.

Powers' treatment of these pieces, however, marks a milestone in Catholic writing. In his book we are suddenly aware of the fact that the Church in this country has passed beyond a period of immaturity during which it was self-consciously on the defensive.

In a family that has not arrived socially there is great care exercised to keep up appearances before guests, but in a family that is accepted socially, the members rib each other good-naturedly and frankly. They can afford to be sincere and honest about each other.

Much of our timidity in American writing in the past has stemmed from Irish influence. For many years the Irish suffered the terrible privation of having no priests. When they came to America, they not only gave their sons in great numbers to the Church but developed a kind of unwritten law that a curse would fall upon the head of anyone who dared to express the least criticism of a priest.

In so far as this attitude expressed a reverence for Holy Orders, it is a tradition to be cherished. Powers never loses its spirit. He is an Irishman, though not born on the auld sod. His affinity for priests is in his Irish blood as is his joyous sense of humor, but his attitude marks the passing of timidity, insecurity, fear. He is at home in the Church. And because the Church is his home he feels free to ask a little more holiness in priests, not because he is a carping critic, but because he loves the beauty for which the priesthood stands.

Powers writes about priests because he wants characters who are devoted to something besides earning a living. To him priests are seekers of the Grail; in fact they hold the Grail in their hands. Their spiritual dedication gives to all they do, their failure as well as their success, a depth and a resonance which Powers values above everything else.

In two of his stories Powers makes a study of the relationship of priests to women—housekeepers and nuns. "The Valiant Woman" shows the priest dominated by the housekeeper; "The Lord's Day," the priest dominating the nuns. Powers articulates no connection, but the reader is tempted to make a delicious generalization.

The housekeeper, Mrs. Stoner, is, according to Powers' habit of isolating types, all the dominating housekeepers who have ever ruled parishes and priests rolled into one. One of the funniest of all

Powers' humorous passages occurs when the henpecked Father Firman looks up the section in Canon Law regulating the choice of housekeeper, in order to see where the catch is. But at the end of the day the two play honeymoon bridge and all their bottled wrath is expressed in how they play the cards. Powers says:

> She was awful in victory. Here was the bitter end of their long day together, the final murderous hour in which all they wanted to say—all he wouldn't and all she couldn't—came out in the cards. Whoever won at honeymoon won the day, slept on the other's scalp, and God alone had to help the loser. (171)

J.F. Powers uses symbols adroitly. In this story, the mosquito—"only the female bites"—becomes a kind of Greek chorus in which the whole miserable relationship of the man and woman is counter-pointed in whine and sting, and at last in the futile efforts of the priest to swat the insect.

The fifth of the stories about priests is a classic, the best thing Powers has written, "Lions, Harts, Leaping Does." It is one of the mysteries of creative genius how a young man in his middle twenties could probe so deeply the subtle spiritual problems of an aged Franciscan. Here are socratic wisdom, maturity, tenderness, and a precocious understanding of the spiritual life. Yet the story will remain caviar to the general and presents difficulties not encountered elsewhere in Powers, except in "Renner."

Of special interest to Catholics there are, finally, the three stories about Negroes. "He Don't Plant Cotton" enters sympathically into the Negro temperament; "The Eye" examines lynching; "The Trouble" concentrates on a race riot, with a fleeting but unforgettable glimpse of the failure and responsibility of Catholics in the crisis.

To Powers, pigmentation is indeed an accident, in the Thomistic sense. He may deal with riots and lynchings, but the Negro is never to him merely a symbol of someone to whom wrong has been done. His Negroes are all people first and Negroes second. In his craft as an artist he wields a stronger stick for justice than in exhibiting the wrongs of the Negro.

What Powers sees as an artist coincides exactly with what the Church teaches in her doctrine of the Mystical Body. Here is the perfect integration of the artist and the Catholic.

The Catholic Literary Revival has been slow in getting under way in America. But we may point with just pride to our poets,

Jessica Powers and Thomas Merton. And now we have J.F. Powers in Catholic fiction. Every nation gets the book it deserves. The most certain way of deserving great books is to welcome with enthusiasm the best we have. *Prince of Darkness* is a test and a challenge.

## Notes

1 Mariella Gable, O.S.B., "Catholic Fiction Arrives in America," *Today*, 30 April 1947, 12. Reprinted in Mariella Gable, *This is Catholic Fiction* (New York: Sheed & Ward, 1948).

# Chapter 8

---

# New Boundaries[1]

*The Heart of the Matter* is a magnificent book. Since its publication, reviewers have praised its powerful union of substance, insight, and artistic expression. Its greatness, however, is understood only if one recognizes to what a degree Graham Greene has expanded the boundaries of the English novel.

It is nearly incredible that it has taken the English novel two centuries to discover that the most important fact about human beings is their relationship to God. During those two centuries boundaries have been extended many times, but always outward toward peripheries. At the utmost edge have been explored the maggots of obscenity and perversion. Cretins, idiots, and morons have been our heroes. Psychiatry has recently opened new territories. But if we are regarded merely as a victim of our sub-conscious, we are no longer interesting as protagonists. Life is sound and fury signifying nothing.

Now all areas of experience lie wide open to the artist who is free to deal with reality wherever it is found. But there is a vast difference in value between the peripheral realities of the pus and bubonics of human nature and those which lie at the heart of the matter. It is Greene's distinction that he has chosen to write of the reality of realities—the relationship of human beings to God. Not in the pious tradition that has always been over-simplified, but in the courageous statement that the choice of mortal sin by an informed

Catholic can involve complexities in the sinner's relationship with God apparently unprovided for by the copy-book rules. Greene is a pioneer in his analysis of the peculiar nexus between the moral and spiritual order.

Beside *The Heart of the Matter* the pale spirituality of *Brideshead Revisited* is as old-fashioned as a Victorian wig, and a Victorian classic like *Middlemarch* (Bulstrode's temptation to kill Raffles, which is examined only on an ethical level) reads like a child's primer. Even an acute study of conscience such as is found in Kate O'Brien's *For One Sweet Grape* only skirts the complexities examined in Greene's new book. Bernanos and Mauriac have, of course, long ago made the human relationship to God their central themes. But Greene has explored a part of that center as yet untouched by the French.

This book serves notice that the English novel has at last achieved maturity. It is a challenge to the literary world stating in no uncertain terms that the English novel will no longer be content with a limited and inadequate view of humanity, nor with anything less than the center of realities.

Let us see what *The Heart of the Matter* says. The hero, Scobie, is a good man—by his very nature honest, dependable, and deeply compassionate. But circumstances lead him to many grave sins—among them adultery, sacriligious communions, and suicide. His faith never wavers. He knows all about mortal sin. He knows that he is choosing damnation. He knows that he is offending God.

He commits sin out of mistaken pity for his wife and mistress, believing that he spares them suffering by his sin. But he chooses his sins with agonizing regret. The pages of the book describing what goes on in Scobie's mind as he receives communion in mortal sin and as he decides to kill himself constitute the heart of the matter.

Scobie says to God: "I love you . . . If you made me, you made this feeling of responsibility that I've always carried about like a sack of bricks . . . I can't make one of them suffer so as to save myself." And concerning his bad communions: "I love you and I won't go on insulting you at your own altar" (289-90).

The complexity of what goes on in Scobie's heart is so great that mortal sin and love of God *seem* to coexist.

Greene spares no pains to underline this conclusion. Into the mouth of Father Rank he puts these comments after Scobie's suicide: "The Church knows all the rules. But it doesn't know what goes on in a single human heart . . . It may seem an odd thing to say—when a man's as wrong as he was—but I think from what I saw of him that he really loved God . . . A priest knows only the unimportant things . . . I mean the sins . . . A man doesn't come to us and confess his virtues" (306).

Now if all this says that mortal sin and love of God are co-existent, the book is heretical. I am not a theologian, and the judgment as to the theological soundness of the book can come with authority only from a theologian. I will, therefore, let the famous English Jesuit, Father C.C. Martindale, make the decision. Father Martindale says:

> I am glad that prudent priests and experienced laymen think as I do—that this is a magnificent book, both theologically accurate and by a layman who "knows as much as any man can know about human nature." I know one, a hard-headed man, to whom this book has given the last necessary stimulus to becoming a Catholic and many who like me will continue to draw from re-reading it a deeper love of suffering, distraught humanity, and God.

But Father Martindale does not have the full chorus of Catholic critics with him. A shudder of unease has gone through the ranks. If some critics are not ready to brand the book unsound, they do indicate that they regard it as a theological impropriety. Would it not be better to maintain the popular impression that there are clear boundaries between black and white? Is it not more discreet to ignore the grays?

Sensitive and intelligent readers cry out No, a thousand times No. They recognize what goes on in Scobie's conscience to be true—they know it by their own experience. They realize that for a novelist to explore this reality is a magnificent expansion of the boundaries of truth and they rejoice at that expansion. They know also that the norms for judging mortal sin are true, that they all seem to be fulfilled in Scobie's case, and that mortal sin and love are mutually exclusive.

Furthermore, readers are certain that they are here dealing with a paradox, not a real contradiction. It is like the conflict that seemed to exist between faith and science when the theory of evolution cast certain of the faithful into a panic. But sensitive readers feel no panic whatsoever. They know that truth is one and that the truth of science, whether it be biological or psychological, can never conflict with the truth of theology.

But why should a novelist be regarded with the theologian and the scientist as contributing to the expansion of a human being's knowledge of reality? What is a novelist? A novelist as a seer knows human destiny and the laws which govern its achievement—not as abstractions, but by the infinite mutations of the human heart receiving, evading, or breaking that law. The artist's gift of understanding the human heart is as special as the scientist's microscope or telescope. Artists' intuitions are as dependable as a test tube. Their world is the individual and the concrete. Their wisdom is that of the first observers before the law was promulgated. Theirs is the power to recreate the individual and the concrete in beauty and in order so that less sensitive souls may share their wisdom and the fruit of their contemplation.

By very definition we see that a novelist is a Catholic. For who but a Catholic knows fully human destiny and the laws that govern its achievement? Novelists who take a materialistic, naturalistic, or deterministic view of life by that very fact cancel their status as novelists. Greene himself has indicated as much by dividing his own books into two classes. He regards as novels only those stories which are profoundly Catholic, those which probe the human heart in pursuit of its spiritual destiny. All others he calls merely entertainments.

By definition a novel is serious. It weds art and theology. But until now the novelist and the theologian have been in conflict. In *Theology and Sanity* Sheed summarizes thus: ". . . the theologian finds the modern novel chaotic . . . . But if the theologian dismisses the novelist's world as lacking shape, the novelist dismisses the theologian's world as lacking flesh and blood." Sheed goes on to point out that the theologian needs the novelist for his own development. He says, "The theologian may well have something to gain from the novelist . . . . There is much to be learned by sharing the fruit of the experience of others by reading, not simply reading philosophy, but the works of men especially gifted to react to reality," i. e. the novelist.

It would be the most egregious affrontery on my part to say anything about what theologians need for their own good. But I do wish to underline here one of the greatest needs of the faithful at the present time—the need for the theologian who is at the same time a literate reader of fiction. There are literal readers and literate readers. The literal reader never understands the implications of fiction. According to Father John P. Murphy in the *London Universe*, *The*

*Heart of the Matter* is just another book about sin, and he dismisses it with a shrug and one cynical question: Why write it?

Now this sort of criticism does a great deal of harm. It is an acute trial to the faith of the intelligent reader who would wish the critic to see at least what the problems are which lie at the heart of the matter. And even if the critic were right in his supposing that the novel is just another book about sin, he ought to be on his knees thanking God for it. The very greatest heresy of our age has been its denial of the fact of sin. Our fiction has been filled with people falling off the floor, no height of salvation from which to descend, no depth of hell into which to fall. Critics who want a Catholic fiction to be free from sin are unwittingly contributing to this modern heresy. A book like *The Heart of the Matter*, which handles sin explicitly as damnation with its tragic loss of heaven, is even on its literal level a great contribution to the Catholic cause.

But we need the critic who will handle it on its literate level. Incidentally I should say that the one single thing that would do most to promote the glorious development of our Catholic Revival would be the introduction of strong courses in literature into every seminary in the country. Then the average parish priest, who by his very office must guide the reading of his flock, would be a literate reader and also a theologian—a combination which we cannot longer do without. In fact, we must see that our age is an age of new unity. All around us barriers are being broken down. We can no longer endure to have novelists, theologians, critics, and sensitive readers in water-tight compartments. We all need each other. *The Heart of the Matter* would not, however, be a better book if Greene had been a trained theologian. But this review would be better if I were one. The double requirement cuts both ways. We need the theologian critic.

The theologian critic would not investigate irrelevancies such as whether or not Greene thought Scobie a saint. Or whether or not Scobie repented of his suicide after he took the sleeping pills. He would come with adequate explanation to the central paradox as I have outlined it, the seeming coexistence of mortal sin and love for God. Assuming that Father Martindale was right in affirming the soundness of the book, he might say, for example, that this book is a challenge to theology to catch up with the artist. That the book asks for the expansion of the boundries of theology. Such a thing is not inconceivable. Theology is not a science incapable of development. Jacques Maritain has repeatedly pointed out the need for extending its boundaries. He has devoted his whole life to the application of Thomistic thought to problems about which it has not as yet been explicit.

Upon the utter incompatibility of mortal sin and love of God, the Church has, however, been explicit. May no one suppose that the extension of the boundaries of theology presumes that the sharp distinction of this teaching, which is the very core and essence of morality, would be in any way blurred. To extend a boundary never means the sell-out of the area enclosed. So precious is this center of truth that *The Heart of the Matter* would be a very dangerous book if it led the reader to suppose that just because Scobie habitually felt a love for God and a natural pity for his neighbor, this same habit of heart would by some alchemy slide him into heaven in spite of his mortal sin.

Mortal sin. There is the rub. Judging another's conscience may be impossible. The inward dispositions of a sinner, either in fiction or in life, may be so complicated that even the most astute theologian abandons passing judgment on the precise spiritual condition of the soul. He leaves that to God. The Church does have a process of canonization, but there is none for eternal condemnation.

It is the complicated psychology of the sinner which creates the effect of a gray area—not the blurring of the sharp distinction between the black of mortal sin and the white of love of God. And it is in this area that extension might be possible—though the theologian might very well point out that such an extension is of psychology, not of theology. Or that in the application of theology to psychology there will always be as many problems as there are souls. Which is no news to even the most elementary theologian.

Very well, then. There is Scobie's special case. As an artist Greene is content to present the complexities of Scobie's conscience without theological analysis. He seems content to say—please note that there is this area of gray and that it should fill us with compassion for the sinner and horror of making a judgment on the basis of appearances. Still the reader clamors for a theologian's judgment because the issues matter so terribly.

Thus it is that we now have the question before the answer—a most healthy condition. The real weakness in our Catholic education has been giving answers before students had the questions. The birth of worthy Catholic fiction such as is *The Heart of the Matter* may change all that.

Finally, the critic-theologian may have to say that there is some unsoundness in the book.

If so, I shall still believe that there is no conflict between art and theology. For there is one artistic flaw in the book. The reader does not quite believe the urgency of Scobie's problem. From that same artistic flaw will be seen to stem, I believe, whatever objection can be found with the book—if any. And because of this same flaw *The Heart of the Matter* is not so great as is *The Power and the Glory*, which, though dealing less explicitly with comparable spiritual complexities, does convince us that its hero, the priest, must have been thus and not otherwise.

Finally, it should be noted that in these two novels as well as in Greene's greatest entertainment, *Brighton Rock*, Greene deals with the problem of pity. Pinkie entirely lacks pity and is damned here and in the life to come. If he were a day older than seventeen the reader would not believe in his hardness, for only the young can utterly lack pity. But the two novels deal with pity as a central theme. Pity is love which must give and not take. It is love that is based not on the beauty or excellence of the beloved but only on his need.

True pity would never, however, suppose that it could help another by breaking the law of God. In weakly letting his good impulse betray him into sin, Scobie himself becomes the most pitiful of men. He looks up at the stars and thinks that they must be like the lighted windows of a hospital which look so cheerful and bright but behind which there throbs such suffering. Everywhere in the world there is pain. Over it broods the divine pity.

Something of this cosmic understanding, which is pity, enters the heart of the readers in spite of all unanswered vexing questions. They will be filled with compassion for all sinners, remembering how closed and secret are the complexities of many consciences. And judging anyone else without warrant will seem what it is—the silliest thing in the world.

## Notes

1. Mariella Gable, O.S.B., "New Boundaries," *Today*, October 1948, 20. Reprinted in Mariella Gable, *This is Catholic Fiction* (New York: Sheed & Ward, 1948).

# Chapter 9

---

# Prose Satire and the Modern Christian Temper[1]

In the literary arsenal satire is perhaps the most potent weapon for dealing with evil. If the big guns of vituperation and abuse do not blast an evil, the A-bomb of satire may topple it with hilarious amusement, contempt, and scorn. Strong defenses are necessary to withstand ridicule.

Since ridicule is the weapon of satire, it is well to remember that it has a double aim. It aims to destroy; it also aims to suggest that the opposite of the thing destroyed is desirable. This positive nature of satire, the power to suggest a desirable alternative, gives it a precious value. One cannot be angry with an abuse unless one is deeply convinced of the value of its opposite. Satire is, therefore, a positive thing. Its art is constructive as well as destructive.

In an age of crisis such as the twentieth century has been, when old values seem to be perishing and a new world unable to be born, it is not surprising that many excellent satires have been written in poetry, drama, and fiction. Though the writings of the modern world are scarcely so dominantly satiric as were those of eighteenth-century England, still the amount of satire in our own day is considerable. But the most striking thing about it is its positive content, the fact that it holds up to admiration and approval the Christian values of our culture which seem to be most in danger of being lost. And this defense of Christian principles comes sometimes from those who have repudiated all formal religious connections. Such a satirist is George Orwell, who makes one of the most eloquent defenses for human freedom in literature. But many of the best satirists of this century are Catholics. Those positive values in prose fiction which are in accord with the Christian ideal will be examined in this paper, no matter what the religious persuasion of the satirist. It will be found that the prose satires argue, as with one voice, for the validity of Christian principles.

The period of time covered by the word, "modern," must be clearly determined. Most critics agree that modern literature came into being somewhere around the year 1914 with the cataclysm of World War I. That date will be accepted without argument and this study will carry us down to the present moment.

Since we begin this study with the year 1914, the first important satire to be looked at is *South Wind* by Norman Douglas, which was published in 1917. This satire is directed forcefully *against* Christianity with all its spiritual and moral implications. It stands, therefore, outside the stream of modern satire, which has already been described as dominantly Christian. It is perhaps well that we have this glaring exception. For it helps to point up by contrast the changed character of the satires which followed it.

What is *South Wind*? It is an argument for hedonism. It is an argument against Christianity as a hindrance to a full enjoyment of Epicurean pleasures. Douglas is a kind of belated Omar Khayyám whose jug of wine and loaf of bread are augmented not by a book of verse but by arguments against faith, against the Bible as "the most intemperate book I have ever read,"[2] against the decalogue,[3] and specifically against such virtues as "charity, purity, sobriety."[4] It regards those who practice such restraints as masochists.[5] It defines Christianity as a religion for those who wish to grovel.[6] In fact, grovelling along with superstition and ignorance become the earmarks of the Christian.

The book is, however, just in some of its satire. It is just in holding up to ridicule those perennial abuses of religion—Puritanism, intolerance, and persecution—which dog the steps of religion wherever it becomes proud and self-regarding instead of God-centered.

In order to communicate this effectively Douglas invents a plot in which an Anglican bishop, stopping at the sensuous isle of Nepenthe, is so changed that he accepts murder. Douglas himself says, "How to make murder palatable to a bishop, that is the plot. How? You must unconventionalize him, and instill into his mind seeds of doubt and revolt. You must batter his old notions of what is right."[7] So effective is this battering in *South Wind* that Bishop Heard loses his Christian convictions in twelve days.

Consistent and logical in his atheism, Douglas produced three satires against the three absolutes:[8] against the beautiful in *They Went* (1921), against the true in *In the Beginning* (1928), and against the good in *South Wind* (1917). By far the most important and popular of the three was *South Wind* with its formal protest against the traditional goodness of the Christian order.

How was it possible for Douglas to write a satire dedicated to the pursuit of personal comfort during the frightening years of World War I when the very foundations of Western civilization were ominously shaken? Perhaps because this belated Victorian abhorred politics and world affairs; perhaps because he could fly from the catastrophe around him to the sweet island of Capri, stuff his ears against the roaring of the war, and believe in all sincerity that the major task of human beings was to discover maximum pleasure in this life and to make human comfort the goal of their striving. He wrote of a dream-world of earthly happiness in the same spirit as did Morris in *News from Nowhere* and Bellamy in *Looking Backward*.

But after World War I that kind of dreaming seemed childish, foolish, and hopelessly dated. In the new satiric allegory there is a terrible awareness that the very foundations of society are in jeopardy. Before 1917 it was possible to feel that the Christian religion might inflict curbs on self-indulgence which the hedonist would wish to shed. After 1917 the satiric allegories depict the nightmare which lies ahead if society as we know it now continues to develop toward its logical conclusion.[9] The satires before 1917 may be called visions, those after that date, antivisions.[10] Where we used to speak of utopias we now speak of distopias.[11]

The two most important distopias are Huxley's *Brave New World* (1932) and Orwell's *Nineteen Eighty-Four* (1949). In their implications they read like tracts for Christianity and for that humanism which is embraced and completed by Christianity. Some values they defend in common. Finally they part company and identify in opposite extremes the threat to civilization.

The three values which these satiric allegories defend in common are major and basic values. First, they both present a horrifying picture of the omnipotent state. Western culture has, since the founding of Christianity, conceived society as cared for by two powers, Church and State. These satires demonstrate what happens when the State is unchecked by any power other than its own. This is satire by omission. And in the case of Orwell, a man consciously repudiating any religious affiliation, the potent implications of the omission of the Church as a check may have been unconscious. They are nonetheless powerful. An observation made by Stephen Spender is relevant here. He thinks the current return of interest in the Church may be explained because "the individual needs the authority of the Church to strengthen him against the increasing secular authority of the State."[12] The two satires under discussion simply show the horror of the omnipotent State unchecked by any power. They do not suggest any power able to prevent the State from abusing its omnipotence, for there is none other than the Church.

The second value defended by these two satires is that of freedom. In both satires human personal freedom has been quashed as one would step on a caterpillar and observe only a minute writhing in the perishing creature. Both satires regard loss of freedom as the major calamity that could befall a human being.

The freedom of the individual is one of the rights of human beings strongly defended by the Christian world. It is true, of course, that freedom found its rational basis in the Greeks.[13] But Judeo-Christian ethics with its strong emphasis on freedom of the will joined forces with Greek tradition, amalgamated with it, and gave to rational tradition the sanction of religion. That religious sanction of freedom has gone far to establish its Christian temper. The two basic commands of the decalogue are based on human beings' free rendering of love to God (doing God's will) and their free charity to neighbors, which makes human beings gentle, helpful, and respectful of neighbors' rights also as free human beings. "Here if anywhere is the fundamental root of Western freedom," remarks Barbara Ward, "in this metaphysical sense of the infinite value of each human soul before God and the infinite respect each man owes to his neighbor's liberty and well-being."[14] In defending freedom Huxley and Orwell are defending a basic right which derives not only from reason but also from the Judeo-Christian religion.

In the third place, they both make a strong plea for a return to value judgments. Christians believe in a hierarchy of values and the obligation to make an appropriate response to value.[15] But many social scientists of our day, the pragmatists, ask that only what *is* be reported and studied, not what ought to be. Martin Kessler has made so close a study of *Brave New World* and *Nineteen Eighty-four* as a protest against that sort of pragmatism that one cannot do better than to quote his conclusion verbatim:

> Both Huxley and Orwell present systems which work perfectly. In both satires there is no value scheme against which either system can be measured. It is against this operational determinism that Huxley and Orwell rebel. Both are pleading for the right of individuals to be aware of and act upon apolitical values. And in *Nineteen Eighty-Four* and *Brave New World* they have shown what is likely to happen when that right is destroyed.[16]

This is what the two major distopias have in common. Their difference lies in the purpose for which the omnipotent state has deprived human beings of their freedom. Huxley himself puts it this way: "In *Nineteen Eighty-Four* the lust for power is satisfied by inflicting pain; in *Brave New World* by inflicting a hardly less humiliating pleasure."[17] Happiness and unhappiness are equally horrible, for the conclusion is that no one can end as a human being.

Huxley's society, then, is dedicated to making life entirely comfortable and pleasant. The comfortable and the pleasant are substituted for blessedness and happiness. Huxley points out that total dedication of society to comfort is made possible by technology. "Industrial civilization is only possible where there's no self-denial. Self indulgence up to the very limits imposed by hygiene and economics."[18] Further, regarding the daily doses of *soma* to relieve the slightest tension and discomfort, the text reads: "Christianity without tears, that's what *soma* is."[19] Now, of course, Christianity without tears is Christianity without the cross, an impossibility, a contradiction in terms. Huxley's satire demonstrates that a human being without suffering is indeed no human being. Huxley belongs with the writers of Greek tragedy who concentrated on the problem of suffering in this world. The Greeks showed the dignity of human suffering. Huxley shows the indignity of human beings deprived of suffering. His satire is a shrill warning about the destiny of a technological society dedicated to making human beings entirely comfortable.

Orwell makes an equally grim discovery of evil as evil. Big Brother and the Party are not bad because they are politically reactionary or because they are totalitarian, but because their lust for power is actually a lust for pure evil. They desire power only to hurt and humiliate others. No other writer approaches Orwell in his isolation of evil as pure evil, nor so arouses horror in his readers. Spender thinks that "Big Brother is really anti-Christ." And further he points out that "the tragedy of Orwell's world is that man—Big Brother—turns himself into God."[20] With no God except the human being who is uninhibited by moral or spiritual brakes, the unlimited power of human beings becomes such a nightmare as we can scarcely contemplate.

Whether one contemplates in either of the satiric allegories the spectacle of an omnipotent state ruining human beings by excessive comfort or by excessive torture, the prognostic is terrifying. Evil stalks the world. It cannot be conquered except by first safeguarding the freedom of the individual.

We turn now from the satiric allegories to those novelists who portray society in the twentieth century as they see it to be—Evelyn Waugh, Aldous Huxley, Kingsley Amis, Aubrey Menen, Angus Wilson, and Muriel Spark. Since this study is limited to writers of England, this list omits such remarkable satirists as the Americans, Randall Jarrell, J.F. Powers, and Flannery O'Connor. The British writers named above train their cameras on that area of human conduct where morals, values, manners, and taste overlap. They each take the same picture but from a slightly different angle. However, no matter what their angle of vision, they agree that the society they depict suffers grave disorder. In a disordered society merely accurate portrayal with precise honesty as to the life depicted can be the sharpest satire. Perhaps *A Handful of Dust*[21] may stand as an example. Brenda and her crowd, in their casual acceptance of adultery, symbolize the shedding of the moral imperative; Tony Last, Brenda's husband, those who suffer from that betrayal. From the barbarism of that society which took Brenda from him and ruined his world, Tony ends up in the jungle where he must wear out his days reading Dickens to a lunatic. He has exchanged one barbarism for another, one jungle for another. The book sees human beings as helpless in the face of modern savagery.[22]

The implication in the satires written by the above named novelists is that we must concern ourselves anew with the old basic problems of right and wrong. We must re-examine the society in which we live, and with some freshly apprehended notions of right and wrong change the new barbarism into a new civilization. Perhaps the satirists would all agree with Harry Wesley in *The Fig Tree* (1958) when he says, "It seems to me that the time has come to wake people up. They've got to start thinking about right and wrong again, just as they had to a couple of thousand years ago when the Christians took over the Greeks and the Romans. We've got to start using our brains."[23] So well have fiction writers, especially the satirists, used their brains that Amos Wilder in his book, *Theology and Modern Literature,* points out that the moral problems of modern humanity have been explored more thoroughly in literature than in theology.[24] He recommends that the theologians catch up with the writers.

Among the writers Aubrey Menen is a dedicated satirist who is perpetually posing such problems as shall make the reader sit up and reconsider deeply and freshly all sorts of moral dilemmas. In his double heritage of Oriental and Occidental thinking he has been thrust into a position where he has to contend with difficult problems. With an Irish Catholic mother and an Indian father, with an education which began in the British public school and continued in India under an aristocratic grandmother, he has seen what most of us need to see: that one of the great problems of our time is the capacity for the Oriental and the Occidental to find a common ground on which to stand. This is not so simple as some might think. Out of his seven full-length satires the first one, *Prevalence of Witches* (1948), is the best. It focuses upon the Oriental-Occidental moral problems (with good nature and hilarious laughter). By assembling four oddballs to discuss the most crucial ethical problems, he makes readers do some thinking for themselves. Such is the technique of the modern satirist. He will present a cluster of stimulating and sometimes unorthodox views asking readers to make their own decisions.

But Menen is capable of making up his mind on many points. In *The Prevalence of Witches* his mind was made up on the necessity for all of us to do serious thinking on ethical problems. In *The Stumbling Stone* (1949) he derides the professional social worker who is not motivated by Christian charity. In *The Duke of Gallodora* (1952) he pokes fun at human foibles in general. In *Ramayana* (1954), the retelling of an ancient Oriental story with variations, he indicates the need to view life then and now with skeptical realism. In *The Backward Bride* (1955) his satire demonstrates how against human nature, especially feminine nature, is promiscuous sexual behavior. For good measure he tosses in incidental satires on existentialism, psychiatry, and world politics. In *The Abode of Love* (1956) he satirizes the relationship of religion and sex, and in *The Fig Tree* (1959) his satire is directed against the freedom of the scientist from moral obligations in his research as a scientist.

In the last named satire the successful scientist, not a Catholic, because he is so disturbed about the possible damage to society that may take its rise from his discovery of a powerful aphrodisiac makes the following appeal to the Vatican:

> I want to ask you to tell all—everybody who'll listen to you—and that will be hundreds of millions—that we stand in great danger. We stand in danger of having our lives twisted, our souls and our bodies destroyed by men [the scientists] who boast that they are above right and wrong.[25]

The book argues for curbing the free investigation of scientists. It is characteristic of Menen's occasional superficiality that he does not distinguish here between science which is free to discover all it can about the universe, and the technologist who is not free to make a bad use of science. Science can indeed always be used for either good or ill.

Current satires have much to say about the invasion of the scientific method into those areas of social life where the strict scientific method seems inadequate and often dangerous. For instance, in *The Stumbling Stone* Menen regards professional do-gooders as "those busy-bodies making a living out of others' misfortune."[26] They behave as if their making of tabulations and records actually were a relief to human misery.[27] Why do they do good? Prynne says, "Instead of the agony of saving our own souls, we prefer the pleasure of saving other people's. We are grateful for the wicked; we are thankful for the unfortunate and both for the same reason. They save us the trouble of looking into our own hearts."[28] They leave Chas, a young boy they have accepted as a "case," to die when he attempts to commit suicide. He is, however, rescued by a slightly wacky old woman who has always loved the boy and who has a deep, simple faith in God.[29]

Continuing with recent satire, which deplores having science invade social and human areas, we come to the brilliant novel,

*Memento Mori* (1959) by the Catholic writer, Muriel Spark.[30]  Spark is the most thoughtful, subtle, artistic, and Christian of modern satirists.  She presents us with Alec Warner, the scientific collector of data on old people.  He has tons of such data.  But his method for obtaining his information is highly discreditable.  He is perfectly capable of giving a helpless old person very disturbing news so that he may make accurate records of blood pressure and temperature when the old person is under special emotional stress.  In fact, some say he was born to make trouble, but he did not realize it.[31]  When Alec's apartment burns down with all the facts collected over many years, readers are left to contemplate the ironies of his loss.  Could it symbolize a universal conflagration due to fall upon a scientific world unsupported by suitable moral and spiritual values?  Perhaps human values?

But Alec Warner one day stumbles upon an interesting observation.  His discovery lies precisely at the core of what most of these satires are trying to tell us.  He is visiting a ward filled with old people, but he is not on one of his scavanger hunts for data.  Then he suddenly begins to wonder why scientific observations differ from human ones.[32]  He has in a sudden flash discovered that the human is indeed different from that which can be measured, charted, and tabulated by the scientific method.

The book contains many other thrusts at the vulgar invasion of science into the area of human life.  For instance, geriatrics: a poor old lady in the state ward complains about the doctors who keep her alive long after life's natural span when she would rather die in peace.[33]  To this remarkable book we must return.  For the present the subject of science in human affairs must be continued.

What about science in education and scholarship?  Surely the scientific method in scholarship has enormously extended the boundaries of knowledge.  But in Angus Wilson's *Anglo-Saxon Attitudes* (1956) grave doubts are raised about a life dedicated to discovering more and more about less and less.  Professor Gerald Middleton reflects on the issue of the whole book: how to explain the appearance of a fertility figure in the tomb of Bishop Eorpwald: "was it not after all a small point of historical truth that mattered very little to medieval specialists and nothing, but absolutely nothing at all, to anyone else?"[34]  He has lost confidence in his profession, though he is not quite so dim a figure as Scott-King in his scholarly devotion to old Bellorius."[35]

Bellorius is, of course, so intrinsically unworthy of intelligent attention that Scott-King's dedication to him resembles nothing so much as the stupidity of a moth mistaking a candle flame for that which must be embraced at all costs. Equally hilarious is Waugh's satire on professors and the whole atmosphere of the school at Llanabba Castle.[36] Menen ridicules the whole tribe of Brahmins by pointing out:

> . . .[they] were the top dogs. They made the laws, taught the ignorant, dictated morals, controlled the temples, terrified the king. . . . Any man could become a Brahmin provided he set himself up to know better than his fellow men, and was sharp enough to get away with it.[37]

Menen thumbs his nose with even more boisterous contempt at the English literary classics, praised by professors but discovered by Menen himself to be insupportably dull and stupid.[38]

This sort of contempt for "higher education" is, of course, not a new thing. One remembers the Colleges of Unreason in *Erewhon* where the professors would not communicate anything except through quotations.[39] Excessive devotion to the past was effectively satirized by Shakespeare when he created the schoolteacher-type military officer, Fluellen, who grieves that the warfare at Agincourt is not manipulated according to the standards of old Rome.[40]

The implication in this satire on sterile research and excessive devotion either to the past or to the minutiae of the past is that there are transcendent values which it is the obligation of the educator to examine. He prostitutes his position as educator when he pours out his energies on less than the true, good, and beautiful.

In Kingsley Amis a new type of satire on education comes into focus. This is because a new type of teacher has emerged—the fellow from the lower ranks of society who looks at his academic betters with envy while his personal taste is often on the level of the gutter. We see the academic life through the eyes of Lucky Jim Dixon, an irreverent and amiable opportunist, who is teaching on probation under Professor Welsh.[41] If Professor Welsh and his colleagues represent a decadent scholarship and absurd social life, there is certainly little choice between them and Jim Dixon. Somerset Maugham regards Lucky Jim as ominous: "He represents a new class of people going to the university on government grants. They do not go to the university to acquire culture, but to get a job, and when they have got one they scamp it."[42]   Maugham looks upon himself as fortunate that he will not be alive to see this type prevail.   Through the double vision of the phoney as seen through both Lucky Jim and Welsh, the reader is made to see a new stereoscopic depth in integrity. Integrity is the value Amis consistently underlines.

One of the ways in which science has invaded educational tools is by way of the intelligence test.   Michael Young's *The Rise of the Meritocracy* (1959) deflates our confidence in these tests.   He pictures a society from 1870 to 2033 in which men are sorted for education and for work precisely on the basis of their intelligence.   He resents such a society as harassed by the worst sort of class distinction.   But a rebellion arises in the year 2009 which denies that one individual is in any fundamental way the superior of another.   Certainly mere intelligence does not make a better person.   The rebels want everyone ". . . to be respected for the good that is in him . . . . It is the function of society to discover it and know it, whether it is genius at making pots, growing daisies, ringing bells, caring for babies or even (to show their tolerance) genius at inventing telescopes."[43]   All this is set forth in the "Chelsea Manifesto" which says:

> Were we to evaluate people, not only according to their intelligence and their education, their occupation and their power, but according to their kindliness and their courage, their imagination and their sensitivity, their sympathy and generosity, there would be no classes.   Who would be able to say that the scientist was superior to the porter with admirable qualities as a father?   . . .The classless society would be the tolerant society, in which individual differences were actively encouraged as well as passively tolerated, in which full meaning was at last given to the dignity of man.[44]

This positive interest in human dignity is one of the significant aspects of very recent satire.

Amis lays great stress on a return to moral integrity.   For instance, in *That Uncertain Feeling* (1956), John Lewis has nearly wrecked his marriage by committing adultery.[45]   However, he resolves to live by the moral law.   To insure that he shall do so he gives up his work and moves to a new town where his work is humbler than any he had known.   Suddenly at a party he is confronted by Lisa Watkins, another predatory female. The dispatch with which he flies from her, totally lacking in social poise, would do credit to a medieval hermit confronted by the devil. Some critics have poked fun at this moral ending. But Amis knows where he wished the emphasis placed. In the early chapters of the book he shows how the woman with whom Lewis has been unfaithful to his wife is managing a frame-up so that Lewis will get a better job. When he is indignant at such underhand maneuvering, she points out how inconsistent he is to cavil at mere wire-pulling when he has just committed adultery with her. He resolves deeply on reform. His clear vision about the need to keep on trying no matter how often he fails is so old that it is almost new. This moral emphasis is not satire, but its appearance in a satire on contemporary society strikes a significant positive note. Richard Chase in *Commentary* calls this view "provincial, anti-intellectual, Protestant moralism."[46]

One of the themes through which the return to values is particularly emphasized is death. *Memento Mori* has already been viewed as satirizing excessive confidence in science, especially when science invades the area of strictly human experience. The main theme of the book, however, is the theme of death. The plot is very simple. Someone uses the telephone anonymously to call up various aged persons and announce: "Remember you shall die." The variety of ways in which people respond to this news, along with their deepest personal history, makes this book a profound satire on contemporary society and human nature in general. Most of the persons receiving the message feel great consternation, as if death were news. Dame Lettie Colston concentrates on having the detectives discover the identity of the caller, as if such an identification could alter in the least the fact of death. Through her insane precautions Dame Lettie actually brings about her brutal murder in bed. But before that event the reader is treated to ironies aplenty. The chief inspector who is asked to discover the anonymous caller points out to Lettie that to keep death daily before one's eyes intensifies his life. In fact, without the thought of death, life becomes insipid, like living "on the whites of eggs."[47]

On notes of various pitch the satirists combine to make a veritable symphony of protest against the evasion of death and the implications of death. Ronald Firbank is particularly interested in the macabre situation which is bound to present itself at a death bed when the dying person demonstrates that as you live so you shall die. In

*The Flower Beneath the Foot* (1921) Firbank presents the worldly and shallow archduchess who even during the administration of Extreme Unction is distracted by considering ways and means for constructing inside toilet facilities for dogs.[48]  Here is something like the sardonic wit and humor which prevail in Waugh's *The Loved One* (1948).[49] This satire lampoons the mortuary custom of making death look like life, especially as this custom prevails in the slumber rooms of Whispering Glades where corpses are on exhibit radiant as if bouyantly alive.  Here death is not faced; it is defaced.  And some of the bitterest satire in *Brave New World* is delivered when the savage, John, watches his mother die.  The nurse explains to him, "We try to create a thoroughly pleasant atmosphere here—something between a first class hotel and a feely-palace, if you take my meaning."[50]  The ward is maggoty with children who are being conditioned to accept death as quite jolly.  Huxley shows the whole evasion of death as a violation of decency.

Either life ends the only life we shall ever know, or it opens another life.  In either case, say the satirists, it deserves to be faced for what it is, a solemn reality.

Looking back over the satires of the modern era we find them seeming to say:

1. Unchecked by the Church the State goes hog-wild.

2. The State inflicts intolerable sufferings on humanity.

3. Freedom is being lost; it must be saved.

4. Science can discover the secrets of only a material universe; we need wisdom which science cannot give.

5. Relying only on the scientific method in human and social areas is inadequate and dangerous.

6. The grave danger of becoming less than human confronts a society dedicated to the pursuit of comfort and pleasure.

7. A technological society needs particularly to be balanced by spiritual and moral norms.

8. Learn to detect sham; re-examine life with an eye to integrity; face death with integrity.

9. Without spiritual and moral norms a terrifying barbarism prevails.

The implications are that human beings must concern themselves now with the ideals of Christian humanism.  The satires themselves say that such a humanism has already begun.

# Notes

1. Mariella Gable, O.S.B., "Prose Satire and the Modern Christian Temper," *American Benedictine Review* (Mr-Je 1960): 21-34.

2. Norman Douglas, *South Wind* (New York, 1939), 350.

3. Ibid., 240.

4. Ibid., 239.

5. Ibid., 251.

6. Ibid., 240.

7. *Alone.* Quoted in Ian Greenlees, *Norman Douglas* (New York, 1957), 22.

8. Constantine Fitzgibbons, *Norman Douglas* (London, 1955), 25-26.

9. Ellen Douglas Leyburn, *Satiric Allegory: Mirror of Man* (New Haven, 1956), 107.

10. Stephen Spender, *The Creative Element* (New York, 1954), VII.

11. Martin Kessler, "Power and the Perfect State: A Study in Disillusionment as Reflected in Orwell's *Nineteen Eighty-Four* and Huxley's *Brave New World*," *Political Science Quarterly*, LXXII (December 1957): 567.

12. Spender, *The Creative Element*, 186.

13. Aristotle *Ethics, 3.5.I.*

14. Barbara Ward, *Faith and Freedom* (New York, 1958), 277.

15. Dietrich von Hildebrand, *Liturgy and Personality* (New York, 1943).

16. Kessler, "Power and the Perfect State," 577.

17. Aldous Huxley, *Brave New World Revisited* (New York, 1958), 52.

18. *Brave New World*, 284.

19. Ibid., 285.

20. Spender, *The Creative Element*, 137.

21. Evelyn Waugh, *A Handful of Dust* (New York, 1934).

22. Frederick J. Stopp, *Evelyn Waugh, Portrait of an Artist* (Boston, 1958), 100.

23. Aubrey Menen, *The Fig Tree* (New York, 1959), 192.

24. *Theology and Modern Literature* (Cambridge, 1958), 100.

25. *The Fig Tree*, 188.

26. Aubrey Menen, *The Stumbling Stone* (New York, 1949), 241.

27. Ibid., 80-81.

28. Ibid., 35.

29. Ibid., 253.

30. Muriel Spark, *Memento Mori* (New York, 1959).

31. Ibid., 218.

32. Ibid., 218.

33. Ibid., 176.

34. Angus Wilson, *Anglo-Saxon Attitudes* (New York, 1956), 164.

35 Evelyn Waugh, *Scott-King's Modern Europe* (London, 1947).

36. Evelyn Waugh, *Decline and Fall* (London, 1928).

37. Aubrey Menen, *The Ramayanna* (New York, 1954), 3.

38. Aubrey Menen, "Party of One," *Holiday* (July, 1959): 8.

39. Samuel Butler, *Erewhon*, 227.

40. William Shakespeare, *Henry V*, Act III, Sc. 2; Act IV, Sc. 1.

41. Kingsley Amis, *Lucky Jim* (New York, 1954).

42. Review of *Lucky Jim* by Kingsley Amis, London *Sunday Times*, 25 December 1956.

43. Michael Young, *The Rise of the Meritocracy* (London, 1958), 135.

44. Ibid., 135-36.

45. Kingsley Amis, *That Uncertain Feeling* (New York, 1956).

46. *Commentary*, XXII (September, 1956): 263.

47. Spark, *Memento Mori*, 153.

48. Ronald Firbank, *Five Novels* (London, 1949), 189.

49. Evelyn Waugh, *The Loved One* (Boston, 1948).

50. Huxley, *Brave New World* (New York, 1950), 238.

MARY GABLE,
POSTULANT, 1916

NOVICES MARIELLA GABLE, RONAYNE GERGEN, 1916

1920S
MARIELLA GABLE AND ST. BENEDICT'S STUDENTS

MARIELLA GABLE NEAR SACRED HEART CHAPEL,
COLLEGE OF ST. BENEDICT, 1930S

TERESA HALL TOWER
ST. BENEDICT'S

REMBERTA WESTKAEMPER, MARIELLA GABLE, 1930S

MARY (MARZOLF) AND JOSEPH GABLE,
PARENTS OF MARIELLA GABLE

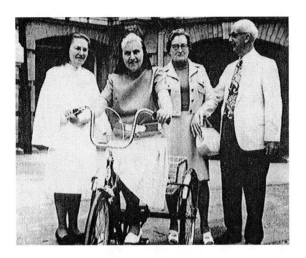

MOTHER HENRITA OSENDORF, MARIELLA GABLE,
CEIL CLIFFORD GABLE AND JOHN GABLE
(MARIELLA'S SISTER-IN-LAW AND BROTHER), 1970S

# Chapter 10

---

# The Past Made Present[1]

An event of the first magnitude in the history of Catholic fiction occurred during the current year when Knopf published for the English-speaking world a translation of the Spanish novel, *The Cypresses Believe in God*. In introducing this two-volume novel to the public, *The Commonweal* said: "The search for the great Catholic novel of contemporary life can end. It was published in Spain in 1953 and now appears in English. *The Cypresses Believe in God* is a work of such power, compassion, and significance for our century that its publication in the United States is a major literary event."

It was indeed. But not just because it was a great book and of our own times. We had long been waiting for a Catholic novel that would combine those two requirements. A still more important fact about that book, as I see it, is that it is a historical novel. It presents the Civil War in Spain during the 1930's. The complex issues of that war are remarkably fleshed out in the various members of the Alvear family, and through these people what seemed like the abstractions of politics become moving personal issues. The Civil War is our problem, our cataclysm.

Why is it significant that this great new Catholic novel should be a historical novel? Because the historical novel has all along seemed to dominate Catholic fiction. This new book brings added weight to the generalization. Perhaps we should, therefore, at this time face some basic questions. Why are so many Catholic novels historical? Is there anything in the Catholic character which makes an author turn to history for his materials for fiction? What does this preoccupation with history mean?

Before undertaking to answer some of these questions, perhaps it is necessary to indicate to what extent the historical novel dominates in Catholic fiction. The three greatest landmarks in Catholic fiction are all historical novels. The very first Catholic novel ever written, *The Betrothed*, by Manzoni in 1825, captures in its pages not only one of the most exciting stories ever told (Manzoni found the story in old historical records and realized that fact really is stranger than fiction) but also the whole texture of life in seventeenth century Italy. It is a fascinating story, loaded with spiritual values, accurate historically, and a world classic. A century later came Sigrid Undset's *Kristin Lavransdatter* (English translation 1923-27), a trilogy of the same magnificent stature, anchoring its monumental study of marriage firmly in the life of medieval Norway. Now, *The Cypresses Believe in God*.

Between Manzoni and Undset, about a century, the period is largely one of growth and preparation. Though Manzoni's novel itself may certainly not be regarded as a preparation, it is a major achievement. Outside of Manzoni we look first at Newman, the father of the Catholic literary revival in England. No one took a more sour view than did Newman of the sheer impossibility of having a Catholic (Christian) fiction. For he equated sinlessness with the essence of Christianity—an amusing confusion in view of the place held by the confessional in all Catholic churches. This is what Newman said: "I say if literature is to be made a study of human nature you cannot have a Christian literature. It is a contradiction in terms to expect a sinless literature in a sinful world."

Yet when Newman wanted to interpret for the world his own struggle to find the light, he turned to the past and wrote *Callista*, a historical novel of third-century Christianity, in which the heroine's finding of the faith is his own. Cardinal Wiseman did a comparable piece of work in *Fabiola*. Neither of these novels is great literature. The Catholic Pole, Sienkiewicz, gave our grandparents, who cherished it with deep affection, *Quo Vadis*, a tale of the time of Christ. And Robert Hugh Benson, as the nineteenth gave way to the twentieth century turned again and again to the historical novel.

Then came *Kristin Lavransdatter*, winner of the Nobel prize, and so superb an achievement that it ranks as a classic outside as well as inside the Church. The time of growth was fairly well over; the time of achievement had come. In the three decades between *Kristin Lavransdatter* and *The Cypresses Believe in God* we are no longer shamed by the appearance of the tractarian novel. Gironella rejoices in the Introduction to the American edition of *The Cypresses* that his countrymen have found him "implacable"—that is, he does not succumb to the "temptation to adulterate truth" in order to make a point. The mature Catholic novel demonstrates a comparable integrity throughout this second period.

What are some of the fine historical novels of this period? Josephine Ward's *Tudor Sunset*, Gertrude von LeFort's beautiful *Song at the Scaffold* and *The Pope of the Ghetto*, scholarly Helen Waddell's *Peter Abelard*, and the best novel Graham Greene ever wrote, *The Power and the Glory*, which so anchors the story of the Mexican priest in the conditions of the Mexican revolution that without the conditions of that time and place the story is inconceivable. Then there are the various historical novels of Helen C. White and of her sister Olive White. There are the many stories in which a saint becomes the central character—a field of writing in which the first name to come to mind is that of Louis de Wohl. But others, too, have succeeded in making the saints live: Franz Werfel in *The Song of Bernadette*, Evelyn Waugh in *Helena*, Charles Brady in *Stage of Fools*. Massive and memorable in their achievement are the *Golden Warrior* by Hope Muntz and *The Man on a Donkey* by H.F.M. Prescott. A very incomplete list, but sufficient to indicate to what an extent the historical novel dominates in Catholic fiction.

What does this dominance of the historical novel mean? Perhaps nothing special, for the spate of historical novels among secular fiction is likewise very great. Every once in a while someone says that the historical novel is dead. But the appetite for it among all readers continues to be demanding. Perhaps the dominance of the historical novel among Catholic novels is only part of the normal, general interest in the form.

Personally, I think it is more than that. But before I tabulate the four meanings I see in the tendency of the Catholic to produce historical novels, a word about the form in general. Let us brush away some of the cobwebs blown into our eyes by irresponsible book reviewers: "a not quite reputable form," "the happy hunting ground of lesser talent." An historical novel, like any other piece of fiction, can be either good or bad. But at its best it is truer than history. No mere historian can make the past live as can the expert novelist. The dry bones of fact become the living flesh of human beings. A good historical novel is a magnificent achievement. And those whose gifts are not quite first-rate have found in history a support giving their work a value beyond that of their native creative power—witness for instance *The Four Rivers of Paradise*.

The development of science has been a boon to writers of historical novels. We know more about the past now than ever before; the card-catalogue makes that knowledge easily accessible. Manzoni studied for years to make every detail in *The Betrothed* accurate; now such accuracy is easier. New novelists aim to be right about every garter, button, epaulet, and spangle. They had better be or the critics will catch them. They had better be right, too, about the implications of history, the conclusions they draw from the past.

And that last consideration brings us to the Catholic novelist. It helps us to answer the main question: What is the significance of the fact that the historical novel seems to dominate Catholic fiction? As I see it there are four parts to the answer.

1. In turning to history to find what conclusions may be drawn from the past, the novelist discovers that history vindicates the Catholic position. The novelist needs to perpetrate no manipulation of events; the actual flow of history is on the side of light. That is why our own times have seen superb Catholic historical novels written by non-Catholics: *The Golden Warrior*, a magnificent vitalizing of the persons of Harold of England and William the Conqueror along with the cataclysmic events of the Norman Conquest. Muntz prepared for this work by sixteen years of concentrated study. Because she lets facts and truth be her guides, the novel projects the values of the ages of faith. The same is true for the massively beautiful *The Man on the Donkey*, by a trained historian, H.F.M. Prescott.

At this point a question may arise. If we are having Catholic historical novels written by non-Catholic authors, what about some of the best-sellers like *The Robe*, by Lloyd Douglas, a Lutheran clergyman, and *The Silver Chalice*, by Costain, a Baptist turned Episcopalian? These novels do not qualify for the reason that a cardboard house is not a home, plastic bread not a food, painted water not a drink.

The Reformation struck a terrible blow at Catholics. Because the records show the venality of some churchmen, Catholics found themselves often on the defensive. In fact, Catholics developed a defensive mentality. They neglected the total, overall view which vindicates the Catholic position. It was Hilaire Belloc at the turn of the century who summoned Catholics with tremendous energy to the long overdue historical counterattack. History itself furnishes the ammunition. The skilled novelist furnishes the art by which the gun is fired. The shot hits the center of beauty and truth.

2. History appeals to Catholics because the past is thoroughly defined. Catholics are disciplined souls, completely at home under the restrictions of the commandments of God and of the Church. By temperament they are then attuned to the past period upon which they have a perspective which shows that thus and so were its meanings and not otherwise.

3. By the discipline of religion Catholics find it impossible to understand the present except by the light of the past. Catholics know that to describe their status accurately they may not call themselves Christian, but more precisely Judeo-Christian. For it is only in the light of the Old Testament that the New reveals itself as prepared for, long waited for, constituting a fulfillment of promise. By deepest training and most intimate emphasis they know that the past is the present and that in understanding the past they make a contribution to contemporary problems.

The greatest problem confronting contemporary human beings stems from this resistance to the fact that they need God. But now, having tried secularism wholesale, they have found it husks for swine. In the popular return to God, at the moment, we have the beginnings of what may well be the greatest world event in four centuries. About its significance Catholic novelists exploring history can throw indispensable lights.

4. Catholic novelists are able to interpret history adequately. They know how to read the past. They know that God is as necessary to them as water to the parched explorer in the desert. They know that there is only one struggle in life as there is only one conflict in fiction: good versus evil.

Goodness and holiness are tremendously important in life. Novelists who can present them adequately touch beauty. They render a profound service to humanity. Among the finest contemporary novels are those which confer life on the heroes of goodness, the saints. To take a canonized saint as the hero of a novel is a very smart choice. Goodness, difficult as it is to communicate, takes care of itself if novelists let the records of the past determine their story. Such a wise novelist is Louis de Wohl, well known for his historical novels in which the saints live again: St. Thomas in *The Quiet Light*, St. Augustine in *The Restless Flame*, St. Francis Xavier in *Set All Afire*. His most recent novel, *The Spear*, reverently explores the story of the persons who figured in the death of Christ, especially that of Longinus who pierced Christ's side.

De Wohl has recently put his finger on the service rendered by the historical novel.[2] He asks the question, "What is the purpose of the historical novel?" If it is properly executed, it makes the reader aware of the fact that the "problems of a past period are the problems of his own period too; that the great saints have provided their solution; and that in their emulation lies the solution of his own problems."

There is no other solution for the problems of the world. In clearly seeing that, Catholic novelists focus the spotlight of their art on a truth so important that the recognition of it or the refusal to recognize it can make or break the world.

With what an overwhelming stab of clarity the Jewish novelist, Franz Werfel, saw this when in 1940, distraught and breathless, flying from the pursuing Nazis, he made brief sanctuary at Lourdes. There he vowed, should he be delivered from the enemy, to write *The Song of Bernadette* in order that he "might magnify even in our inhuman times the divine mystery of holiness in man." The divine mystery of holiness in human beings! Nothing else so beautiful. Nothing else so strong to save. Nothing else to support people in their darkest hour. Like Muntz and Prescott, Werfel was not a Catholic. Also like them he wrote a Catholic novel by being a conscientious historian—as well as a fine artist. Many Catholic artists have achieved success by the same method.

But what of a novel like *The Cypresses Believe in God* ? The history of the Civil War in Spain, the history of the 1930's? Is there a place in our modern times for the heroically holy? Yes, and with a tender and at the same time dramatic beauty. Cesar Alvear, a sixteen-year-old boy, is a holy martyr. Even as one writes these words one is suddenly reminded of those dreadful stories of martyrs read to the little boy in Graham Greene's *The Power and the Glory*—horrible concoctions of saccharine sentimentality. They were not history; they were lies. How far have we come from such stupidity in the character of Cesar Alvear.

We have had an opportunity to watch him from his tenth to his sixteenth year—entering a seminary, giving his whole heart to God, having a burning need to help the poor, even if it be so low and humiliating a job as shaving them without cost. Then Spain goes wild in its revolution. Gerona is emptying its ciboriums onto church floors and burning churches. Cesar sees the suffering of his country as caused by sin. And he offers his life to God in reparation for the sins of his countrymen. He could have remained at home protected in the bosom of his family. But he goes to the churches to save the Blessed Sacrament from desecration. Thus, he is caught and lined up with many other citizens to be shot. As he stands facing the firing squad, he reflects that he has received Holy Communion some sixty times that day. He has carried one host with him which he plans now to swallow slowly and reverently. But Corbera, next to him, is exploding with rage against his executioners. Cesar offers him the host. He blinks in amazement, understands, receives it. Cesar feels something pierce his skin. Then his heart closes.

Out of the history that our own times is making will come many more sublime moments in the new historical novel. The concentration camps are making martyrs. The present is a new age of spiritual heroism. As the present becomes the past and as the past is made present in great fiction, the wheel comes full circle. We have greatness to look back upon. We have greatness to look forward to. Our times are great.

### Notes

1. Mariella Gable, O.S.B., "The Past Made Present," *Today*, December 1955, 14-17.

2. Louis de Wohl, "The Problems of a Historical Novelist," *Books on Trial* (November 1955): 113-14.

# Chapter 11

---

# Ecumenic Core in Flannery O'Connor's Fiction[1]

To be alive at this moment in the history of the world is a
privilege. We are as fortunate as the apostles to whom the Holy Spirit
came like a rushing wind. Pius XII called our age a springtime in the
Church,[2] John XXIII a New Pentecost,[3] and Cardinal Augustin Bea
described America's response to Pope John's loving concern for the
unity of all Christians as a "benevolent explosion."[4]  One observer
called it a tidal wave which will change the face of the world.[5]

It would be strange indeed if literature did not concretize this
new ecumenical spirit.  As a matter of fact it has spoken with power
and originality in the fiction of Flannery O'Connor.  A Catholic from
the South, O'Connor is well known among the literary elite as "one of
the most important writers of our age."[6]  The author of two novels,
*Wise Blood* and *The Violent Bear It Away*, of a novella, *The Lame
Shall Enter First*, of a collection of short stories, *A Good Man Is
Hard To Find*, and of eleven uncollected stories in the literary
quarterlies of the *haut monde*, O'Connor is still a young writer in her
mid-thirties.[7]  She is a totally committed Catholic.  To her the dogmas
of the Catholic Church are not something she accepts grudgingly, but
they are the sun-bright center from which shines the light that lifts her
work to sheer greatness.  No truck for her with the dimness of half-
faith or the darkness of unbelief, though like an expert painter she
consistently brushes into her fiction the dead black of modern

secularist culture to highlight by contrast the white splendor of the Incarnation.

To communicate the profoundest Catholic dogmas she uses the non-Catholics of the Bible Belt. Why? Because these people have grown up with Scripture, lived with it, breathed its maxims and its stories until they are marinated in the words of God.[8]

One would think so clear a situation could not be misunderstood. But some Catholic readers resent her use of non-Catholic characters to project religious problems. Robert Bowen in *Renascence* condemns, with table-thumping fury, O'Connor's fiction as flagrantly anti-Catholic, deterministic, presenting "a thorough point-by-point dramatic argument against Free Will, Redemption, and Divine Justice."[9]

I believe that an understanding of the ecumenic core in O'Connor's fiction can dissipate the perversity of such judgments. She is a John the Baptist crying in the wilderness of an unbelieving world.

## A SOUTHERN EXPOSURE

How has O'Connor come by her ecumenism? Possessing a marked integrity, she would be the last person in the world to dream of leaping onto a popular bandwagon to take advantage of ecumenical drums and trumpets. Through her own intimate experience with the non-Catholic Christians of the South she has discovered firsthand, and with the wonder of discovery, that her own people are perfect tools through which to communicate the Catholic truths about which she cares so much.

Perhaps a professor of fundamental theology at the University of Bonn, Germany, Joseph Ratzinger, describes as well as anyone the particular ground for ecumenism which appears in the fiction of O'Connor. In an address after the first session of Vatican II, January 18, 1963, he said:

> Ecumenical means that one ceases to see non-Catholics merely as opponents against whom one must defend oneself; that one tries to recognize them as brothers, with whom one speaks and from whom one learns something. Ecumenical means that one respects the truth which the other possesses and the important Christian values which he can uphold even when he is separated from us in error.[10]

The first great truth O'Connor has learned from her separated brethren is respect and reverence for their dedication to Scripture. But her own Scripture-anchored fiction seems strange to Catholics. Concerning this problem she has said:

> The fact that Catholics don't see religion through the Bible is a deficiency in Catholics. And I don't think the novelist can discard the instruments he has to plumb meaning just because Catholics are not used to them. You don't write only for now. The biblical revival is going to mean a great deal to Catholic fiction in the future. Maybe in fifty years or a hundred Catholics will be reading the Bible the way they should have been reading it all along. I can wait that long to have my fiction understood. The Bible is what we share with all Christians, and the Old Testament we share with all Jews. This is sacred history and our mythic background. If we are going to discard this we had better quit writing at all. The fact that the South is the Bible Belt is in great measure responsible for its literary pre-eminence now. The Catholic novelist can learn a great deal from the Protestant South.[11]

Back in the thirteenth century St. Bonaventure wrote, "Scripture describes the totality that has to be known for salvation."[12] Today Cardinal Bea has told us: "The field of Scripture studies is central to ecumenism. The scholar and teacher of Holy Scripture must show that the teachings, the sacraments, and the hierarchical structure of the Church are rooted in Scripture and harmony with it."[13] And Ignatius Hunt, O.S.B., put it the simplest of all, "Scripture is the foundation stone of ecumenism."[14] On this foundation stone O'Connor takes a firm stand; she regards it as a safe rock from which she can sort out from the bewildering richness of the deposit of faith those truths which are central, those we have always known but which we have ceased to regard with awe and dedication.[15]

For her the whole meaning of life centers in the Incarnation:

> I see from the standpoint of Christian orthodoxy. This means that for me the meaning of life is centered in our Redemption by Christ and that what I see in the world I see in relation to that. I don't think that this is a position that can be taken half way or one

that is particularly easy in these times to make transparent in fiction.[16]

Indeed it is a terrifyingly difficult task, particularly since O'Connor does not write especially for believers, least for all for Catholics, but for the millions of committed secularists. These are the deaf people to whom one must shout in order to be heard, the nearly blind for whom one draws enormous figures. Thus is explained the violence in her writing.[17]

But in and under and through that violence burns her passionate concern for faith such as we have not had in American fiction since Hawthorne, unless one excepts so fine a Christian novel as Faulkner's *Light in August*. Ours is an age of case histories. Characters in fiction are not responsible to a Supreme Being; they simply have experiences. And we are so accustomed to stream-of-experience fiction that coming upon the astounding faith in O'Connor's novels is "as startling, as disconcerting as a blast from a furnace which one had thought stone cold but which is still red hot."[18]

## SIX CONVICTIONS

In her fiction this red-hot blast of faith, the ecumenic core, is concretized in six key convictions:

1. Scripture is the history of salvation; it is true.

2. Christ redeemed all human beings and this is the core and center of the meaning of life. In "The Displaced Person" O'Connor with the subtlest irony makes clear that all who do not believe in the redemption are displaced persons. Their native country is Christianity.[19]

3. Redemptive grace is available to all.

4. Human beings are free to use this grace or to reject it. Scorning the interpretation of human beings as creatures controlled by stimulus-response psychology, she underlines the fact of human free will. Sumner Ferris believes that the central place given to free will in her fiction accounts for its greatness. He says that "she has shown that a Christian tragedy can be written; for in her novel, *The Violent Bear It Away*, fate and doom do not conspire against man. Either struggling against grace or opening his arms to it, his choice is his own."[20]

5. The devil exists. He tempts us to unbelief. But he is a fool who by over-reaching himself contributes to our salvation. This

is the theme of *Paradise Lost*—God bringing good out of evil. Nothing in our day could be less congenial to people than taking the devil seriously. O'Connor even suggests that juvenile delinquency might very well be explained by the power of the devil.[21]

      6. Modern humanity has elected to choose, instead of redeeming grace, four kinds of fool's gold:

> a. Rationalism. Those who claim to have no illusions have the most. The great illusion is to trust reason and science to the exclusion of revelation.
>
> b. Humanism. The professional do-gooders are hollow tin Jesuses.[22]
>
> c. Psychology. Pinning pseudo-scientific labels onto experience explains experience.
>
> d. Quantifying. The quantifiers pin their faith to tests of intelligence, aptitude, preference, and think to discover truth by inspecting questionnaires.

## THE VIOLENT BEAR IT AWAY

      Let us see by what craft these six tenets are developed in O'Connor's fiction. Only her three most important works will be examined here, and these only superficially. The first of these is *The Violent Bear It Away*.[23] Concerning the writing of a novel O'Connor has made the following relevant observation:

> I don't think you should write something as long as a novel around anything that is not of the gravest concern to you and to everybody else, and for me this is always the conflict between an attraction for the holy and the disbelief that we breathe in with the air of the times.[24]

This statement pinpoints the conflict in *The Violent Bear It Away*—the conflict suffered by Tarwater, a fourteen-year-old boy, in choosing between a life totally dedicated to Christ and a life of unbelief. Overtly he opts for atheism, but redemptive grace brings him back to his vocation as a prophet. It is so obviously a study in the gravest vocation of all, the vocation to choose Christ, that it is difficult to see how Robert Bowen could have gone so wildly astray in the adverse criticism already quoted. When I gave *The Violent Bear It Away* to the student sisters at Marillac College, they said, "That's an easy one;

it's about vocation. We understand it because we ourselves did not
like having a vocation of total dedication to Christ. We tried to run
away from it, but God caught up with us and here we are." During
O'Connor's visit to Marillac College she expressed delight in this
accurate description of her intention. In a recently published
interview she named these same sisters as among her best readers and
added with appreciation: "That's all the understanding you could ask
for."[25]

## THE ECUMENIC MESSAGE

Tarwater had been raised to be a prophet by his great uncle,
Mason Tarwater, because Mason was a builder of faith. Old Tarwater
was a prophet, not in the vulgar sense of one who foretells the future,
but in the biblical sense of one totally committed to the will of God.[26]
In a letter to me O'Connor said:

> . . . the prophet is a man apart. He is not typical of a group. Old
> Tarwater is not typical of the Southern Baptist or the Southern
> Methodist. Essentially, he's a crypto-Catholic. When you leave
> a man alone with his Bible and the Holy Ghost inspires him, he's
> going to be a Catholic one way or another, even though he knows
> nothing about the visible church. His kind of Christianity may
> not be socially desirable, but it will be real in the sight of God.

Then she added significantly, "If I set myself to write about a socially
desirable Christianity, all the life would go out of what I do."[27]
Mason Tarwater, as a prophet, is not socially desirable. He is
that nearly extinct creature, the religious fanatic, who behaves as
unpredictably as an Elias, Eliseus, Amos, Habacuc, or Osee. Where
else except in the South, that "breeding ground for prophets," could
O'Connor find the vitalized faith she needs for her ecumenic
message?[28]
Old Tarwater is a prototype of human free will. He acts. He
abhors faith that cannot act. And so we see him acting crazily
according to our standards—kidnapping two of his male descendants
to baptize them and raise them as Christians. One of these, Rayber,
escapes. He deliberately, clearly, and with the most patent exercise of
free will, chooses atheism. In the detailed analysis of his choice we
see his rejection of faith as also a rejection of love. For his idiot son,

Bishop, he feels a mysterious love.  But he steels himself against so irrational an attachment, realizing that if anything ever happened to Bishop, he would find the whole world his idiot child.

It is to this unbelieving uncle that young Tarwater flies when the old prophet is dead.  He had been raised to do two things:  baptize Rayber's idiot child and bury the old prophet with a cross to mark his grave.

"Jesus is the bread of life," the prophet had taught him (21).

But Tarwater had not wanted Jesus.  "In the darkest, most private part of his soul, hanging upsidedown like a sleeping bat, was the certain, undeniable knowledge that he was not hungry for the bread of life" (21).  Yet faith is not something that can be turned off like an electric switch.  Tarwater finds his atheist uncle irritating.  Rayber admits that once he tried to drown Bishop, a perfectly logical thing to do if one is an atheist.  But he could not do it.  With devastating logic young Tarwater points out, "You can't just say NO, . . . You got to do NO.  You got to show it.  You got to show you mean it by doing it.  You got to show you're not going to do one thing by doing another" (157).  Tarwater shows that he can act NO by actually drowning Bishop.  But in the act of drowning the child he baptizes him.  The words slip out, completely astonishing their speaker.  Upon this single incident Robert Bowen bases his charge that O'Connor's fiction is opposed to free will when the whole context of her writing is aggressively packed with examples of human beings making free choices and acting by them.

Throughout Tarwater's stay with Rayber in the city he is consumed by mounting physical hunger, for he finds dry cornflakes and hamburgers an unsatisfactory substitute for the good food his prophet uncle had served him—a patent symbol for his spiritual starvation.  Rayber himself is a symbol of a modern man settling for only what reason and science can tell him.  He is a school teacher dedicated to testing, to quantifying the unmeasurable.  "At his high school he was the expert on testing.  All his professional decisions were prefabricated and did not involve his participation" (114).  After a study he once made of the old prophet he arrived at this psychological conclusion:  the old man's fanaticism came from insecurity.  He wanted to be called; therefore, he called himself.  To O'Connor this sort of jargon is the hollowest absurdity.

Rayber's wife, the do-gooder O'Connor despises, is a social worker who cannot endure the humiliation of an idiot child, tells others how to cope with abnormal children, leaves her husband without a divorce lest the court allot the care of the idiot child to her, and then upbraids Rayber for not putting the idiot in an institution.

## A VIEW OF THE DEVIL

O'Connor projects the devil convincingly in this book as a voice carrying on a conversation with young Tarwater from the moment of the prophet's death.  He speaks Tarwater's dialect and the situation is so managed that temptation seems to coalesce from two roots:  human beings' own evil impulses plus the suggestions of the devil.  After Tarwater drowns Bishop and is returning to Powderhead, the devil is concretized as a homosexual who violates Tarwater.  Here the devil overreaches himself and does God's work in spite of his diabolical intent.  For the effect of his outrage is to drive Tarwater sickened and chastened back to his vocation as a prophet.  I have it on O'Connor's word that this is the particular view she wishes to give of the devil.  Tarwater expresses the violence of his disgust by setting fire to the spot where he was violated and to the surrounding forest.

When he gets back to the charred ruins of the prophet's home which he thought he had burned with the corpse in the house, he finds the prophet's grave marked by a cross.  Near it stands a Negro friend, Buford, who says with terrible scorn, "It's owing to me he's resting there.  I buried him while you were laid out drunk. . . . It's owing to me the sign of the Saviour is over his head" (240).  Here is accomplished all that Tarwater should have done himself.  The inscrutable Providence of God.  Stunned, the boy gazes in a trance while the Negro goes his way.  He who rejected the Bread of Life stares at the field where an inward vision of unimaginable beauty shows the old prophet eating of the loaves and the fishes, and Tarwater discovers that his insatiable hunger is for the very Bread of Life he had tried to reject.  "He felt his hunger no longer as a pain but as a tide. . . . He felt it building from the blood of Abel to his own, rising and engulfing him" (242).  And in this sacred moment he is aware that a fire in a red-gold burning tree was the fire that "encircled Daniel, that had raised Elijah from the earth, that had spoken to Moses and would in the instant speak to him.  He threw himself to the ground and with his face against the dirt of the grave, he heard to command.  GO WARN THE CHILDREN OF GOD OF THE TERRIBLE SPEED OF MERCY" (242).

Note that it is the terrible speed of mercy, not justice. The old prophet had used the word justice in the same context, but in the New Pentecost it is the terrible speed of mercy.

Tarwater takes dirt from his great uncle's grave and smears it on his forehead. Exhausted as he is and physically starving, he moves steadily on, ". . . his face set toward the dark city, where the children of God lay sleeping" (243). The exile has returned to God.[29]

## WISE BLOOD

Not only in this novel but also in that vital comic creation, *Wise Blood*,[30] O'Connor articulates the same theme: human beings try to run away from God but redemptive grace saves them from apostasy. In *Wise Blood* Hazel Motes, a man of terrifying sincerity who has lost faith while in the armed services, preaches a new church, The Church of Christ without Christ. He is a modern man exposed in comic relief with all his absurdities. Insofar as he chooses atheism and looks upon a car, which he uses as a pulpit, as the very essence of the good life, he does symbolize modern humanity. But he is not literally of our times. A backwoods hayseed, he has no slick polish. It is O'Connor's boast that her characters are usually poor, deprived people and that she finds these hicks entirely adequate for communicating her essentially Christian convictions. What Hazel Motes does have to an astonishing degree is an absolute integrity of spirit. The book swarms with various religious charlatans, in particular an itinerant preacher, Aza Hawks, who poses as a blind man. Once he had promised the people that as a witness to Christ he would publicly blind himself with quicklime. Failing in courage at the last moment, he only scarred his cheeks; these scars plus a pair of black glasses are sufficient, however, to maintain his public posture as one who heroically blinded himself for Christ.

But when Hazel loses his car, apparently God's way of saying that he does not like the Church of Christ without Christ, Hazel Motes immediately blinds himself with quicklime. He spends the rest of his life doing terrible penance for his defection.

"His grandfather had been a circuit preacher, a waspish old man who had ridden over three counties with Jesus hidden in his head like a stinger" (20). And Hazel "knew by the time he was twelve years old that he was going to be a preacher. Later he saw Jesus move from tree to tree in the back of his mind, a wild ragged figure motioning him to turn around and come off into the dark where he was not sure of his footing, where he might be walking on the water and not know it and then suddenly know it and drown" (22).

In her extraordinarily helpful "Author's Note to the Second Edition" of *Wise Blood*, 1962, O'Connor says:

> . . . Hazel Motes' integrity lies in his trying with such vigor to get rid of the ragged figure [Christ] who moves from tree to tree in the back of his mind. For the author Hazel's integrity lies in his not being able to. Does one's integrity ever lie in what he is not able to do? I think that usually it does, for free will does not mean one will, but many wills conflicting in one man. Freedom cannot be conceived simply. It is a mystery and one which a novel, even a comic novel, can only be asked to deepen.[31]

Not only does O'Connor render a service to literature by refusing to confuse free will with a single will, but also by dramatizing the force of an apparently dormant will surviving from early childhood. For Hazel Motes there is ineradicable conviction that for sin one does penance. Just as in childhood he placed stones in his shoes and walked a mile because he had looked at a lascivious sideshow, so now after his great defection, he walks several miles a day on the glass and sharp stones he has placed in his shoes.

His return to faith and penance is handled with the utmost delicacy. By nature uncommunicative, under constant questioning from his landlady, he makes only two avowals when she asks over and over again why he blinded himself. "I'm not clean," he says (224). This cryptic statement recalls vividly an earlier remark when Hazel had been insulted by a wench for not being clean. "I AM clean, . . ." he declared. And then ruefully, "If Jesus existed, I wouldn't be clean, . . ." (91). Now that he admits he is not clean we know that he believes in Jesus. And we know it from his second equally cryptic remark that he blinded himself to atone. His penance includes sleeping with barbed wire about his chest, living in the greatest poverty, suffering the ravages of consumption, and finally wandering about in the cold of a driving winter storm. But the final beauty of the book bursts through the fascination of the materialistic landlady for him because in his blind face glows an inward vision like a point of light—like the star which guided the Magi to Christ. The only appropriate end for Hazel Motes is his ignominious death in a ditch at the hands of two callow officers of the law.

Even in his overt atheism there was something unmistakable in his bearing. Said the sniveling Enoch Emery to him: "I knew when I first seen you you didn't have nobody nor nothing but Jesus. I seen you and I knew it" (58). And the vicious Sabath Lily Hawks, who posed as a child preacher but pursued Hazel Motes with evil intent, exclaims in exasperation: "I knew when I first seen you you were mean and evil, . . . I seen you wouldn't never have no fun or let anybody else because you didn't want nothing but Jesus!" (188).

To want nothing but Jesus lies at the core of the simple faith celebrated by O'Connor as humanity's greatest need. She comes back again and again to faith as the greatest good available to human beings.

## THE LAME SHALL ENTER FIRST

In the short novel, *The Lame Shall Enter First*, O'Connor shows that a terrible sinner, if he keeps the Christian faith, is infinitely preferable to the "good" pagan.[32] In this story we see an atheist social worker, ironically called Sheppard, interviewing Johnson, a young juvenile delinquent with a club foot. He is sure that the foot explains Johnson's evil acts, but he asks the boy why he is so destructive. "Satan, . . . He has me in his power," the boy answers, whereupon Sheppard immediately supposes that his ideas have been formed by stupid billboards: "DOES SATAN HAVE YOU IN HIS POWER? REPENT OR BURN IN HELL" (450-51). Because Johnson is very bright, an IQ of 140, Sheppard takes a great interest in him, inviting him to come and live in his own home. Sheppard's ten-year-old son, Norton, extremely lonely since the recent death of his mother, seems to his father to be very selfish and he thinks having Johnson in the home will help the child to be less selfish. To bolster Johnson's self-confidence he gives him the key to his house. But Johnson feels only contempt for such softness. He despises Sheppard's patronizing unction in having him fitted for a new shoe for his club foot and on two occasions perpetrates the most violent destruction in the neighborhood. When the police come to complain, Sheppard defends Johnson and will not believe that he has betrayed his confidence. Trust a villain thoroughly and he will not betray that trust; this is the psychology by which Sheppard operates. Johnson despises his weakness. Sheppard buys a microscope and then a telescope for his adopted renegade.

Soon Johnson steals a Bible and explains the elementary Judeo-Christian beliefs to Norton, who has never heard the good news of human redemption. The little boy is comforted immeasurably to know that his mother's spirit lives on. He would rather believe her in hell than that she does not exist at all. Sheppard is outraged that his son should be so contaminated. Johnson sneers: "Whoever says it aint a hell, . . . is contradicting Jesus. The dead are judged and the wicked are damned." Johnson insists that if Norton's mother believed in Jesus she is saved on high, "but you got to be dead to get there" (461-62). With terrible wisdom Johnson goes on to tell the little boy: ". . . Right now you'd go where she is, . . . but if you live long enough, you'll go to hell" (462).

The child begs Johnson to repent so that he will not go to hell. Whereupon Johnson answers: "If I do repent, I'll be a preacher, . . . . If you're going to do it, it's no sense in doing it half way" (476). With insolence Johnson assures Sheppard, "Satan has you in his power, . . ." (477). And concerning the Bible he announces: "Even if I didn't believe it, it would still be true. . . ." (477). He chews and eats a page of the Bible remarking: "I've eaten it like Ezekiel and it was honey to my mouth" (477).

Later when Sheppard goes to the attic to check on his son who is looking through the telescope, the child declares ecstatically that he can see his mother in heaven. Sheppard sends him to bed. But he does not go.

When Sheppard returns downstairs, the police are at the door with Johnson who declares loudly that he got caught on purpose. Why? With acid scorn he explains: "To show up that big tin Jesus! . . . . He thinks he's God. I'd rather be in the reformatory than in his house. . . . He's a dirty atheist, . . . He said there wasn't no hell . . . I lie and steal because I'm good at it! My foot don't have a thing to do with it! The lame shall enter first! The halt'll be gathered together. When I get ready to be saved, Jesus'll save me, not that lying stinking atheist, . . ." (480).

The police take him away. Stunned, Sheppard reflects, "I have nothing to reproach myself with, . . . I did more for him than I did for my own child" (481). Suddenly he realizes how gravely he had neglected his own little boy and the depth of his own selfishness: "He had stuffed his own emptiness with good works like a glutton. He had ignored his own child to feed his vision of himself. He saw the clear-eyed Devil, the sounder of hearts, leering at him from the eyes of Johnson. His image of himself shrivelled until everything was black before him" (481).

He feels an overwhelming new love for his neglected son. Dashing to the attic full of dreams of making up to the child for past neglect, he finds that little Norton had hanged himself to be with his mother.

A summary of so profound a story cannot do justice, of course, to Flannery O'Connor's art. Yet these aspects of the ecumenic core in her writing must be clear:

   1. Belief in the primacy of Scripture.

   2. An illustration of St. Paul's statement that "wherein thou judgest another, thou condemnest thyself."[33] Sheppard saw the small selfishness in his little son, but he could not see the engulfing selfishness in his whole program of do-goodism.

   3. Through the devil in Johnson, however, Sheppard does have the grace to recognize this selfishness for what it is.

   4. Little Norton receives the redemptive grace of faith (baptism of desire) which saves him from the nearly certain damnation which would be his if he continued to live with his atheist father. This grace, too, came through the devilish Johnson.

   5. A sinner, Johnson, who clings to the faith is infinitely preferable to Sheppard, an atheist dedicated to public welfare.

   6. It is Johnson, the devil, who declares Christ. This may shock us but O'Connor explains:

> In the gospels it was the devils who first recognized Christ and the evangelists didn't censor this information. They apparently thought it was pretty good witness. It scandalizes us when we see the same thing in modern dress only because we have this defensive attitude toward the faith.[34]

## THE ECUMENIC CORE

The task remains for us now to pinpoint accurately just how this ecumenic core in the writing of Flannery O'Connor is indeed ecumenic. Our best help comes from Father Yves Congar, O.P., who clearly distinguishes three levels of ecumenism, describing only the third level as "authentic ecumenism." He describes it carefully to mean "that we renew our doctrinal positions at the deepest sources of biblical revelation and the great Catholic tradition." And he adds significantly: "This is not a suggestion of liberalism, far from it; neither is it a minimal way, but rather a maximum measure, a path of conversion which is both spiritual and intellectual. . . . This is the way of authentic ecumenism."[35]

Now this "path of conversion" which is a "maximum measure" of return to essentials is O'Connor's ecumenism. We are accustomed to hearing this renewal described as an emphasis "less canonical," "less juridical,"[36] as "making sacrifice of those non-essentials which tend to confuse non-Catholics,"[37] and as "cutting through the non-essentials of faith to its Gospel center . . . cutting through centuries of legalism and stale tradition to somewhere near the heart of what it means to be Christian."[38] To Flannery O'Connor with her gift for simplicity and directness it is "recalling people to known but ignored truths."

## AN APOSTOLIC URGENCY

This recalling people is shot through and through with apostolic urgency. If there are those who think that ecumenism is not apostolic they have missed its deepest intention, its widest implication. Its modern upsurge began with the embarrassment felt by zealous Christian missionaries who could not present to unbelievers the image of the united Christendom.[39] Furthermore, in the reopening of Vatican Council II, Pope Paul VI named four areas in which the council is to advance the life and wisdom of the Church. The fourth of these is purely missionary: the Church's relation to the modern world.[40]

Finally, there is a close relationship between the religious mystery of the Incarnation, so central to O'Connor's thinking, and the art of fiction, which incarnates or concretizes the mysteries of life. Concerning this relationship of the abstract to the concrete in fiction she says with the utmost wisdom:

> I know that the writer does call up the general and maybe the essential through the particular, but this general and essential [what I have ticked off as her six points] is still deeply embedded in mystery. It is not answerable to any of our formulas. It doesn't rest finally in a statable kind of solution. It ought to throw you back on the living God. Our Catholic mentality is great on paraphrase, logic, formula, instant and correct answers.

We judge before we experience and never trust our faith to be sujected to reality, because it is not strong enough. And maybe in this we are wise. I think this spirit is changing on account of the council but the changes will take a long time to soak through.[41]

But even while they take a long time to soak through, Flannery O'Connor's fiction, years ahead of the new emphasis which is certain to come out of Vatican II, throws us back on the living God. I am grateful to have had this opportunity to point, even with an unsteady finger, at that ecumenic core which explains somewhat her tremendous accomplishment.[42]

## Notes

1. Mariella Gable, O.S.B., "Ecumenic Core in Flannery O'Connor's Fiction," *American Benedictine Review* (June 1964): 127-43.

2. Quoted by Godfrey Diekmann, O.S.B., in *Come, Let Us Worship*, Benedictine Studies II (Baltimore 1961), 21.

3. John XXIII, *The Pope Speaks*, VIII, 4 (1963): 402.

4. Interview with Archbishop J. Hallinan, Atlanta, Georgia, quoted in the St. Cloud *Visitor*, 30 June 1963, 1.

5. The Reverend Frederick Grant, Anglican observer at Vatican Council II, *The Catholic Hour*, NBC-TV, 4 August 1963.

6. Caroline Gordon, "Flannery O'Connor's *Wise Blood*," *Critique*, II, 2 (Fall 1958): 6.

7. O'Connor is working on what she hopes will become a novel, *Why Do the Heathen Rage?* a portion of which was published in *Esquire*, LX (July 1963): 60-1.

8. An amusing quarrel between old Mr. Fortune and his nine-year-old granddaughter, Mary, is couched entirely in biblical terms:

Grandfather, despising Mary's father, says: "Do you think I give a damn hoot where that fool grazes his calves?"

Mary: "He who calls his brother a fool is subject to hellfire."

Grandfather: "Jedge not, . . . lest ye be not jedged."

As she continues to be difficult he refuses to drive her home in his car and says: "Walk home by yourself. I refuse to drive a Jezebel."

Mary: "And I refuse to ride with the Whore of Babylon." O'Connor,

Flannery, "A View of the Woods," in *The Complete Stories of Flannery O'Connor*, intro. Robert Giroux, (New York, 1981), 342-43.

9. Robert Bowen, "Hope Versus Despair in the Gothic Novel," *Renascence*, XIII (Spring 1961): 147.

10. Joseph Ratzinger, Davenport *Catholic Messenger*, 20 June 1963, 12. If one prefers a definition rather than Father Ratzinger's description, cf. the seven definitons of "ecumenical" in Gustave Weigel, S.J., *A Catholic Primer on the Ecumenical Movement* (Westminster, MD., 1959): 73. These definitions correspond to seven periods in Church history, the one appropriate to our times being: "the quality or attitude which expresses the consciousness of and desire for Christian unity."

11. Joel Wells, "Conversation with Flannery O'Connor," *Critic*, XXI (September 1962): 4.

12. Quoted in George H. Tavard, *The Catholic Approach to Protestantism* (New York, 1955), 148.

13. Augustin Cardinal Bea, "The Ecumenical Responsibility in Teaching Theology," lecture at the University of Freibourg, Switzerland, quoted in the *Ecumenist*, I (February-March 1963): 41.

14. Ignatius Hunt, public lecture, College of St. Benedict, St. Joseph, Minnesota, 2 July 1963.

15. A study of Miss O'Connor's "sensitive, perhaps sub-conscious use of Scripture parallels" has been made by Sister Bertrande Meyers, D. C., "Four Stories of Flannery O'Connor," *Thought*, XXXVII (Autumn 1962): 140 ff.

16. Flannery O'Connor, "The Fiction Writer and His Country," in Granville Hicks, ed., *The Living Novel* (New York, 1957), 162.

17. Flannery O'Connor's precise words are: "When you have to assume that your audience does not hold the same beliefs as you do then you have to make your vision apparent by shock—to the hard of hearing you shout, and for the almost blind you draw large startling figures." Ibid., 163.

18. Gordon, "Flannery O'Connor's *Wise Blood*," 6.

19. "Almost all her people are displaced persons and some are either aware of it or become so. But it is not a sectional or regional condition; it is a religious condition, common to North and South alike, common indeed to the world we live in. The stories not only imply, they as good as state again and again, that estrangement from Christian plenitude is estrangement from the true country of man." Robert Fitzgerald, "The Countryside and the True Country," *Sewanee Review*, LXX (Summer 1962): 394.

20. The full text of Ferris's comment is instructive: "Miss O'Connor's world is a violent one, but the violence is ultimately spiritual, inflicted by

characters on themselves. Her theology is, furthermore, Catholic (although none of her characters are). God neither saves or damns the characters who have free will; although He provides that the helpless Bishop be baptized and thus saved, He does no more than give Rayber and Tarwater the opportunity to work out their own salvation or damnation. And it is this character that makes *The Violent* not only a subtle and profound and disturbing study of spiritual states but a great religious novel. Miss O'Connor has shown that a Christian tragedy can be written; for in her novel fate and doom do not conspire against man. Either struggling against grace or opening his arms to accept it, his choice is his own." Sumner J. Ferris, "The Outside and the Inside: Flannery O'Connor's *The Violent Bear It Away*," *Critique*, III, 2 (1960): 19.

21. The juvenile delinquent in "The Lame Shall Enter First" knows he is in the devil's power. To John Hawkes who made a study of "Flannery O'Connor's Devil" in *Sewanee Review* (Summer 1962) Miss O'Connor wrote: "I want to be certain that the devil gets identified as the devil and not simply taken as this or that psychological tendency." Note from editor: I have used the following source for "The Lame Shall Enter First" and changed the references to fit: *The Complete Stories of Flannery O'Connor* (New York, 1981), 445-82.

22. Sheppard in "The Lame Shall Enter First" is her most impressive example. In "The Comforts of Home," *Kenyon Review* (Fall 1960), a woman who decides to take a nymphomaniac into her home is described as one who "pursues goodness with such mindless intensity that everyone involved is made a fool of and virtue itself becomes ridiculous."

23. Flannery O'Connor, *The Violent Bear It Away* (New York, 1960).

24. C. Ross Mullins, Jr., "Flannery O'Connor, An Interview," *Jubilee*, XI (June 1963): 34.

25. Ibid.

26. O'Connor is interested in prophets without caring in the least about their affiliation to any sect. "I'm not interested in sects as sects; I'm concerned with the religious individual, the backwoods prophet." Granville Hicks, "A Writer at Home with Her Heritage," *Saturday Review*, XLV (12 May 1962): 22.

27. Flannery O'Connor to Mariella Gable, O.S.B., 4 May 1963. *The Habit of Being: Letters of Flannery O'Connor*, ed. Sally Fitzgerald (New York, 1980), 517.

28. Arthur Mizener quoted in M. J. Friedman, "Another Legend in Southern Fiction," *English Journal*, LI (April 1962): 242.

29. The critics do not all agree with this interpretation: "The call that

Tarwater hears and obeys at the end of the novel, after he discovers that his great uncle has after all been buried, is thus a specious one, a capitulation to the circumstances rather that to God; for although he has fulfilled God's will, he has rejected God's ways. It is with the passion of fanaticism and despair, not of religion, that hellfire behind him and darkness before him, he begins to walk back to the city." Ferris, "The Outside and the Inside," 18.

30. Flannery O'Connor, *Wise Blood* (New York, 1962).

31. Ibid. Author's Note to the Second Edition.

32. *The Complete Stories*, 445-82.

33. Romans 2:1.

34. Flannery O'Connor, to Mariella Gable, 4 May 1963, *The Habit of Being*, 517.

35. The full text of Father Congar's three-fold discrimination is as follows:

Ecumenism may be understood on three levels, where the third includes the second and the second the first, so that passing from one to the other is like growing in depth and authenticity. The first level consists in an attitude of benevolence with the intention of avoiding anything that would needlessly hurt others. This means that we uphold and propose doctrinal propositions in their classical or even in their scholastic formulations, without an attempt to improve them; we simply try to present them in their best light and make up for their harshness by gestures of charity or words of friendship. This is good but not enough.

On the second level of ecumenism we take into account the positive values and the difficulties of "the others" and try to recognize the misconceptions from which these others suffer when they represent our position to themselves. Here we try to answer their real difficulties by an effort of adaptation. This is better but not good enough.

We must advance to a further level of ecumenism by accepting, in the very area of our Catholic truth, the salutary shock produced by the dialogue with "the others" and by renewing our own doctrinal positions at the deepest sources of biblical revelation and the great Catholic tradition. This is not a suggestion of liberalism, far from it; neither is it a minimal way, but rather a maximum measure, a path of conversion which is both spiritual and intellectual. Spiritual it is because a radical self-criticism puts its finger on our attitude of being in possession, on our comfortable conscience, on our self-justification and our apologetical and confessional triumph; and intellectual it is because the effort to pass beyond the easy and closed possession of truth without problems attempts to integrate into an equally traditional but larger conception the aspects of the truth which the questions of the other oblige us to acknowledge. This is the way of authentic ecumenism. *Informations Catholiques Internationales*, 15 December 1962, 3. Quoted in *The Ecumenist*, 1 (April-May 1963): 66.

36. Bernard Leeming, S.J., English theologian and correspondent for the Secretariat of Christian Unity. Quoted in *The Catholic Messenger*, 9 November 1962, 1.

37. Cardinal Bernard Alfrink, *Twelve Council Fathers* by Walter Abbot (New York, 1963). Quoted in *The Catholic Messenger*, 20 June 1963, 8.

38. James O'Gara's summary of Pope John's program for ecumenical renewal, "Good Pope John," in *The Commonweal*, 28 June 1963, 366.

39. The "confusion and scandal" of a divided Christendom to an apostolic missionary is described by Gustave Weigel, S.J.: "In the missions there was reduplication of work, an alienating bewilderment in the minds of non-Christians on hearing conflicting conceptions of Christianity, and bitterness between the missionaries who should have been united in the charity which led them to the mission fields." *A Catholic Primer on the Ecumenical Movement* (Westminster, Md., 1959), 27.

40. Gregory Baum, "New Spirit at the Council," *The Commonweal*, 25 October 1963, 126.

41. Flannery O'Connor, to Sister Mariella Gable, 4 May 1963. *The Habit of Being*, 516-17.

42. Gable Collection, St. Benedict's Convent Archives. Gable's handwritten note on the original manuscript reads: "Flannery was delighted with this article and told the novelist, Richard Coleman, that it did her greater justice than any previously published article. `It makes sense of what I'm doing.'"

# Chapter 12

## Feather in the Wind[1]

I put down the *New Yorker* very reluctantly.  It was the issue of August 19, 1961, and my fingers lingered over it in a kind of ecstatic unbelief.  For here in black and white was a short story I thought I should not live to see either in a Catholic or a secular magazine—"Pigeon Feathers" by the Lutheran, John Updike, a clear, brilliant, amazing announcement that the Age of Nada was passing and that with us was the daybreak of a new Age of Faith.

The Age of Nada—it was the Hemingway period which saw human beings as so many ants on a log waiting in the fire to be roasted or steamed to death.  The meaningless horror of this life could, of course, be faced with courage, the courage to accept it and not whimper, but this stoic "heroism" could be achieved only through detachment and non-commitment to others.  In perfect accord with this chill view of life was the stripped Hemingway style.  It ticked off cold, accurate details with clinical accuracy in primer-short sentences.  Let us not care.  Since there was no God to care, why should we batter our breasts with compassion?

Yet as one of the most perceptive analysts of the Age of Nada demonstrated, there was a kind of pseudo-compassion in the outcropping of all sorts of organized charities.  This is how the great French novelist, Georges Bernanos, explained the situation: Human beings lost their faith in the most essential part of the Christian religion. They no longer believed in Heaven or Hell. Even nominal Christians did not believe in heaven or hell. They made their heaven on earth by surrounding themselves with all the comforts of a technological society. Yet they were tortured by a gnawing subconscious sense of guilt for their unbelief. To assuage the pain of their guilt they threw themselves into all sorts of corporal works of mercy, all kinds of organized charity, as if substituting acts which should be the fruit of faith could compensate for the Monstrous Betrayal.

John Updike's "Pigeon Feathers" trumpets the news that the Monstrous Betrayal is passing. He himself must have realized its importance, for when he collected his second volume of short stories in the spring of 1962 he pointed to this story as special by naming the volume, *Pigeon Feathers and Other Stories*. Of this book Granville Hicks, himself an agnostic, said: "We hear talk now and then of a breakthrough in fiction, the achievement of a new attitude and hence a new method; something like that seems close at hand in *Pigeon Feathers*."

Not close at hand, but here, a breakthrough heralding a Christian Revolution, which though it cannot be realized in full immediately, is substituting various Christian attitudes for the presuppositions of the Age of Nada.

In spite of the embarrassing inadequacies of summary, let us see what Updike does in "Pigeon Feathers." This story is indeed a feather in the wind. It concerns David Kern, a fourteen-year-old boy who has been sent regularly to Lutheran Sunday-school and who by nature and grace has the gift of faith in Christ. In a household upset by moving into a primitive farm home, David casually picks up from his mother's book box a copy of H.G. Wells' *An Outline of History*. He reads the snide account of the life of Jesus:

> He had been an obscure political agitator, a kind of hobo, in a minor colony of the Roman Empire. By an accident impossible to reconstruct, he (the small "h" horrified David) survived on his own crucifixion and presumably died a few weeks later. A religion was founded on this freakish incident. The credulous imagination of the times retrospectively assigned miracles and supernatural pretensions to Jesus; a myth grew and then a church, whose theology at most points was in direct contradiction of the simple, rather communistic teachings of the Galilean. (118-19)

David was horrified and stricken at this denial of Christ's divinity. The reader of the story is suddenly thrust back into the 1920's when society took such smug nonsense seriously. In the light of the stunning advances made today in Scripture studies by both Catholic and Protestant scholars, no person of intellectual stature can doubt the historical records of Jesus. But David's mother, father, and his minister are all blighted by the age which is passing away and are revealed in the story as symbols of an obsolescent culture.

David does not turn to them for help but eats out his heart in terrifying fear. And that fear is one of the most remarkable theological insights in the story. Fear of death! If Christ is not divine, not able to rise from the dead, then there is no immortality. It is as if the Gospel statement, "If Christ be not risen, then indeed is your faith vain," had found in this story a perfect embodiment. David feels with terrible certainty the truth of Pascal's observation: "Take away Christ and we know neither what death is, nor what life is, nor what God is, nor what we ourselves are." No summary can even suggest the delicacy with which David's psychological anguish is manifested to the reader.

And those who have not the faith, David's parents and his minister, with what quiet irony Updike demolished them. David first asked Reverend Dobson:

> "About the Resurrection of the Body—are we conscious between
> the time when we die and the Day of Judgment?"
> "No, I suppose not . . . ."
> "Well, where is our soul, then, in this gap? . . ."
> "I suppose you could say our souls are asleep. . . ."
> ". . . Where will Heaven be?" (132-33)

And here the stupidity of Reverend Dobson reaches a climax. He says: "David, you might think of Heaven this way: as the way the goodness Abraham Lincoln did lives after him." The shame of these words overwhelms David. To hear Christianity betrayed in such frivolous unfaith!

When his mother notices his distress and begs him to tell her why he is depressed, he reluctantly repeats Dobson's observation about Lincoln, breathlessly waiting for her to be shocked. She merely asks casually why he didn't like it, whereupon he bursts out with the terrible truth: "Well, don't you see? It amounts to saying there isn't any Heaven at all." She has nothing to give him. In her own lack of faith "she had assumed that Heaven had faded from his head years ago. She had imagined that he had already entered, in the secrecy of silence, the conspiracy that he now knew to be all around him" (136).

She is the symbol of the modern unbeliever, willing to send her child to church as a formality and utterly dismayed to discover that he takes his faith seriously. Good heavens! How long is it going to take the boy to discover that there is no heaven?

His intuitions, however, make theological strides she is utterly unable to follow. He says, "Mother, good grief. Don't you see . . . if when we die there's nothing, all our sun and fields and what not are all, ah *horror*? It's just an ocean of horror" (137-38).

This she cannot see. All David wants is "a word, a gesture, a nod of certainty"—some little signal from his elders that they do believe. His father fails him with a hearty, "Hell, I think death is a wonderful thing. I look forward to it. Get the garbage out of the way. If I had the man here who invented death, I'd pin a medal on him" (139).

David is given a rifle for his fifteenth birthday and asked to kill the pigeons in the barn. Fearing death he does not wish to kill anything. But he shoots the birds and when he has to bury them, he takes time out to look at their feathers. He looks at them as he had stared at the perfection of his dog's hair, at his ear-whorls, at the texture of his nostrils. Sensitive, he had seen in all these humble manifestations of nature a mystery of beauty and design. And now he sees the feathers, so beautiful, so ordered, so superbly colored—slate blue, lilac, gray. As he contemplates the order and beauty of these birds, bred by the millions and exterminated as pests, a great certainty clothes his whole being; "the God who had lavished such craft upon these worthless birds would not destroy His whole creation by refusing to let David live forever" (150).

The story seems to say clearly: If the unbelievers of the recent past cannot give the assurance in faith needed by the new faith-hungry generation, then these young people can grasp out of the order and beauty of the universe a witness to the existence of God. It seems to say, moreover, that there is with us a new generation of young people with intuitive faith who make their elders seem as antiquated as an antimacassar.

In Updike's other books there is a persistent vein of intuitive faith along with a considered criticism of the modern do-gooder who

operates without Christian love.  His first novel, *The Poorhouse Fair*,
1958, pictures the inmates of the poorhouse discussing their ideas of
heaven.  Outstanding for dignity and fineness among them is Hook, a
ninety-four-year-old retired school teacher who consistently reads the
Bible.  In stating his position he seems to be stating Updike's:

> When you get to be my age—and I shall pray that you never do, I
> wish it in no one, but if you do—you shall know this: there is no
> goodness without belief, there is nothing but busyness.  And if
> you had not believed, at the end of life you shall know you have
> buried your talent in the ground of this world and have nothing
> saved to take into the next.

Hook directs these words to the superintendent of the poorhouse who
has no interest whatever in the "next life." He is too busy providing
cold, impersonal care for the inmates of the institution, and when they
stone him, their rebellion is like the rising up of society against the
whole fabric of public welfare administered without a personal
Christian love.

We see something akin to this criticism of "charity" in the novel,
*Rabbit, Run*, which might offend some readers by the intimacy of its
sex montage.  However, one of the very significant highlights in the
book is the picture of the Reverend Eccles, Episcopalian, who wears
himself out in an effort to influence his parishoners.  He sits up late in
a drug store to listen to teenagers who want to know how far they can
go with petting and still love Jesus, visits everyone who has a
problem, and invites Rabbit to play golf with him in the hope that he
can persuade him to leave a prostitute and go back to his pregnant
wife.  When he calls on a Lutheran clergyman to ask his assistance in
bringing Rabbit back to his wife, the Reverend Kruppenbach tells him
off in no uncertain terms:

> You think your job is to be an unpaid doctor, to run around and
> plug up the holes and make everything smooth . . . . I don't think
> that is your job. . . .a minister selling his message for a few
> scraps of gossip and a few games of golf. . . .You don't know
> your role or you'd be home locked in prayer. That's your role to
> be an exemplar of faith. There is where comfort comes from: not
> what little finagling a body can do here and there . . . . There is
> nothing but Christ for us. All this busyness and decency is
> nothing. It's the devil's work. (154-55)

All this sounds as if Updike were a didactic writer, but he is not primarily apostolic. Though he was raised a Lutheran, he lists himself today as a Congregationalist, in deference to his wife's preference. He is always gently biographical evoking his details of American life with magic accuracy. Yet his constant regard for faith, for immortality, for goodness, "Only goodness lives, but it does live" (*The Centaur* 297), his conviction that joy belongs to the Lord and that wherever true joy abides, there is God (*The Centaur* 296)—all these indicate a new Age of Faith.

After a half-century of boredom, bitterness, and defeatism in fiction, Updike's voice is like the first sweet whistle of the redbird after a grim, gray, snowless winter.

Is this voice a lone cry or are there others forming a small but significant chorus? The supporting voices are impressive: Flannery O'Connor whose fiction has enthralled the literary elite and the two most popular writers of the present moment, J.D. Salinger and William Golding. Let us look at the contribution of each.

Flannery O'Connor, regarded as "one of the most important writers of our age," is much more apostolic than Updike. She is certain that the Incarnation is the most important event in history and that human beings must so regard it and live by it. Carolyn Gordon is much impressed with the quality of faith in O'Connor's fiction, which comes as a great surprise in an Age of Nada. She points out how unbelievers have been content with a mere chain of experience and that in this milieu of unfaith O'Connor's fiction is "as startling, as disconcerting as a blast from a furnace which one had thought stone-cold but which is still red-hot."

A red-hot Roman Catholic, Flannery O'Connor reserves in her fiction first place for the basic verities: faith, redemptive grace, free will, death, the importance of the poor and the deprived, the reality of the devil, and the absurdity of the professional do-gooder when he is not animated by Christian charity. Hers is the craft of saying all these things without ever manipulating reality in violation of art in order to teach a lesson. Usually no Catholic character figures in her fiction. Her characters are the people of the Bible Belt who have grown up saturated in Scripture, whose whole lives have been permeated by the word of God. She usually does not even identify them as Baptists or Methodists or Church of God. With the hicks and the hayseeds of her native South she finds that she can very well communicate the greatest

Christian truths and in this she demonstrates a strong ecumenical spirit—the spirit which recognizes truth wherever it exists. She has deeply realized in her fiction the truth spoken by Ignatius Hunt, O.S.B.: "Scripture is the foundation stone of ecumenism." Regretting the ignorance of Scripture in the average Catholic, O'Connor is yet hopeful that the new world-interest in Scripture will bring Catholics closer to the Bible and ultimately enable them to appreciate what she is doing in her fiction.

Though O'Connor is the darling of the quarterlies of the literary *haut monde*, many average readers are thoroughly acquainted with her celebration of redemptive grace in her novels, *Wise Blood* and *The Violent Bear It Away*. These novels seem to say that even though Hazel Motes and Frances Tarwater tried to run away from God, redemptive grace caught up with them in their flight and brought them back to faith in Christ. Both of these characters apparently symbolize our society which is being brought back to faith in spite of its Great Defection.

No one should miss her stunning novella, "The Lame Shall Enter First," even though it has not yet been published in hard cover. It can be found in the *Sewanee Review*, Summer 1962, and is well worth a half-day's trip to the library. Not often does a story skyrocket so high in human interest and burst into a shower of stars that glitter with the primacy of Scripture, the absurdity of un-Christian charity, and the truth that even a very great sinner, if he keep the faith in Christ, is infinitely preferable to the good pagan.

We turn now to the two most popular writers of our decade, J.D. Salinger and William Golding.

Ever since 1951 the public has been having a love affair with Salinger. Only recently does that ecstatic embrace seem to be relaxing. It did credit to those readers who were apparently charmed by Salinger's idealism.

What was that new idealism? First, an incisive criticism of our society which was found to be phony to the core. So phony that two of his main characters, Holden Caulfield and Franny Glass suffered breakdowns in contemplating it. For Holden it was the way people today never listen when others talk, the way they pretend to be delighted to receive guests whom they hate. It was materialistc educators who expect boys to study so that they will be able to buy a Cadillac some day or to die of grief if their team loses. It was a school society where all they talk about is girls, liquor and sex all day

and everybody sticks together in dirty little cliques. For Franny it
was the whole shallow show of college life. She was suffocated by
seeing that everything seems meaningless, tiny, and "sad-making."
Some have thought that Salinger's enormous popularity took its rise
from the relish young people feel in identifying their elders as phony.
But that is to underestimate the sharpness of young readers in catching
his main idea which is nothing less than the Gospel message of perfect
charity, which asks us to love the sinner though we hate the sin. If
Holden had not been so repelled by the sins of his teacher, Antolini,
that he could not accept his good advice about accepting an imperfect
world (even though this truth came clothed in pomposities), he might
have saved himself a breakdown.

Franny is restored to peace in her minor collapse when her
brother reminds her that as Quiz Kids on the radio they used to shine
their shoes for the Fat Lady. And the Fat Lady was everyone in the
audience—the vulgar, the critical, the absurd—everyone. But
Everyone is also Jesus Christ, and unless, says Salinger, you can
accept and love Christ in everyone in spite of their limitations, you
are doomed. As Auden says, "We must love each other or die."
Salinger himself took from Dostoevski the motto in his most beautiful
story, "For Esme With Love and Squalor" and which also permeates
everything he writes: "Fathers and teachers, I ponder what is Hell? I
maintain that it is the suffering of being unable to love."

The collective response of millions of young readers to this
message has been heartening. I do not take seriously the recent anti-
Salinger mood led by Mary McCarthy and "her thumbing her nose at
Salinger in a kind of bitchy pique . . . . To McCarthy's Hemingway-
fed generation Salinger is a bad writer because he is the opposite of
Hemingway."[2] Salinger likes to write about sensitive, gifted people
who have a flair for contemplation. His warm subjective style is the
opposite of Hemingway's. But the anti-Salingers are like a bull in a
Glass shop enjoying the clatter of broken crystal. Even *Today*
recently joined the wrecking party straining out gnats of facts and
ignoring the great camel of charity about which Christian
commentators could be expected to rejoice.[3]

Salinger, as everyone knows, takes his inspiration from two
oriental sources, the Bible and Zen Buddhism. In his amalgamation
of Zen with the Judeo-Christian message, he does a great service to
those who have not yet discovered that ecumenism means finding the
truth in the oriental religions as well as in the disparate Christian

denominations. As Bede Griffiths, O.S.B., pointed out in a recent visit to America, the oriental religions are filled with the contemplative spirit. From this Christians must learn, but they must also show the orientals how Christianity can supplement their grave needs. Salinger's fiction often shows those areas of truth which the orientals and Christians have in common.

If his work is dedicated to charity, integrity, and the celebration of the sensitive, contemplative personality, William Golding's contribution is of a more basic order. His most popular book, *The Lord of the Flies* makes a strong case for original sin. When this book was published in America in 1955 it was passed over. But England saw its value. When Golding was invited to America as a visiting professor in 1961-62, we finally recognized *The Lord of the Flies* with such tumultous acclaim that for the first time Salinger's place as prime favorite was challenged.

As everyone knows, this is the story of a pack of school boys, aged six to twelve, stranded on a desert island during an atomic war. They divide into two camps, Jack the leader of the rebels clearly symbolizing the ruthless dictator. Here in an idyllic tropical setting these children have an opportunity to prove the truth or untruth of Rousseau's theory that society makes people evil; that sweet children would develop into reasonable persons if not perverted by social institutions. According to Golding's own words, he has made "an attempt to trace the defect of society back to the defects of human nature"—in other words to state anew the doctrine of original sin.

Let F.E. Kearns, Father Egan and Thomas Coskren, O.P., squabble all they like as to whether this book describes a depraved nature or a deprived nature. What delights the millions of young people is its basic truth described thus by Brother Luke M. Grande:

> In a world that tends to equate evil with unfavorable environment, Golding sees instead man's inner responsibility for choosing between good and evil; in a world that defines personality as a functional phenomenon, Golding emphasizes the substantive reality and absolute value of each human being. Finally, in a world that can affirm at one and the same time a belief in human perfectibility and in instinctive and natural depravity, Golding projects the timeless predicament of man who despite his moral weakness, struggles to attain heroic ideals.[4]

The proportion of *The Lord of the Flies* beautifully underlines the possibilities for good. Out of four important boys featured, only Jack is frighteningly evil, while the other three, Ralph, Piggy, and Simon stand for humankind guided by good impulses. "Three-to-one seems like an impressive ratio favoring at least a limited goodness in the human community." The same critic just quoted makes a brilliant analysis of Simon as a Christ figure. He encounters the beast and does not succumb to the beast's temptation to despair. This encounter is the boy's Gethsemane: he comes face to face with evil, recognizes it for what it is, and despite the horror and agony of the meeting, he is neither defeated nor intimidated by it. This is the same beast who frightened Hemingway into the despair of the Age of Nada. Immediately after his confrontation with evil Simon climbs the mountain to free the dead pilot, whose parachute lines have become entangled in the rocks. In other words, Simon climbs the mountain to free fallen humanity.

He returns to the boys to announce the good news: they need no longer fear the beast.

But the group will not listen to him. Like the One in whose place he stands symbolically, Simon is murdered during a religious festival.

*The Lord of the Flies* says many things. In its final message it presents the awesome picture of the world which, not satisfied with murdering Simon, continues to neglect the significance of his sacrifice.[5]

In view of this admission that the world had rejected the truth of the Redemption through Christ, the students during Golding's recent visit to America asked if he thought there were any hope for society. Golding answered YES.

Yes indeed. There is at the moment a hope for society world-shaking in its promise. It is the ecumenical movement, rolling forward like a tidal wave that will change the face of the world. A tidal wave is a power shrouded in mystery which gathers its incredible force long before it crashes upon the waiting shore. It has been long in coming, long in preparation. So too is the literature of the Christian Revolution, part of the ecumenical movement, which reaches back from Manzoni and Sigrid Undset through the great European novelists like Georges Bernanos right down to Marie Jose Gironella's *One Million Dead*.

One age overlaps another. The Age of Nada has not disappeared, nor will it perish very soon. Perhaps not ever. Yet when truth and falsehood are locked in mortal combat, truth carries the lethal dagger. The truth of the supernatural is winning a struggle to the death.

That struggle is a return to the Sources of Truth. No one has created a better analogy for understanding the ecumenical movement than Barbara Ward. She sees the people of various Christian persuasions like persons on opposite sides of a river who wish to cross over to each other. But the river is too wide, too turbulent. So they all walk upstream, farther and farther to the Source. There the stream can be crossed by a single step.

Going to the Source! The immutable eternal truths are discovered fresh and new. The barriers between Christians are falling; the barriers between East and West, and most happily, the barriers of custom which have been made to look in the past like the laws of God are also falling.

Naturally literature captures this new ecumenical spirit. The four writers presented in this essay all express some aspect of it. Many more authors might have been cited. But one glance at the spread of truth communicated by these four is a heartening experience: the correct notion of basic human nature, the condition of original sin; the primacy of faith in Christ, of Scripture, of free will, of redemptive grace; a new respect for goodness and joy, a lyric longing for immortality; a detestation of the phony in society and a clear summons to make our own the charity which embraces Christ in all people.

As Chesterton said: "Like the white lock of Whistler, that lit our aimless gloom/ Men showed their own white feather as proudly as a plume."

## Notes

1. Mariella Gable, "Feather in the Wind," *Today*, January 1964.

2. Donald Costello, "Salinger and His Critics," *Commonweal*, 25 October 1963, 1.

3. *Today*, November 1963, 19.

4. Luke M. Grande, *Commonweal*, 25 January 1963, 457.

5. Thomas Coskren, O.P., "Is Golding Calvinistic?" *America*, 6 July 1963, 18. I owe much to Coskren's interpretation here.

MARIELLA GABLE, 1950S
MARIELLA GABLE, 1970S

MARIELLA GABLE, REMBERTA WESTKAEMPER, 1977

# Chapter 13

---

# The Concept of Fame in Teilhard de Chardin and Dante[1]

Let us consider human work. It is both a curse and a blessing. It is a soporific which drugs human beings into unawareness of the passing of time. They who work with intense interest come to the end of the day before they know it has begun. They who toil with heart-absorbing interest speed the arrival of death. Death surprises them in the midst of consuming interests. Work is also a life-saver. Those to whom retirement is imminent fear like the plague the day they will not go to work. The only alternative to work for them is suffocating boredom. Yet their work harasses them. They long to leave it for play, agreeing with Tom Sawyer that "work consists of whatever a body is obliged to do; play consists of whatever a body is not obliged to do." And it is in being obliged to stick to continuous effort that many people feel work to be a curse.

In fact, Charles Lamb who hated his work as a clerk in a counting house asked ruefully: "Who first invented work, and bound the free / And holiday-rejoicing spirit down. . . / To that dry drudgery of the desk's dead word?" No one escapes entirely the experience of "dry drudgery" in daily work.

Whichever way we look at it, work presents a problem. And so it is that we might well listen to one of the greatest modern thinkers when he presents to us a view of work which transfigures it with splendor and beauty. Such a thinker is Pierre Teilhard de Chardin.

In the ten years since his death the volume of critical works on him attests to the global interest in his contribution to the thinking of modern humanity. A dedicated American student[2] of Teilhard noted recently "The flood of Teilhardian literature undoubtedly will continue to swell." A European scholar[3] noted that "The output of studies on the thought of Teilhard de Chardin shows no sign of slackening." In fact, his thought is like a harvest of wheat purring steadily between two millstones. There are no indifferent readers of Teilhard. There is going on an intensive grinding of his thought between the millstones of the negative thinkers who are disturbed by his discontinuities and the positive thinkers who appreciate the sweep and truth of his cosmic view. I say that this grinding is excellent. For out of this cracking apart of the virgin wheat, the fine white flour of truth will be sifted from the bran of errors and mistakes.

Time, of course, is the judge who holds the golden scales and weighs the value of world visions. The balancing is a long process. We are only in the midst of it. But it is my own guess that the great system of Teilhard de Chardin will make all thinkers of the past kick the beam—even such giants as Plato, Aristotle, and Thomas Aquinas. Nor should this surprise us. For we know now so much more than we have ever known before. A cosmic view of the universe asks for a Christianity viewed in proportion to that universe.

## TEILHARD AND THE NEW AGE

Teilhard saw with great clarity that we are entering a new age, not in the sense that rationalism or romanticism or the industrial revolution marked new ages. But in the sense that human beings, who have for over a million years continued in the Neolithic period,[4] are now moving into an entirely different period. Into what?

Into a period which should bring all who see it truly, great joy and great hope. He speaks first of all to those persons who have been troubled by an apparent cleavage between what is true scientifically and what is true in the area of faith. For them he has achieved a synthesis of faith and science. He sees a marvelous unity in which humanity can no longer be torn between the claims of the spirit and the "seduction" of matter. He is, first of all, a synthesizer.

He was trained in anthropology, paleontology, geology and various branches of biology. Spending a lifetime in research, he was able to bring the findings of all the sciences to bear upon the human problem in the cosmos. Moreover, as a Jesuit, he had suitable initiation into theology and philosophy. Besides, he was a mystic and a poet. He brought all these competencies to bear at once on whatever problem he attacked.

No longer is it possible to suppose that truth can be attained by keeping disciplines segregated. Truth is one and requires a synthesis of all disciplines. Educators feel the new thrust. The vast changes in curricula throughout the country testify to a new urgency to synthesize learning.

The whole world is being drawn like iron filings to a magnet by Teilhard's system of thought. In the ten years since his death his teaching has spread like wildfire. And the very mention of fire reminds me of one of his pertinent observations: "Let truth appear but once to a single soul, and / nothing can ever stop it invading everything and / setting everything ablaze."[5] Perhaps not even a *monitum* from the Holy Office can halt the spread of such a fire. We ought to note that the *monitum* of June 30, 1962, which was signed by Sebastianus Masala and which warned that the *Phenomenon of Man* might not appear on the open shelves of seminaries did *not* (and in this it was unlike many other documents from the same office)—it did *not* carry the explicit approval of the reigning pontiff, John XXIII.[6]

In fact, when Pope John was presented with documents condemning Teilhard, he refused to sign them. "What," said he, "do you want me to have another Galileo on my hands?" He further declared that he regarded the *monitum* as "very regrettable."[7] Our reigning pontiff, Paul VI, has also described the writings of Teilhard as "indispensable for the thinking of modern man."[8] Indispensable!

Scholars are neither discouraged by the *monitum* nor elated by the admiration of Popes John and Paul. A man of the stature of Teilhard asks simply for the patient analysis and understanding of scholars.

Teilhard's thinking forms a system so perfectly integrated that it is like a carefully wrought design woven into a rug. You pick up the corner of the rug and you lift the whole design. This paper proposes a rather modest lifting of the corner of the rug which investigates Teilhard's philosophy of work. It can transfigure our daily toil with immeasurable beauty and radiance.

What has our daily work to do with fame? Fame is the public reputation which follows our work. Whether we like it or not, each of us lives in a circle of fame—limited surely, but valid. One is known for thoroughness, another for creative vision, a third for easy public relations while shirking productive labor. Another is a slave driver who makes others carry the load. There are as many types of fame as there are individuals in the world.

Teilhard is always a positive thinker. He is concerned with excellence in work and with the aura of fame which surrounds that excellence as certainly as a glow surrounds a candle flame. Fame for him is the good fame of the one who unites making and loving.

Western thought has for centuries troubled itself deeply over the question: Ought we to pursue fame? Milton expressed a typical ambivalence when he spoke of the appetite for fame in "Lycidas." He called it "the last infirmity of noble minds." "Infirmity" suggests a weakness; "noble" suggests strength. Teilhard's thought banishes all such ambivalence.

But we must fit his thinking into a long history. Ever since Newman's great book, *The Development of Christian Doctrine*, the Church has more and more explicitly accepted the idea that there is a continuous development in the human understanding of truth. There is a perpetual unfolding. To grasp fully the fact of unfolding spares us many a shock at discoveries in the past. We see why things were as they were.

Let us turn back now to Saint Augustine in the fourth and fifth centuries. We find that he took a very sour view of the pursuit of fame. He saw a total cleavage between the City of God and the City of Man. To be concerned with the City of Man, with the material world, was the devil's work. It was, in fact, a sin.[9] But we cannot judge Augustine too harshly. He was the product of his own times. He was greatly influenced by Platonism and Manichaeism.[10]

I believe that Alfred North Whitehead expressed a true evaluation of most of our Western philosophy when he said it was nothing but a collection of footnotes on Plato. But there it has been for centuries—a disturbing dichotomy between matter and spirit. In helping to destroy this dichotomy I believe Teilhard has perhaps made his greatest contribution to humanity and to Christianity. It might be noted here, however, that the destruction of this dichotomy has been assisted by other forces such as the renewed studies in Sacred Scripture and in Hebrew thought.

When we make the long leap between Saint Augustine and the thirteenth century, we find that Saint Thomas took a much more mellow view of the pursuit of fame. In effect, he asked that humanity seek fame under just two conditions: (1) Recognize that your gifts come from God and give God the honor; (2) Use your gifts for the good of humankind.[11] This is basically the position of Teilhard de Chardin. But he deepens and expands this point of view so that the whole pursuit of excellence in work is suffused with a new luminous splendor.

Close to Saint Thomas in time and in vision was Dante. Dante was nine years old when Saint Thomas died. He was tutored by a pupil of Saint Thomas, and his *Divine Comedy* embodies much of the thinking of Saint Thomas.

I want to make special use of Dante's views on fame in this paper for three reasons:

> 1. We all know how irritating it is to listen to abstract generalizations if they are not supported by concrete examples. Teilhard de Chardin clearly shows that human beings have habitually made three wrong answers to the problem of fame and that there is only one right answer. Since Dante illustrated in his *Divine Comedy* all four of the attitudes toward fame which Teilhard presents, I find that I can considerably illuminate this paper, that I can concretize its concepts, by using the examples from Dante.
> 2. Dante knew by intuition the right attitudes. We have had to wait until Teilhard for a clear statement as to *why* they are right.
> 3. During this year we are celebrating the seven-hundredth anniversary of the birth of Dante. What more fitting tribute to his memory than to demonstrate how impressively his thinking was just seven hundred years ahead of his time?

## TEILHARD'S PHILOSOPHY OF WORK

Now to the main business of this paper: Teilhard's philosophy of work. I take it mainly from that beautiful little book, *The Divine Milieu*,[12] 139 pages, but pages of pure gold. His other translated works, however, including *The Phenomenon of Man*, *The Future of Man*, and *The Hymn of the Universe* have been consulted. I draw on them for confirming evidence of Teilhard's teaching.

First of all, I want to share with you Teilhard's own clear, honest statement of the dilemma human beings face when looking at fame or at work in this life: "How can man, who believes in heaven and the Cross, continue to believe seriously in worldly occupation?"[13] This question is simple, clear, honest.

Next, Teilhard tabulates three faulty answers humanity has made to this dilemma.[14]  Finally he presents his own brilliant, heart-warming answer to the problem.  I will take up now in order these answers to the problem, both wrong and right, and as I promised you I will conflate them with illustrations from the *Divine Comedy.*  So let us begin with the three false solutions to the dilemma.

1. In Canto 24 of the "Inferno" Dante describes himself as utterly exhausted by the labors of writing his great poem.  He lets the difficulty of climbing a steep embankment in his approach to the thieves symbolize his weariness in work.  He says of himself: "The breath was so exhausted from my lungs when I was up / that I could no farther; nay I seated me at my first arrival."  Virgil is outraged at this spectacle of one permitting something like personal fatigue to deflect his pursuit of fame.  He administers a sharp rebuke to Dante: "Now it behooves thee thus to free thyself from Sloth. . . / For sitting on down, or under coverlet, men come not into fame;" And then he adds a general comment on fame which is of capital importance.  He says: "And without fame, who so consumes his life, leaves such / vestige of himself on earth as smoke in air or foam in water. / Therefore rise...and act that it may profit thee."  Dante, who consistently shows the most profound respect for the opinions of Virgil, immediately rises up and "in order to make believe he had more breath than he had, he even went on speaking that he might not seem faint."[15]

Here we have clearly symbolized the human being who sees only the material present without any reference to the supernatural.  If life without fame is only smoke in air or foam in water, then as Teilhard points out we are dealing with a materialist, who "will dismiss the evangelical counsels to lead what seems to him a complete human life."[16]  For Teilhard there is possible no true humanism without the supernatural.  Let us note that this first false solution to the dilemma was offered in Hell.

2. The second false view appears in the "Purgatorio," Canto II. Here on the terrace where pride is punished we meet Oderisi, an artist remembered for his illuminating.  At first we see him generously willing to share his honor with a fellow artist, Franco Bolognese—a

generosity of which he would not have been capable while alive. But then comes the significant passage—a bitter outburst against the pursuit of fame simply because fame does not last. He cries out: "O empty glory of human powers! How short the time / its green endures upon the top. . . ." He shows how Cimabue thought to hold the first place in painting and was with great speed superseded by Giotto, how one poet sits for a moment in the public eye as the greatest, only to be shoved aside by a better poet. He concludes that earthly fame is nothing but a breath of wind. He asks dramatically what difference it will make after a thousand years whether any one dies as a child or grows up to do one's work. He argues that because the glory of fame is ephemeral one should not work for it.[17]

Teilhard says this viewpoint is typical of Christians who will force themselves to concentrate "on purely religious objects only"[18] —to the exclusion of the largest possible number of worldly objects. This is a kind of Platonism.

3. Teilhard singles out the undecided as representative of the third wrong way to meet the dilemma. The undecided are the fence-straddlers who cannot make up their minds as to the claims of matter and spirit. Dante had a special horror for these trimmers. He expressed this horror by locating them *outside* Hell, for if he had placed them *in* Hell the devils would have lorded it over them; the devils at least made up their minds.[19] "Because you are neither hot nor cold I will vomit you out of my mouth."[20] Dante further suggests the utter damnation of the trimmers by keeping them anonymous. Nowhere else in the "Inferno" does he refuse to name individuals. His disgust for the spirit of those who cannot decide is total, furious, and frightening.

Teilhard de Chardin is also hard on the undecided. He finds them "imperfect in their own eye and insincere in the eyes of men." They are to be deplored because they have "become resigned to living a double life."[21]

4. Now we come to the only appropriate solution to the dilemma, which, as we have seen, postulates some opposition between matter and spirit. Teilhard once and for all rules out this dichotomy by showing that our problem is not either-or, not either matter or spirit. It is both-and, both matter and spirit. Both matter and spirit united inseparably deserve our total dedication. Why? As Teilhard saw it, Christ is present in matter the way light irradiates a crystal.[22] The light is not the crystal and the crystal is not the light. But they

are united in the way that light irradiates a crystal— "without immixture, without confusion."[23]   His critics like to accuse Teilhard of being a pantheist; repeatedly Teilhard denies that he teaches pantheism.[24]

## THE EUCHARIST AND CHRIST'S PRESENCE IN THE UNIVERSE

Through a lifetime of thinking Teilhard arrived at his Christology, based solidly on Saint Paul and Saint John.  He began with the presence of Christ in the Holy Eucharist.

In the *Hymn of the Universe* Teilhard includes three beautiful little *contes* in which as early as 1916 he made his thinking clear.  In a mystical vision he saw the host at exposition expanding to embrace the whole cosmos.  Christ's presence

> overran everything.  At the same time everything, though drowned in this whiteness, preserved its own proper shape. . .for the whiteness did not efface the features or change the nature of anything, but penetrated objects at the core of their being. . . .  It was as though a milky brightness were illuminating the universe from within and everything were fashioned of the same kind of translucent flesh. . . .So through the mysterious expansion of the host, the whole world had become incandescent, had become itself like a single giant host.[25]

As to the relationship between the Eucharist and Christ's presence in the whole universe Teilhard asks the following:

> But how can we avoid going further and believing that the sacramental action of Christ, precisely because it sanctifies matter, extends its influence, beyond the pure supernatural, over all that makes up the internal and external ambiance of the faithful, that is to say that it sets its mark upon everything which we call 'our Providence?'
> If this is the case, then we find ourselves (by simply having followed the 'extension' of the Eucharist) plunged once again precisely into our divine milieu. . . .  Christ reveals Himself in each reality around us, and shines like an ultimate determinant, like a center, one might almost say like a universal element.  As

our humanity assimilates the material world, and the Host
assimilates our humanity, the eucharistic transformation goes
beyond and completes the transubstantiation of the bread on the
altar. Step by step it irresistibly invades the universe. . . .

In a secondary and generalized sense but in a true sense the
sacramental Species are formed by the totality of the world, and
the duration of creation needed for its consecration.[26]

Though such a passage is somewhat unsatisfying because it
depends upon a rhetorical question and assertion, we shall see in a
moment how much stronger becomes his argument when he invokes
the evidence of St. Paul.  But first let us note this.  Teilhard
recognized that his doctrine of the omnipresence of Christ was
different from "the unusual speculation which is current concerning
the presence of God," and that this difference lay in the idea that "the
presence of God reaches the elements of the world only through and
in the Body of Christ."[27]

## THE ONENESS OF COSMOGENESIS

This doctrine of the omnipresence of Christ was of capital
importance to the whole system of Teilhard de Chardin.  Of the
evolution of the universe from the beginning of matter to our own
time he had what seems to be persuasive evidence.  By an extremely
probable extrapolation he sees that this same evolution, which has as
its aim the emergence of humanity, is destined to continue in the
direction of the ever more spiritual development of humankind.  This
continued evolution of the material universe he calls cosmogenesis.
He also sees that this cosmogenesis is bringing with it a new era of
the unification and convergence of humankind in love and
compassion.[28]  He cannot believe that this ultimate in the
cosmogenesis is separate from or different from the Christogenesis of
the universe—in which all will be one in Christ.

Teilhard is particularly eloquent in asserting the oneness of
cosmogenesis and Christogenesis.  He says, for instance, "The world
can no more have two summits than a circumference can have two
centers."[29]  And again he declares, "To build the City of Man is
already to build the City of God."[30]

Teilhard saw that the development of science asked for an
interpretation of Christ concomitant with the extensiveness of the

cosmos. He asked with great concern: "Is the Christ of the gospel imagined and loved within the dimensions of the Mediterranean world capable of still embracing and still forming the center of our prodigiously expanded universe? Is the world not in the process of becoming more vast, more close, more dazzling than Jehovah? Will it not burst our religion asunder—eclipse our God?"[31]  It was for the millions of human beings who see the development of science as a threat to faith that he made the supreme effort to bring together science and faith.  The culmination of this union Teilhard names the Omega point.

Now this Omega on the scientific level is an extrapolation reached only from phenomena.  It is an assumption and a conjecture which cannot provide the necessary guarantee of cosmogenesis.[32] Teilhard felt the need to bridge the gap.  He needed to show how the Christ of revelation may be identified with the Omega of evolution. In order to bridge this gap he drew on Scripture, specifically on Saint John and Saint Paul.  He repeatedly made use of what Dr. Christopher Mooney calls the three cosmic texts of Saint Paul.  These texts, according to Mooney, have "received relatively little attention and almost no development since the time of the Greek Fathers. . .it is only in recent years that the so-called cosmic texts have emerged as subjects of discussion and debate."[33]  I might remark here that Father Christopher F. Mooney has explored in complex detail Teilhard's whole treatment of the Body of Christ in *Theological Studies*.[34]  This study is of special value since Father Mooney as a member of the *Institut Catholique* of Paris has been able to consult sources not available to American scholars.  He saw that the question with which we have to deal here is simply this: "To what extent can Paul be said to extend the physical relationship between Christ and mankind to the whole creation, including therefore all that is material?"[35]

## ST. PAUL'S COSMIC TEXT

The sources on which one relies for an answer are extremely limited.  They are the three cosmic texts of Saint Paul: Rom. 8:19-23, Col. 1:15-20, and Eph. 1:9-10, 22-23.[36]  These passages have usually not been approached by the exegetes with the precise aim of determining Christ's relationship to the material world.  But there is a new direction now being taken by a number of authors who are aware that they must discover what Paul might have meant about the presence of Christ in the material universe.

Father Mooney gives an interpretation favorable to Teilhard's view. He shows how in Col. 1:15-20 Paul "goes back to the pre-existence of Christ in the Father, in whose image *(eikon)* He is the source as well as the instrument and final end of creation. The Incarnation, crowned by the triumph of the Resurrection, is seen as placing the human nature of Christ at the head not only of the whole human race but also of the entire created universe."[37] Father Mooney's concluding analysis lends superb support to the use Teilhard makes of this passage of Saint Paul. He says:

> For many people today the "Plenitude" of Christ in this extraordinary text, His Pleroma, represents in Paul's mind the extension of Christ's work of redemption to the whole cosmos, the whole of creation. . . . Christ is God, and through his work of redemption He unites himself not only to redeemed humanity. . .but also to the whole of the cosmos which is humanity's dwelling place."[38]

The limitations of this paper do not permit me to examine the other cosmic texts of Saint Paul. We should note, however, that exegetes are not at one in their interpretation of Saint Paul and that interpreting the cosmic texts is still an open question to theologians.[39]

But for Teilhard, Christ's physical presence in the universe was a basic tenet. He believed with overwhelming faith that "God is in some sort at the tip of my pen, my spade, my brush, my needle."[40] By doing my work, whatever it is, I become a co-creator with Christ in the continued evolution of the cosmos toward the Pleroma. What I do does not matter. If I know that I am doing Christ's work I must enter into it with creative joy and enthusiasm. Sometimes the humblest labor undertaken with total dedication can lead to the most astonishing discoveries.

## EXAMPLES OF DEDICATED LABOR

I think, for instance, of a novice at Königskloster in 1843. It was young Gregor Mendel, an Augustinian monk who later became Abbot and who never could pass the examination for the teaching profession. As a novice he asked for permission to plant tall peas and dwarf peas in the monastery garden. He cross-fertilized them and kept accurate records. Later he published his findings in a scientific journal to which the world paid not the slightest attention. Not until thirty-four years after his death did scientists awaken to the great importance of his discovery of Mendel's Law, which "laid the foundation for the science of genetics."[41]

But it does not matter whether you are a Father Gregor Mendel or an ordinary botany student entering with the fullness of joyful enthusiasm into the problems of taxonomy.

I think of Maria Montessori trained as a teacher. She used to look at little boys and girls in rows in a classroom and think they were like dead butterflies mounted on a bulletin board. She thought they deserved a better education. Then she received her first assignment: to teach a group of mentally retarded children. To her this was a great blow. But she met the challenge with such creative energy that her defective children passed the state examinations in reading and writing for normal children.[42] Now, thanks to her, educators are widely introducing something we call the Montessori method. But in the same class with her is the young religious sister who enters into her practice teaching with total creative zest and enthusiasm. Christ's evolutionary plan for the cosmos is served well both by those whose excellence wins for them great fame as well as by those who win small fame.

Christian workers always say "yes" if at all possible when they are asked to perform a task. That they are placed in a situation where their gifts are asked for is indication that it is the will of God that they perform what they can.

Christian workers never indulge in discontent with present circumstances. They do not dream of a different place, a different superior, of different circumstances. This moment, this work, this spot—here and now—these are God's will for me and deserve my most creative effort. There were those who advised Teilhard to become a secularized priest since his order exiled him from France for nearly a lifetime in China. But this he would never consider. For him the Jesuit order was the "Divine Milieu," and he would not entertain the thought of leaving it. In fact, "Divine Milieu" means simply the presence of Christ in the universe.

Now what about the cross? No Christian can neglect it. It has, however, often been grievously misunderstood. Being co-creators with Christ requires of us unflagging effort. Fatigue, boredom, and weariness are the ordinary price one has to pay for a job well done. Effort means carrying our cross with painful perseverance. It means renouncing personal comfort and slothful ease. If we are engaged in *creative* effort, our days are dogged by continual rejection of trial efforts and scores of new beginnings.[43]

Finally, there is the whole important area of diminishment.[44] God has many ways of requiring the diminishment of the individual: personal illness, or the envious obstruction of our work by the malice or the misunderstanding of others, or the approach of old age—a diminishment no one can escape. The list could be extended indefinitely. All of them the co-creator with Christ bears in perfect peace of soul. But no one has the right to diminish self for the sake of diminishing self.[45] He continues to do his utmost. Homer and Milton were both blind. Beethoven was deaf. Not one of them discontinued his creative work because of his personal diminishment. The co-creator with Christ is forever at peace, united to God not only by intention but also by the attention given to every moment of work. This attention becomes a kind of adoration. The co-creator with Christ is forever spared the hardest cross of all to bear, the pain of being divided between the material and the spiritual world.

## DANTE AND THE PROBLEM OF FAME

Dante saw all this very clearly. In the opening canto of the "Paradiso" Dante prays to Christ, under the name of Apollo, begging for the grace to write of Heaven well.[46] He explains to Christ that if he can communicate only a shadow of Heaven, then he will come to the laurel tree to be crowned by Christ for success.[47] Then he bursts out with a bitter complaint against those who do not aim at fame. In a sense he argues with Christ in favor of those who do their utmost. He says: "So few times, Father, is there gathered of it (the laurel of fame) for triumph of Caesar or of poet—fault and shame of human wills—that the Penian frond should bring forth gladness in the joyous Delphic deity when it sets *any* athirst for itself."[48] Notice that he mentions both politics and poetry as fields in which we should be seeking fame. He shows how important it is to aim for the highest since "one great man inspires another to greatness."[49] And on the basis of this argument he begs for personal success.

Dante comes much more directly to the problem of fame, however, in Canto 17 of the "Paradiso," the canto in which he meets Cacciaguida, his own great, great grandfather, who is both a martyr and a saint. First of all, the old man prophesies with great clarity

Dante's exile from Florence and how he shall have to leave behind him all his dear ones as well as to suffer the continued humiliation of living among strangers: "Thou shalt make trial how salt doth taste another's bread / And how hard the path to descend and mount another's stair."[50] This is Dante's diminishment. He accepts it without complaint. But his poem, the *Divine Comedy*, his life work, is another matter. How can he save that for humankind? How can he win fame? He has a specific problem. He has been shown things in his journey through Hell and Purgatory which people will not like to hear: perhaps his vision of the popes in Hell suffering for simony. Dante says that if he tells his whole vision of the next life accurately, it will have a "strong-bitter flavor to many."[51] And he knows precisely what the cost to him will be if he does not tell the whole truth as it has been revealed to him. He says: "If to truth I am a shrinking friend, I fear to be / forgotten in ages yet unborn."[52]

In other words he will miss winning fame. His saintly grandfather puts his heart at rest: "Every lie set aside. Make thy entire vision / manifest, and let them scratch where is the scab."[53] The great artist communicates truth as he knows it and he who dares to be true dares to be great. Teilhard thought that our own age needs people who are willing to die for truth. He himself suffered greatly for truth. In fact, both Teilhard and Dante were exiles, Dante for political reasons and Teilhard because he would not say less than the truth as he saw it about evolution.

Dante even provided a very special heaven in the planet of Mercury for the "good spirits who were active that honor and that fame might come to them."[54] Intuitively he knew he had the truth. But we had to wait for Teilhard to explain *how* it is true, how we are by our work co-creators with Christ. However, it might be pointed out that now there are a goodly number of progressive theologians, men like Karl Rahner, DeLubac, and Mersch who are bringing the force of their thinking to bear in the same direction.

Let us take a quick glance at that heaven which Dante reserved for "those good spirits who were active that honor and that fame might come to them." Side by side in this heaven of Mercury he featured two things: (1) The success of a Roman Emperor, Justinian, who codified Roman Law, the exemplar of the man who has worthily sought fame;[55] (2) Immediately following the account of Justinian's fame comes the "chief theological discourse in the Paradiso."[56] It is on the Incarnation and the Redemption—as if Dante had felt with

Teilhard de Chardin the need to keep these two concepts together—the concept of excellence in work and the concept of the Incarnation.[57]

## EXCELLENCE IS APOCALYPTIC

Thus far we have noted only correspondences between Dante and Teilhard. They are significant and impressive. Let us look at one difference—a difference perhaps more eloquent than all the correspondences. It underlines the extent to which Teilhard is a spiritual pioneer. Dante's Heaven of Mercury is one of the lowest of Dante's ten heavens. In fact, it is the second lowest. In the final construct of the poem Dante makes it clear that the first three heavens are for those souls who had practiced in an imperfect way the virtues of faith, hope, and charity. In the Heaven of Mercury are those who practiced an imperfect hope. Hope of fame, then, becomes an imperfect thing as compared to hope of Heaven which is a perfect thing. Dante further symbolizes this imperfection by letting a cone-shaped shadow of the earth fall on these first three heavens.

To Teilhard such a concept would be totally deplorable. To him, humans as co-creators with Christ in doing their work well are practicing the highest type of conformity to God's will. He even went so far as to point out that when we once grasp the full import of our work as co-creators with Christ "there would be little to separate life in the cloister from life in the world."[58]

In other words our labor properly understood makes all life religious life. For Benedictines this idea is of profound importance, for we live by the mystique that work is prayer.

It is this religious concept which Teilhard commends to all of us. One works hard, exercises unflagging effort to make one's work excellent, not because one cares about the recognition of others, but because excellence is holy. Excellence is beautiful. Excellence is apocalyptic. Our work assists in moving the cosmogenesis and Christogenesis of this world more swiftly toward the Pleroma, that fullness in Christ which gives meaning to all effort. Teilhard himself recaptured the joyous expectation of the Pleroma which animated the Church in the days of Saint Paul. We are moving with tremendous speed out of noosphere, an envelope of knowing, into the Christosphere, an envelope of loving, in which all humanity will be united.[59] In Christ present in the material universe "we live and move and have our being."[60] We must learn not to resist technological progress but to promote it, for it is part of a magnificent total plan for the consummation of the world.   On both the scientific and Christological level Teilhard's system "allows technological man to feel that henceforth he is on the road (planned by God) to Christianity, and not simply the servant of a dehumanized, accursed world:  thus the modern world of technology acquires value from the invisible world."[61]

"The whole of nature has been groaning until now in an agony of birth."[62]  All workers are co-creators with Christ in assisting at this birth, this becoming, this Pleroma.   This is a view of humankind which "substitutes progressive optimism for static pessimism."[63]  We have now a Christ-centered cosmos in which the heart rises joyously and creatively to the opportunity to spend a life-time of effort in being co-creators with Christ.

## Notes

1. Mariella Gable, "The Concept of Fame in Teilhard de Chardin and Dante," *American Benedictine Review* (Sept. 1965): 341-58.  Also reprinted in Harry Cargas, editor, *The Continuous Flame: Teilhard in the Great Tradition* (St. Louis: Herder, 1969).

2. Robert T. Francoeur, S.J., "Teilhard de Chardin," *Jubilee* (July 1965): 39.

3. William Donnelly, S.J., "Teilhardian Vision," *The Month* (April 1965): 249.

4. Claude Cuénot, *Teilhard de Chardin: A Biographical Study* (Baltimore 1965): 109.

5. Ibid., 373.  From *Le Critique*, page not given.

6. Ronald J. Campion, S.J., "Tired of Chardin," *America*, 15 May 1965, 697.

7. Quoted in a letter by Robert T. Francoeur, S.J., to Sister Jeremy Hall, O.S.B., spring 1964.  I asked Father Francoeur if this quotation could be verified.  He assured me that it was most certainly true but that the ecclesiastic who reported it prefers to remain anonymous.

8. Francoeur, 36.  Father Francoeur says:  As Pope Paul remarked to a high ranking member of the hierarchy last spring, "Le Père Teilhard est indispensable a notre temps, son apologétique est nécessaire!"

9. Mortimer J. Adler and William Gorman, editors, *The Great Ideas: A*

*Syntopicon of Great Books of the Western World*, I, 374.

10. Maurice B. McNamee, S.J., *Honor and the Epic Hero* (New York 1960), 120.

11. Ibid, 125.

12. Pierre Teilhard de Chardin, *The Divine Milieu: An Essay on the Interior Life* (New York 1960).

13. Ibid., 19.

14. Ibid.

15. Dante Alighieri, *The Divine Comedy*, the Italian edited by H. Oelsner, English translation by J.A. Carlyle, Thomas Okey, and P. H. Wicksteed (New York: Modern Library, 1932).

16. Teilhard, *The Divine Milieu*, 20.

17. Dante, "Purgatorio" 11, lines 91-106.

18. Teilhard, *The Divine Milieu*, 20.

19. Dante, "Inferno" 3, line 42.

20. Apocalypse 3:16.

21. Teilhard, *The Divine Milieu*, 20-21.

22. Ibid., 15.

23. Ibid., 23.

24. Ibid., 93. Teilhard says, ". . . the sojourner in the divine milieu is not a pantheist. At first sight, perhaps, the depths of the divine which St. Paul reveals to us may seem to resemble the fascinating domain unfolded before our eyes by monistic philosophies or religions. In fact, they are very different. . . ." The passage develops the difference between pantheism and Teilhard's thought.

25. Pierre Teilhard de Chardin, *Hymn of the Universe* (New York 1965), 48.

26. Teilhard, *The Divine Milieu*, 104-105.

27. Teilhard, *Mon Univers* (1924), 24-25, 26, 49 note 1. Quoted in Christopher F. Mooney, S.J., "The Body of Christ in the Writings of Teilhard de Chardin," *Theological Studies* (December 1964): 587.

28. Pierre Teilhard de Chardin, *The Future of Man*, trans. from the French by Norman Denny (New York 1964): 224.

29. Teilhard, *The Divine Milieu*, 137.

30. Cuénot, 107.

31. Teilhard, *The Divine Milieu*, 14.

32. Mooney, 577.

33. Ibid., 595.

34. See note 27.

35. Mooney, 601.

36. The three cosmic passages are as follows, the translation taken from the Revised Standard Version (Catholic Edition) of the New Testament:

Rom. 8:19-23. "For the creation waits with eager longing for the revealing of sons of God; for the creation was subjected to futility, not of its own will but by the will of him who subjected it in hope; because the creation itself will be set free from its bondage to decay and obtain the glorious liberty of the children of God. We know that the whole creation has been groaning in travail together until now; and not only the creation, but we ourselves, who have the first fruits of the Spirit, groan inwardly as we wait for adoption as sons, the redemption of our bodies."

Col. 1:15-20. "He is the image of the invisible God, the first-born of all creation; for in him all things were created, in heaven and on earth, visible and invisible, whether thrones or dominations or principalities or authorities--all things were created through him and for him. He is before all things, and in him all things hold together. He is the head of the body, the church, he is the beginning, the first-born from the dead, that in everything he might be pre-eminent. For in him all the fulness of God was pleased to dwell, and through him to reconcile to himself all things, whether on earth or in heaven, making peace by the blood of his cross."

Eph. 1:9-10, 22-23. "For he has made known to us in all wisdom and insight the mystery of his will, according to his purpose which he set forth in Christ as a plan for the fulness of time, to unite all things in him, things in heaven and things on earth, and he has put all things under his feet and has made him the head over all things for the church, which is his body, the fulness of him who fills all in all."

37. Mooney, 603.

38. Ibid., 604.

39. Ibid., 606.

40. Teilhard, *The Divine Milieu*, 33.

41. Gregor Johann Mendel, (1822-1884), *Encyclopedia Brittanica*, 1965, XV, 146-7.

42. Maria Montessori, (1870-1952), Ibid., 786.

43. Teilhard, *The Divine Milieu*, 41

44. Ibid., 53-4.

45. Ibid., 73.

46. Dante, "Paradiso," 1, line 13,

47. Ibid., line 25.

48. Ibid., lines 28-34.

49. Ibid., line 34.

50. Ibid., Canto 17, lines 58-60.

51. Ibid., line 117.

52. Ibid., lines 118-120.

53. Ibid., lines 127-129.

54. Ibid., Canto 6, lines 112-114.

55. Ibid., Canto 6 entire.

56. Introductory paragraph to "Paradiso" Canto 6 in Carlyle-Okey-Wicksteed translation. See note 16.

57. To the traditionalist this juxtaposition of the two concepts is just another example of Dante's teaching on Church and State. Justinian represents the State and the Incarnation forms the heart of the Church. I believe this interpretation is valid, but that Dante's whole concept of Church and State takes on new depth and meaning from the implications of the teaching of Teilhard de Chardin.

58. Teilhard, *The Divine Milieu*, 37.

59. Pierre Teilhard de Chardin, *The Phonemenon of Man*, with an Introduction by Sir Julian Huxley, (New York 1959), Bk 4, Chap. 2: "Beyond the Collective: The Hyper-Personal," 254-272.

60. Acts 17:28.

61. Cuénot, 404.

62. Rom. 8:22.

63. Cuénot, 399. This statement is part of a remarkable summary of Teilhard's achievement: "By a master stroke Teilhard, by reconciling twentieth-century man with himself, reconciles Christianity with evolutionist science, substitutes progressive optimism for static pessimism, and finds again a treasure buried since the days of St. Paul and St. Irenaeus, 'the meaning of the cosmic component of salvation,' of Christ, in whom all things are taken up."

# Appendix

# Appendix 1: J.F. Powers

## J.F. Powers' letter on *Prince of Darkness*[1]

Dear Sister Mariella, Arrived home from "the Cities" very late last night to read your letter (also one from my agent: "The Lord's Day" is accepted for *Cross Section*) and to turn over the contents, of which there was plenty for meditation—the good hands John Humphrey is in, the gift for Sister Kristin, which strikes me as inspired, your suggested title for my book or some such title, your approval and Sister Remberta's of "The Lord's Day" and finally your friend's criticism of Fr. Burner. Now then. Since you don't object, the dedication on "The Lord's Day" will stand; that is putting it mildly, I think, by debt, to say nothing of the general account I owe for the good done by me in *Our Father's House* and by it since publication.[2] About a title, I'm afraid I can't see your suggestion for several reasons. The idea of an over-all title is, as you say, the result of having read four or so of my stories; there are a couple which do not concern themselves with the Church and the Negro. In short, I can only see an over-all title as in the case of *Dubliners* or *Winesburg, Ohio*, where there is a unifying factor, geographical or sociological, not anything so vague as the spirit you say you find in my work, especially since you will not find it in some stories, I daresay, at least not in its native dress. Finally, *Candle For Philistines*, has a nice ring, yes, but is a little presumptuous, or at least I would feel that way using it; furthermore, it is my private opinion the word

"Philistine" can never be used again; it is dead of exhaustion, misused by too many hands. I had never shied away from *Prince of Darkness* for any reason except the politic. That is to say I didn't want people to like me who should not like me (the enemies of the Church), nor did I want to offend people with whom I have no difference, but who it seems have to take things, a few things, too seriously and wrongly, so that our relationship must needs cease if it has been good. Some saint says such friendships, such as perish, are not friendships. That is so, I believe, but I wish I did not. I believe in the idea of men of good will if I believe in anything most men are capable of, and so each time I see a little more of it go out of existence it is saddening. And still, coming back, I know it should not be preserved at the price of deceit. It is deceit I should be practicing, I know now, if I picked out a nice holy story, which I haven't got, and called the book by it, and left Fr. Burner and "The Lord's Day" hidden, as it were, between the covers (that does not consider your suggestion for a title at all, and for the reasons given before). In the past months I have been conducting a little poll among people I trust, indeed since Fr. Burner appeared I've been doing it, and there are enough of you who do not object to the story for the only reason I should fear, really fear—that it is an evil story, and though I didn't want to I somehow wrote an evil story—there are enough of you, then, to substantiate my own judgment,and so the book will be *Prince of Darkness*. If I had a better title, I would use it. I am using *Prince of Darkness* because it is the best title I have. I even like it. I had liked *Tower Of Ivory* better, though I seemed to be pretty much alone in that when I was mentioning it around, but in the meantime I've decided to call the story something else, and besides, as Chuck Shattuck pointed out, K.A. Porter's last was a "tower" book, and she is one writer any young writer with self-respect and pretensions to originality might be accused of trying to get himself thought of as an equal with. To conclude this problem, let me quote from Bucklin Moon, my editor at Doubleday: "I think *Prince of Darkness* has a nice sound and is quite appealing, saleswise. Certainly I don't want to stir up a mess between you and less progressive Fathers who review books, but I am very much afraid there will be that kind of storm, regardless of title," and then he goes on to say the title can be changed if I have serious objections to it. Says Henry Volkening, my agent: "My personal feeling is that the title is excellent, and that any possible disapproval in Catholic circles would be more than counterbalanced by approval in other Catholic circles. Furthermore, I think you exaggerate the importance, numerically, of the so-called Catholic reader. In my own judgment, most of the readers of your collection will be from among a small group of discriminating people, of whatever religion, who want to be familiar with the work of a "distinguished new writer." Now about Maude Lowen. If you didn't say she wasn't, I'd say she was Catholic Irish. In any case she is objecting to the whole story itself and I have no intention of dropping it. I would have to read more of her to feel the confidence in her judgment that you feel. She makes no apposite point that I can see. It may be harmful, she says. Yes, and what isn't, or rather as soon as we leave the realm of beauty, the description of it in nature, and enter the human comedy and begin to describe it with the same precision and inspiration, then, look out, for cats will look when let out of the bag. And finally, and this for Maude, it does matter how a man puts his pants on, but I can't see that I made a "point" of it. Now don't think I'm mad at Maude. No, I just can't see much for me in what she says. I see more for you. I see her writing at certain concepts she imagines you to have. I see two friends being friends by mail. But I was interested in what she said, which is why you sent the letter on. Also interested in your review of *The Unbroken Heart*, in one thing particularly: what the priest said about "The Hound of Heaven." Perhaps you noticed that I hint at such heresy in "Prince of Darkness." I have always thought the poem a rackety bore, but when I made Fr. Burner like Thompson over Hopkins, besides handing down an estimate of literature among the clergy, I thought I was the only one, the only Catholic at least with soul so low. There is quite an underbrush of misevaluation where literature is concerned, as you know so well, which Catholics and their voices have perpetuated down the years, until there is almost a tradition of misunderstanding, and something very funny about the reviews, and sad, of course, you see in the diocesan papers and pious little monthlies. And poetry! That new book of Noyes' illustrates the point beautifully. Besides the people not included that the reviewer mentioned, there is Robert Lowell, of the Massachusetts Lowells, a new convert whose conversion was even worse than his pacifism, coming when it did. Lowell, with the possible exception of John Frederick Nims, is the only living Catholic who is seriously regarded by secular critics, and I don't mean the crones who edit *Atlantic*, *Harper's*, etc. And the Catholic critics, they never hear of him, are too busy with Thompson. I asked Paulding to get somebody to review Lowell's book, *Land of Unlikeness*, when it came out last year, but nothing came of it. The book got fine reviews in the little mags, which, after all, publish the only poetry published, and in the liberal weeklies. I think he has another book coming. He is the husband of Jean Stafford who wrote *Boston Adventure*, and had a somewhat Catholic story in *Harper's* a year or so ago.

Jim

Will be over to see you soon.

## Notes

1. J.F. Powers to Mariella Gable, n.d., Gable Collection, St. Benedict's Convent Archives. The context suggests that the letter is written before the publication of *Prince of Darkness* (1947) and after Gable published two of Powers' stories in *Our Father's House* (1945).

2. "For S.M." Powers dedicated "The Lord's Day" to Mariella Gable in the anthology, *Cross Section*, ed. Edwin Seaver, New York: Simon Schuster, 1947, 13.

# *The Trouble*
# by J.F. Powers[1]

"The Trouble" is, according to the author, "an attempt to focus hearts upon the devilish irony of race today; it is my belief that the Church alone, holding within herself divine direction and cure, can combat evil of a preternatural order in its most fierce and subtle forms." How magnificently the author has realized his purpose readers are urgently invited to discover for themselves. May they not pass over in haste the quietly ironic moment when the white man, who has been taking violent part in a race riot, announces to the priest, "I am a Catholic, too." "That is the trouble," answers the priest; and according to Mr. Powers, that indeed is the key to all our grief—the Catholic who does not live according to the sublime doctrine of the Church. Readers are urged to examine the second of Mr. Powers' stories included in this volume, "Lions, Harts, Leaping Does," for there he has developed the theme of personal regeneration, only touched upon here.

J. F. Powers is a Catholic whose concern is first and foremost with profound spiritual truths. Of these he writes as a mature artist. To Charles Shattuck and Kerker Quinn, the editors of *Accent,* belongs the credit of having "discovered" Powers. His stories have also appeared in *The Commonweal, The Catholic Worker, Rocky Mountain Review, Opportunity: A Journal of Negro Life, New Mexico Quarterly Review.* For a WPA project, the Historical Records Survey, he edited two books, and for several years has worked for retail and wholesale booksellers.

James Farl Powers was born at Jacksonville, Illinois, in 1917. At Rockford and Quincy he attended the local parochial schools and spent four years with the Franciscans at Quincy College Academy; he also studied at Northwestern University (the evening school in Chicago). He is one of the very few Catholic writers of fiction who produce "fiction of the center" which is artistically of a very high order. In commenting upon the inclusion of his stories in the present volume, Powers wrote: "I am very happy, and a little surprised to be among those present; recognition from Catholic critics is somehow hardest to come by." Verily. The compiler takes great pleasure in making known to Catholics J.F. Powers, perhaps the most competent of our living Catholic authors who treat in short fiction the issues which really matter.

---

# *Lions, Harts, Leaping Does*
# by J. F. Powers[2]

"Lions, Harts, Leaping Does" is a profound story. With Socratic wisdom it points a steady finger at the prime necessity of knowing oneself. The priest Didymus "had the despicable caution of the comfortable who move mountains, if need be, to stay that way." But he had a memorably luminous moment in which "he saw himself tied down, caged, stunted in his apostolate, seeking the crumbs, the little pleasure, neglecting the source, always knowing death changes nothing, only immortalizes . . . and still lukewarm. In trivial attachments, in love of things, was death, no matter the appearance of life. In the highest attachment only, no matter the appearance of death, was life." It is very late, however, when Didymus becomes fully aware of his condition. He has found it comfortable to obey his rule; he has done the right thing for the wrong reasons; he has refused to visit his aged brother, not because it was contrary to the spirit of his rule, but because he hated the effort to make the trip. Thoughtful readers will find themselves in the shoes of Didymus; for it is only the unthoughtful who maintain that they have no secret and hidden sins from which to be delivered. So packed is this story with wisdom, with subtle character-analysis, with the meaningful contrast provided by the character of Brother Titus, that it deserves many readings. In fact, it is a story that may not be read only once. The superficial reader is hereby advised to skip it.

The title is taken from St. John of the Cross—the text neatly embedded in the story, where the reader may find its far-reaching implications. This story grew out of the author's interest in a group of priests who are engaged in bringing about what Peter Maurin calls "the green revolution"—a revolution which begins within and proposes to regenerate the world by personal sanctification. Its background might well have taken its rise from the four years the author spent with the Franciscans at Quincy College Academy. This story was published in *Accent*, Autumn 1943, and was included in *Best American Short Stories* 1944.

### Notes

1. These notes by Mariella Gable, O.S.B., are from *Our Father's House*, ed. Mariella Gable, O.S.B., (New York: Sheed & Ward, 1945).

2. Ibid.

# Appendix 2: Flannery O'Connor

## Gable's Tribute to O'Connor and O'Connor's letters[1]

Flannery O'Connor was the most gifted American writer of the mid-century endowed with a cluster of dazzling talents which added up to pure genius. A brilliant stylist, she was immediately recognized by the literary *haut monde*, though she was carelessly lumped with other outstanding Southern writers as another purveyor of the gratuitously grotesque. Nothing could have been less true. She somewhere, somehow early in life discovered the magnetic power of truth—that which lies at the vortex of reality and explains the dizzying whirlpool. She saw that the whole meaning of life centered in the Incarnation. She said:

> I see from the standpoint of Christian orthodoxy. This means that for me the meaning of life is centered in our Redemption by Christ and that what I see in the world I see in relation to that. I don't think that this is a position which can be taken half way or one that is particularly easy in these times to make transparent in fiction.[2]

Difficult as it was to make such a viewpoint clear in fiction she did accomplish this miracle over and over again. Particularly in "The Displaced Person" where she makes it transparently clear that all who do not believe in the redemption are displaced persons. Their native country is Christianity.  Robert Fitzgerald points out that her stories "not only imply, they as good as state again and again that estrangement from Christian plenitude is estrangement from the true country of man."[3]

But more than being a committed Christian she was the first great writer of ecumenical fiction anywhere in the world.  Though she was only a month away from death, she exerted herself to tell me that my article, "Ecumenic Core in the Fiction of Flannery O'Connor," came nearer the truth about her writing than any other criticism.  With characteristic humility she said, "I shall learn from it myself and save my breath by referring other people to it."  Her people in and around Georgia and Tennessee were the people of the Bible Belt who lived with Scripture.  They were marinated in the word of God.  She saw with Ignatius Hunt, O.S.B., that Scripture is the stepping stone to ecumenism.  How true was an observation she made in a letter to me:

> I am more and more impressed with the amount of Catholicism
> that fundamentalist Protestants have been able to retain.
> Theologically our differences with them are on the nature of the
> Church, not on the nature of God or our obligations to Him.[4]

Because she saw this truth with great clarity, felt it in the core of her being, she chose her characters from the Bible Belt (very infrequently included a Catholic) yet elicited from her fiction some of the profoundest Catholic truths ever concretized in fiction.  She wrote for an unbelieving world, not for Catholics.  Her fiction was Christian in a new and startling way which shocked and pained many readers.

Like Christ who found the poor suitable for His friendship, she remarked of the characters in her stories:

> When I look at the stories I have written I find they are for the
> most part about people who are poor, who are afflicted in both
> mind and body, who have little—or at best a distorted—sense of
> spiritual purpose, and whose actions apparently do not give the
> reader a great assurance of the joy of life.[5]

People complained about the grotesquerie and ugliness of her stories. Why did she not paint Christianity so that it looked desirable?  In a letter to me she answered this key question with such wisdom that I believe a large part of it should be shared at this time with the public so shocked at her death, still so bewildered by much of her fiction. She who realized that the Incarnation had transformed the whole status of humanity took an incarnational view of fiction so profound in its implications for the artist that it might, if it were suitably apprehended by many, transform the whole aspect of what has been so objectionably called "Catholic fiction." She makes this clear to me in the following letter.

Milledgeville, Georgia
4 May 1963

Dear Sister Mariella,

. . .When they ask you to make Christianity desirable, they are asking you to describe its essence, not what you see. Ideal Christianity doesn't exist, because anything the human being touches, even Christian truth, he deforms slightly in his own image. Even the saints do this. I take it to be the effects of Original Sin, and I notice that Catholics often act as if that doctrine is always perverted and always an indication of Calvinism. They read a little corruption as total corruption. The writer has to make the corruption believable before he can make the grace meaningful.

The tendency of people who ask questions like this is always toward the abstract and therefore toward allegory, thinness, and ultimately what they are looking for is an apologetic fiction. The best of them think: make it look desirable because it is desirable. And the rest of them think: make it look desirable because it is desirable. And the rest of them think: make it look desirable so I won't look like a fool for holding it. In a really Christian culture of real believers this wouldn't come up.

I know that the writer does call up the general and maybe the essential through the particular, but this general and essential is still deeply embedded in mystery. It is not answerable to any of our formulas. It doesn't rest finally in a statable kind of solution. It ought to throw you back on the living God. Our Catholic mentality is great on paraphrase, logic, formula, instant and

correct answers.  We judge before we experience and never trust
our faith to be subjected to reality, because it is not strong
enough.  And maybe in this we are wise.  I think this spirit is
changing on account of the council but the changes will take a
long time to soak through.

About the fanatics.  People make a judgment of fanaticism by
what they are themselves.  To a lot of Protestants I know, monks
and nuns are fanatics, none greater.  And to a lot of monks and
nuns I know, my Protestant prophets are fanatics.  For my part, I
think the only difference between them is that if you are a
Catholic and have this intensity of belief you join the convent and
are heard from no more; whereas if you are a Protestant and have
it, there is no convent for you to join and you go about the world
getting into all sorts of trouble and drawing the wrath of people
who don't believe anything much at all down on your head.

This is one reason why I can write about Protestant believers
better than Catholic believers—because they express their belief
in diverse kinds of dramatic action which is obvious enough for
me to catch.  I can't write about anything subtle.  Another thing,
the prophet is a man apart.  He is not typical of a group.  Old
Tarwater is not typical of the Southern Baptist or the Southern
Methodist.  Essentially he's a crypto-Catholic.  When you leave a
man alone with his Bible and the Holy Ghost inspires him, he's
going to be a Catholic one way or another, even though he knows
nothing about the visible church.  His kind of Christianity may
not be socially desirable, but it will be real in the sight of God.  If
I set myself to write about a socially desirable Christianity, all the
life would go out of what I do.  And if I set myself to write about
the essence of Christianity, I would have to quit writing fiction,
or become another person. . .I probably have enough stories for a
collection but I want to wait and see what this turns out to be that
I am writing on now.  Then perhaps if it ["Why Do The Heathen
Rage?"] turns out to be a long story, I'll put them all together in a
collection. . .[6]

As everyone knows by now, she had completed plans before she
died for a collection of her stories to be published in February 1965
under the magnificent title, *All That Rises Must Converge*, a quotation
from her favorite philosopher, Pierre Teilhard de Chardin.

Fourteen months before she died she wrote me the following
eloquent comment on the point she had reached as a writer.  She had

already begun a new novel, *Why Do the Heathen Rage?* But she felt that she had reached a milestone and that her first great contribution had been completed. Here are her own words: "I've been writing eighteen years and I've reached the point where I can't do again what I know I can do well, and the larger things that I need to do now, I doubt my capacity for doing."[7] Perhaps her doubt indicated that it was not God's will for her to continue to write. About the excellence of her ecumenical fiction she entertained not the slightest doubt. I can still hear her say with the assurance that she had touched eternal truth in *The Violent Bear It Away*: "I can wait fifty years, a hundred years for it to be understood." She noted how readers, even Catholic readers who should have known better, identified with Rayber, the materialist, rather than with the fanatic, Old Tarwater. "It will take a while," she smiled, "for people to see what I mean." Her confidence in her ability to communicate the most important truth in the world was part of her humility.

To talk with her was one of the most unforgettable experiences of a lifetime. Simple, unpretentious, humble, gay with a sense of humor which saw our absurdities as matter for laughter, her direct honesty even made persons who thought they habitually spoke the truth look like liars. I have never known one so habitually at home with truth. God gave her a magnificent work to do. That God took her from us is proof positive that she had completed that work. It remains now for us to understand it truly.

**O'Connor to Gable:[8]**

Milledgeville
5 July 64

Dear Sister Mariella,

Thank you so much for sending the essay. I think Richard [Stern] has read your meaning incorrectly. I don't find anything in it that I could object to. Richard apparently dislikes the people of the Pentecostal religions with a certain vigor and for, I gather, purely personal reasons. I don't know what I said to him to give him the impression he seems to have taken away about my attitude toward them. I have the feeling that all my visitors go away with their own views confirmed. Half the time, I don't know what they're talking about and my answers are vague.

I do very much appreciate what you've put into the essay and I shall learn from it myself. And save my breath by referring other people to it.

The wolf, I'm afraid, is inside tearing up the place. I've been in the hospital 50 days already this year. At present I'm just home from the hospital and have to stay in bed. I have an electric typewriter and I write a little every day but I'm not allowed to do much.

I'll count on your prayers and when I have the strength I'll try to write you and Richard a joint letter about the Catholic Protestant inspiration problem in the stories. When critics get ahold of them the tail usually starts wagging the dog.

Yours,

Flannery

### Notes

1. Mariella Gable, O.S.B., "Tribute to Flannery O'Connor," *Esprit*, University of Scranton, Pennsylvania (Winter 1964): 25-27.

2. Flannery O'Connor, "The Fiction Writer and His Country," in *The Living Novel*, ed. Granville Hicks, 162.

3. *Sewanee Review*, LXX, 394.

4. Flannery O'Connor to Mariella Gable, O.S.B., 4 May 1963, *The Habit of Being: Letters of Flannery O'Connor*, ed. Sally Fitzgerald (New York: Vintage, 1980), 516-18.

5. O'Connor, "The Fiction Writer," 161.

6. Flannery O'Connor to Mariella Gable, O.S.B., 4 May 1963, *The Habit of Being*, 516-17.

7. Ibid., 518.

8. Flannery O'Connor to Mariella Gable, O.S.B., 5 July 1964, *The Habit of Being*, 591.

# Gable's review of *Everything That Rises Must Converge*

*Everything That Rises Must Converge*, by Flannery O'Connor. 269 pp. Farrar, Straus and Giroux. $4.95.[1]

Two human beings looked out from prison bars; one was sin, the other the Omega point. It was with calculated irony that Flannery O'Connor, famous for her portrayals of sinful human beings, chose as the title of her posthumous book of short stories the optimistic promise of Pierre Teilhard de Chardin: *Everything That Rises Must Converge*. To date, say these new stories, there is mighty little convergence. Human beings hate each other.

Though Flannery admired Teilhard's philosophy, and though she was perhaps willing to believe that, some 300 million years hence, human beings would come to love each other in the Pleroma of Christian and scientific unity, still she believed that the author must look at life as *it is* and communicate that vision with terrible honesty. Thus, one might apply equally to this new book the words with which she dedicated her first collection of stories to the Robert Fitzgerald family: "Nine stories about original sin, with my compliments. . ."

Her compliments went out to the Fitzgeralds because she had become very much one of the family during the several years she boarded in the Connecticut home. Robert Fitzgerald, now Boylston professor at Harvard, contributes the Introduction to this book. As a poet whose vital translation of the *Odyssey* has assured him an honored place in the English-speaking world, Fitzgerald has the necessary gifts for writing about Miss O'Connor as she deserves. The humorous yet dedicated young Flannery; her hometown, Milledgeville, Georgia, aghast at her fiction; the ravages of lupus which brought about her death at 39—all are here together with an astute critique of her art. Respectful always of that which the critic cannot pigeon-hole, Fitzgerald nevertheless manages to communicate such insights as could be gained only by a close and perceptive friend. This introduction by one of them will probably remain a classic tribute.

After eighteen years of writing, Flannery O'Connor left to the world two novels, *Wise Blood* and *The Violent Bear It Away*, and two collections of short stories, the second of which is the subject of this review. All are of a piece: her country is the South. Her characters are, to use her own words, "people who are poor, who are afflicted both in mind and body, who have little—or at best a distorted—sense of spiritual purpose, and whose actions do not apparently give the reader a great assurance of the joy of life."

Her viewpoint is that of the Christian who finds modern life filled with repugnant distortions which must be pointed out to an audience used to seeing them as natural. Her method is to shock by the use of the grotesque—like shouting to make the deaf hear. She maintained that in her lifetime the Catholic faith taught her more about writing than she could have otherwise learned in a thousand years. It was her habit to view life *sub specie aeternitatem* so that the grubbiest farm and its deprived people were illumined by a clear shaft of light streaming from the supernatural. Yet she wrote for the atheist, for the non-believer. Very few Catholics appear in her stories. Her believers are usually the Bible-Belt Christians. She abhorred manipulations by the artist to teach a lesson. Nothing but the truth would do. And this truth as she saw it, she delivered with terrifying intensity, tragic awe, and a sense of humor which pervades her work like God's grace in a Waste Land.

The nine stories in *Everything That Rises Must Converge* are all cut to this pattern. The best of them, "The Lame Shall Enter First," "Greenleaf," and "A View of the Woods," are as fine as the best in her first collection. A half dozen of her stories are among the classics of American Literature.

Faith pitted against unfaith is the theme of "The Lame Shall Enter First "as it was of her novel, *The Violent Shall Bear It Away*. To the same extent that her mastery of the short story surpassed her mastery of the novel, "The Lame Shall Enter First" is better than *The Violent Shall Bear It Away*. The story's three characters, Sheppard, Johnson and Norton, are parallels to Rayber, Tarwater and the idiot child in the novel.

An atheist do-gooder, ironically named Sheppard, takes into his home one Rufus Johnson, a violently destructive juvenile delinquent. The boy has a club foot which Sheppard believes to be the cause of his "compensating" evil behavior, while Johnson himself declares that he is simply under the power of Satan. In spite of his misdeeds,

Johnson is a furiously committed Christian. He eats a page of Scripture declaring, "I've eaten it like Ezekiel and it is honey to my mouth." Taunting Sheppard he adds, "Even if I didn't believe it, it would still be true." Sheppard has a son, Norton, who is neglected and lonely for his recently deceased mother. Johnson instructs the boy in the facts of afterlife and swears that the child's mother is in heaven if she believed in Jesus. Little Norton would rather believe that his mother were in Hell than that she did not exist at all—which is the viewpoint proposed by his father. Johnson explains to the child that if he died right now he would go where his mother is, but that if he lives any longer with his atheist father, he will go to Hell.

Detesting Sheppard's soft attitude, Johnson commits crime after crime. When the police ask him why, he shouts before Sheppard, "To show up that big tin Jesus. . . He thinks he's God." Sheppard is suddenly faced with the piercing realization that "he had stuffed his own emptiness with good works like a glutton. He had ignored his own child to feed his own vision of himself. He saw the clear-eyed devil, the sounder of hearts, leering at him from the eyes of Johnson." To soothe the ache of this injured self-love he remembers that he did more for Johnson than he did for his own son. Full of good resolutions for the future, Sheppard goes to the attic where he had left Norton looking through a telescope, hoping to find his mother in the stars. The child has hanged himself, presumably because of what Johnson has told him. No summary can do justice to the persuasiveness of this story which says unmistakably that a Christian believer, no matter how sinful, is infinitely to be preferred to a do-gooder atheist.

In "Greenleaf" the reader is exposed to vices with which he is more at home. The story revolves around Mrs. May, a widow, and Greenleaf, the no-good, shiftless caretaker on her farm. Mrs. May, a woman totally absorbed with hate and self-pity, tries to make Greenleaf kill a stray bull that is spoiling her herd. Although Mrs. May has grown-up sons who live under her roof and eat her bread, they have not the slightest interest in the farm. Greenleaf, whose boys are rising in the world, rubs in the undutifulness of Mrs. May's sons and tells her that his boys would never let their mother tend to all the chores. Mrs. May's sons also taunt her by telling her that when they are ready to marry, they will choose someone like the slovenly Mrs. Greenleaf. Mrs. May reflects: "I work and slave, I struggle and sweat to keep this place for them and soon as I'm dead they'll marry trash and bring it here and ruin everything." In taking the shiftless Greenleaf out to make him kill the bull, she herself gets gored to death. Is it possible that the horn piercing her heart is less tragic that the daily opening of her spirit to spleen, envy, self-righteousness, and the corroding rip of self-pity?

In "A View of the Woods," Flannery O'Connor is at the peak of her power. Old Mark Fortune, nearly eighty, is a cluster of malicious purposes. He tries to realize them through his nine-year-old granddaughter, Mary Fortune Pitts, whom he elaborately favors because she is his spit and image. Fortune keeps the Pitts family in virtual bondage to himself. Though he permits them to live on his farm and to keep what they earn, he delights in reminding them of their dependence on him. When the well runs dry, he will not permit the Pittses to have a deep well drilled. No, they must pipe water from a spring. For he is afraid that if he permits Pitts to pay for the well then when he says to Pitts, "It's my land you're sitting on," Pitts could retort, "It's my pump that's pumping the water you're drinking." Every now and then he gives the Pittses a practical lesson by selling off some of the land which they wanted to buy. One of his prime aims is to instill in little Mary Fortune a contempt for her family. But when he sells the front yard which gave the Pittses a view of the woods (to them a visible symbol of hope and beauty), little Mary sulks openly. Old Mark Fortune attempts to change her mood by taking her to town where he signs a document willing all his property to her. But nothing can shake her resolve to be all Pitts and no Fortune. Before they reach home, she and her grandfather have killed each other, and by due process of law, the land which Fortune had deeded to Mary will go to the Pitts family. This is the very wormwood of irony.

In so brief a review the other powerful stories in the book must be passed over. The unessentials are easier to record—for instance, the fact that three of the stories make full use of current race tensions in the South. But to Flannery O'Connor segregation is only one more facet of the flawed human nature she habitually examines. She plumbs the ignorance which maintains white superiority, the ignorance which lives in Civil War memories and can, on the basis of vanished ancestral wealth, boast, "I know who I am." Among the "nice ladies" of the South, "I know who I am" runs like a weird incantation. Flannery O'Connor is another Socrates reminding all of us that we do not know who we are.

In the title story of the book, Julian's mother exercises a nauseous patronizing condescension to Negroes. She presents, with unctuous friendliness, a penny to a tiny colored boy whose angry mother promptly fells her with a blow from a huge red purse. The outrage of it makes her lose her mind. The main character in "Judgement Day" discovers that he is worse off in the canyons of New York with a daughter who hates him than if he had remained in Georgia to run a still for a Negro—the unspeakable disgrace of working for a colored man.

But there is a crowning vision in "Revelation." Having been called "a wart hog from Hell," Mrs. Turpin is licking the wounds of her self-esteem when she sees a procession into heaven. (Incidentally, she observes this vision from a pig pen.) She sees whole armies of white trash made clean for the first time in their lives, bands of Negroes in white robes, freaks and lunatics shouting and clapping. And then bringing up the rear of the procession a crowd of people like herself, who had always had a little of everything and the God-given wit to use it right. Though they are last in the procession, they chant "with great dignity, accountable as they had always been for good order and common sense and respectable behavior. They alone were on key. Yet she could see by their shocked and altered faces that even their virtues were being burned away."

## Notes

1. Mariella Gable, O.S.B., review of *Everything That Rises Must Converge* by Flannery O'Connor, *The Critic* (June-July 1965): 58-60.

# Gable's Review of *The Complete Stories*

Flannery O'Connor, *The Complete Stories*. Edited by Robert Giroux. Farrar, Straus and Giroux, New York, 1971. Pp. xvii, 555. Cloth, $10.00.[1]

This is unquestionably the most significant book of the year. At a strategic moment in the evolution of our culture it underlines the importance of Flannery O'Connor. And this at a time when we are more prepared to receive her Christian message than ever before.

In this book Robert Giroux, O'Connor's editor since the time of *Wise Blood*, provides a perceptive introduction and bibliographical notes. He also gives us for the first time in book form the twelve short stories written by Flannery O'Connor at the University of Iowa as a partial fulfillment for her MFA degree in creative writing under Paul Engle. Also in chronological order are included her four well-known books, a chapter of a projected novel, and sketches which she later incorporated into her first novel, *Wise Blood*.

Between *Wise Blood* and *A Good Man Is Hard to Find* her craft developed astoundingly. In *A Good Man Is Hard to Find* there were only "nine stories about original sin" which she dedicated to her "adopted kin, Robert and Sally Fitzgerald." Had she trained her sights on quantity rather than quality she might have included the dozen stories from her thesis. They had all been published in prestigious magazines. An astute critic of her own work, she knew how much brighter shines a diamond when not surrounded by rubies.

*The Complete Stories* appears at a most propitious moment in the development of our culture. Technology does not satisfy our deepest needs; it does not answer our profoundest questions about life and death. Bearing witness to the current popular interest in a return to religious values are men as diverse as Arnold Toynbee and Alvin Toffler. Though Flannery O'Connor abhorred the idea of edification at the expense of truth, she once and for all nailed down her major creative concern: "I see from the standpoint of Christian orthodoxy. This means that for me the meaning of life is centered in our

Redemption by Christ and that what I see in the world I see in relation to that." And this analysis of her own work stands, Josephine Hendin to the contrary notwithstanding.

Change is accelerating at so great a rate that our own culture is at the moment turning with dizzying speed to Christianity. I remember in 1962 that Miss O'Connor told me wistfully about the public response to her novel, *The Violent Bear It Away*: "Most people," she said, "identify with the materialist, Rayber. They do not see what my book really says. But I can wait forty years or eighty years for them to discover what I am really saying."

In ten years this hoped-for shift is being made. *The Complete Stories* underlines the importance of Flannery O'Connor as a major writer. How great is she? After her death in 1964 at the age of thirty-nine, Thomas Merton was the only critic who dared to detach her from her peers and place her with the giants. Said he, " I don't think of Hemingway, or Katherine Anne Porter, or Sartre, but rather of someone like Sophocles. . . .I write her name with honor, for all the truth and all the craft with which she shows man's fall and dishonor" (*Jubilee* November 1964). Sophocles? By all means, for her tragedy and the grotesque. But what about grace touching all and sundry? Grandma's hysterical encounter with the Misfit. Mrs. Turpin in the pig parlour. Scores of fireflies light up the swamps of degradation. Only Dante in "Hell" and "Heaven" had anything like so wide a vision. Let us not deny to those who are near us in time an appreciation of magnificent achievement.

## Notes

1. Mariella Gable, O.S.B., review of *The Complete Stories* by Flannery O'Connor, ed. Robert Giroux, *Sisters Today* (April 1972): 512-13.

# Works Cited

Gable Bibliography

Abbott, Walter. *Twelve Council Fathers*. New York: Macmillan, 1963.

Adler, Mortimer and William Gorman, eds. *The Great Ideas: A Syntopicon of Great Books of the Western World*. Chicago: Encyclopaedia Brittanica, 1952.

Alighieri, Dante. *The Divine Comedy*. Trans. J.A. Carlyle, Thomas Okey, P.H. Wicksteed. New York: Modern Library, 1932.

Amis, Kingsley. *Lucky Jim*. New York: Viking, 1954.

-----. *That Uncertain Feeling*. New York: Harcourt, Brace, 1956.

Aristotle. *Ethics*. Trans. D.P. Chase. New York: E.P Dutton, 1950.

-----. *On the Art of Poetry*. Ed. Lane Cooper. New York: Harcourt, 1913.

Baring, Maurice. *Landmarks in Russian Literature*. London: Methuen, 1910.

Barr, Donald. Review of *Island Priest* by Henri Queffelec. *The New York Times*, 28 September 1952.

Barrett, Alfred. *Mint by Night*. New York: America Press, 1938.

Baum, Gragory. "New Spirit at the Council." *The Commonweal*, 25 October 1963.

Bea, Augustin, Cardinal. "The Ecumenical Responsibility in Teaching Theology." *Ecumenist* (February-March 1963).

Bentz, Ida and W.A. Willibrand. "Werner Bergengruen—Aspects of His Life and Work." *Books Abroad*. Norman, Oklahoma: University of Oklahoma, 1958.

Bernanos, Georges. *Joy*. Trans. Louise Varese. New York: Pantheon, 1946.

-----. *Plea for Liberty*. Trans. Harry L. Binsse. New York: Pantheon, 1944.

-----. *The Star of Satan*. Trans. Pamela Morris. New York: Macmillan, 1940.

Bloy, Leon. *The Woman Who Was Poor*. Trans. I.J. Collins. New York: Sheed & Ward, 1947.

Bowen, Robert. "Hope Versus Despair in the Gothic Novel." *Renascence* (Spring 1961): 147.

Brooks, Cleanth, and Robert Penn Warren. *Understanding Fiction*. New York: F.S. Crofts, 1948.

Butler, Samuel. *Erewhon* or *Over the Range*. New York: E.P. Dutton, 1927.

Campion, Ronald J., S.J. "Tired of Chardin." *America*, 15 May 1965, 696-97.

Chase, Richard. *Commentary*. September 1956: 263.

Clancy, W.P. Review of *The Cypresses Believe in God*, by Jose Gironella. *Commonweal*, 15 April 1955, 53-55.

Conger, Yves. *Informations Catholiques Internationales*, 15 December 1962, 3. Quoted in *The Ecumenist* (April-May 1963): 66.

Connolly, James M. "Theology and *The Devil's Advocate*." *America*, 28 May 1960, 312-13.

"The Corn Squeeze Artist." *Time*, 20 June 1960.

Coskren, Thomas M., O.P., "Is Golding Calvinistic?" *America*, 6 July 1963, 18-20.

Costello, Donald. "Salinger and His Critics." *Commonweal*, 25 October 1963, 132-35.

Cuénot, Claude. *Teilhard de Chardin: A Biographical Study*. Trans. Vincent Colimore and ed. Rene Hague. Baltimore: Burns-Oates, 1965.

Davis, Horton. *A Mirror of the Ministry in Modern Novels*. New York: Oxford University Press, 1959.

DeWohl, Louis. "The Problems of a Historical Novelist." *Books on Trial* (November 1955): 113-14.

Diekmann, Godfrey, O.S.B. *Come, Let Us Worship*. Baltimore: Benedictine Studies, 1963.

Donnelly, William, S.J. "Teilhardian Vision." *The Month* (April 1965): 249-52.

Douglas, Norman. *South Wind*. New York: Hermitage Press, 1939.

Ferris, Sumner. "The Outside and the Inside: Flannery O'Connor's *The Violent Bear It Away*." *Critique* III, 2, 1960.

Firbank, Ronald. *Five Novels*. London: Duckworth, 1949.

Fitzgerald, Robert. "The Countryside and the True Country." *Sewanee Review* (Summer 1962): 380-90.

Fitzgibbons, Constantine. *Norman Douglas*. London: Richards Press, 1955.

Flores, Angel and Dudley Poore, eds. *Fiesta in November*. New York: Houghton Mifflin, 1942.

Fowlie, Wallace. "Catholic Orientation in Contemporary French Literature." In *Spiritual Problems in Contemporary Literature.* Ed. Stanley R. Hopper. New York: Harper, 1952.

Francoeur, Robert T., S.J. "Teilhard de Chardin." *Jubilee* (July 1965): 36-39.

Friedman, M.J. "Another Legend in Southern Fiction." *English Journal* (April 1960): 233-43.

Gardiner, Harold C., S.J. *Norms for the Novel.* Garden City, New York: Hanover House, 1960.

Golding, William. *Lord of the Flies.* New York: Coward-McCann, 1955.

Gordon, Caroline. "Flannery O'Connor's *Wise Blood.*" *Critique* (Fall 1954).

Grande, Luke M. Review of *Lord of the Flies*, by William Golding. *Commonweal*, 25 January 1963, 457-59.

Greene, Graham. *The Heart of the Matter.* New York: Viking, 1948.

Greenlees, Ian. *Norman Douglas.* New York: Longmans, Green, 1957.

Griffiths, Bede, O.S.B. *The Golden String.* New York: Kenedy, 1954.

Hawkes, John. "Flannery O'Connor's Devil." *Sewanee Review* (Summer 1962): 395-407.

Hunt, Ignatius. Public lecture. College of St. Benedict, St. Joseph, Minnesota, 2 July 1963.

Huxley, Aldous. *Brave New World.* New York: Harper and Row, 1950.

-----. *Brave New World Revisited.* New York: Harper and Row, 1958.

John XXIII, Pope. *The Pope Speaks*, VIII, 4 (1963).

Kessler, Martin. "Power and the Perfect State: A Study in Disillusionment as Reflected in Orwell's *Nineteen Eighty-Four* and Huxley's *Brave New World.*" *Political Science Quarterly* (December 1957): 565-77.

Kunitz, Stanley I. and Vineta Colby. *Twentieth Century Authors.* First Supplement. New York: Wilson, 1955.

Leeming, Bernard, S.J. *The Catholic Messenger*, 9 November 1962.

Lewis, R.W.B. *The Picaresque Saint.* New York: Lippincott, 1959.

Leyburn, Ellen Douglas. *Satiric Allegory: Mirror of Man.* New Haven: Yale University Press, 1956.

Machen, Arthur. *Hieroglyphics.* In *Literature, the Channel of Culture.* Ed. Francis X. Connelly. New York: Harcourt, 1953.

Madeleva, Sister. *See* Wolff.

Marshall, Bruce. "Graham Greene and Evelyn Waugh." *Commonweal*, 3 March 1950, 551-553.

Masefield, John. "Biography." *Poems of John Masefield.* Ed. Henry Seidel Canby, Frederick Erastus, Willard Highley Durham. New York: Macmillan, 1917.

Mauriac, Francois. *Viper's Tangle.* Trans. Warre B. Wells. New York: Sheed and Ward, 1933.

-----. *Woman of the Pharisees.* Trans. Gerard Hopkins. London: Eyre & Spottiswoode, 1946.

McNamee, Maurice B., S.J. *Honor and the Epic Hero.* New York: Holt, Rinehart & Winston, 1960.

"Mendel, Gregor Johann." *Encyclopedia Britannica* XV, 1965.

Menen, Aubrey. *The Fig Tree*. New York: Scribner, 1959.

-----. "Party of One." *Holiday* (July 1959): 8.

-----. *Ramayanna*. New York: Scribner, 1954.

-----. *The Stumbling Stone*. New York: Scribner, 1949.

Meyers, Bertrande, D.C., "Four Stories of Flannery O'Connor." *Thought* (Autumn 1962): 410-26.

Mooney, Christopher F., S.J. "The Body of Christ in the Writings of Teilhard de Chardin." *Theological Studies* (December 1964): 576-610.

Newman, John Henry. "English Catholic Literature." In *Idea of a University*. New York: Longmans, 1921.

O'Connor, Flannery. *The Habit of Being: Letters of Flannery O'Connor*. Ed. Sally Fitzgerald. New York: Farrar, Straus, Giroux, 1980.

-----. Interview by Joel Wells. "Conversation with Flannery O'Connor." *Critic* (September 1962).

-----. Interview by C. Ross Mullins. "Flannery O'Connor: An Interview." *Jubilee* (June 1963): 32-35.

-----. Interview by Granville Hicks. "The Fiction Writer and His Country." *The Living Novel*. Ed. Granville Hicks. New York: Macmillan, 1957.

-----. Interview by Granville Hicks. "A Writer at Home With Her Heritage." *Saturday Review*, 12 May 1962, 22-24.

-----. "The Lame Shall Enter First." *The Complete Stories of Flannery O'Connor*. Ed. Robert Giroux. New York: Farrar, Straus, Giroux, 1981.

-----. *The Violent Bear It Away*. New York: Farrar, Straus, Cudahy, 1960.

-----. *Wise Blood*. New York: Farrar, Straus, Cudahy, 1962.

O'Donnell, Donat. *Maria Cross: Imaginative Patterns in Modern Catholic Writers*. New York: Oxford University Press, 1952.

O'Gara, James. "Good Pope John." *The Commonweal*, 28 June 1963.

Paton, Alan. *Cry the Beloved Country*. New York: Scribner's, 1951.

Powers, Jessica. *The House at Rest*. Pewaukee, Wisconsin: Carmelite Monastery, 1984.

Powers, J.F. *The Prince of Darkness*. New York: Doubleday, 1947.

Queffelec, Henri. *Island Priest*. Trans. James Whitall. New York: Dutton, 1952.

Ratzinger, Joseph. Davenport *Catholic Messenger*, 20 June 1963, 12.

Reid, J.C. "The Novels of Elizabeth Langgaesser." *Downside Review* (Spring 1960): 117-27.

Review of *Lucky Jim*, by Kingsley Amis. London *Sunday Times*, 25 December 1956.

Robinson, Henry Morton. *The Cardinal*. New York: Simon and Schuster, 1950.

Salinger, J.D. *The Catcher in the Rye*. Boston: Little, Brown, 1951.

-----. *Franny and Zooey*. Boston: Little, Brown, 1961.

Scott, Nathan A., Jr. *Modern Literature and the Religious Frontier*. New York: Harper, 1959.

Sheed, Francis. *Theology and Sanity*. New York: Sheed and Ward, 1946.

Simons, John W. "Salvation of the Novels." *Commonweal*, 25 April 1952, 74-76.

Sorokin, Pitirim. *The Crisis of Our Age*. New York: E.P.Dutton, 1941.

Spark, Muriel. *Memento Mori*. New York: Lippincott, 1959.

Spender, Stephen. *The Creative Element*. New York: British Book Center, 1954.

Stolpe, Sven. *Night Music*. Trans. John Derlin. New York: Sheed, 1960.

Stopp, Frederick J. *Evelyn Waugh: Portrait of an Artist*. Boston: Little, Brown, 1958.

"Studies in Modern Fiction." *Critique* (Fall 1958).

Tate, Allen. "Orthodoxy and the Standard of Literature." *New Republic*, 5 January 1958.

Tavard, George H. *The Catholic Approach to Protestantism*. Trans. by the author. New York: Harper, 1955.

Teilhard de Chardin, Pierre, S.J. *The Divine Milieu: An Essay on the Interior Life*. New York: Harper, 1960.

-----. *The Future of Man*. Trans. Norman Denny. New York: Harper and Row, 1964.

-----. *Hymn of the Universe*. New York: Harper and Row, 1965.

-----. *The Phenomenon of Man*. Intro. Julian Huxley. New York: Harper, 1959.

Updike, John. *The Centaur*. New York: Knopf, 1963.

-----. *Pigeon Feathers and Other Stories*. New York: Knopf, 1962.

-----. *The Poorhouse Fair*. New York: Fawcett Crest, 1958.

-----. *Rabbit, Run*. New York: Knopf, 1960.

Vann, Gerald, O.P. *The Water and the Fire*. New York: Sheed, 1954.

Von Hildebrand, Dietrich. *Liturgy and Personality*. New York: Longmans, Green, 1943.

Ward, Barbara. *Faith and Freedom*. Garden City, New York: Image Books, 1958.

Waugh, Evelyn. *Decline and Fall*. Boston: Little, Brown and Company, 1946.

-----. *A Handful of Dust*. New York: Farrar and Rinehart, 1934.

-----. *The Loved One*. Boston: Little, Brown, 1948.

-----. *Scott-King's Modern Europe*. London: Chapman and Hall, 1947.

Weigel, Gustave, S.G. *A Catholic Primer on the Ecumenical Movement*. Westminster, Maryland: Newman Press, 1959.

Wilder, Amos. *Theology and Modern Literature*. Cambridge: Harvard University Press, 1958.

Wilson, Angus. *Anglo-Saxon Attitudes*. New York: Viking, 1956.

Wolff, Madeleva, C.S.C. "Catholic Literature." *Prose Readings*. Ed. Vincent J. Flynn. New York: Scribner's, 1942.

Young, Michael. *The Rise of Meritocracy*. London: Thames & Hudson, 1958.

Booth, Wayne. *The Company We Keep*. Los Angeles: University of California Press, 1988.

Borgia, Sister Frances. Review of *Many-Colored Fleece*, edited by Mariella Gable, O.S.B. *Insight* (January 1951).

Boyle, Michael, S.J. "Teaching 'Dirty Books' in College." *America*, 13 December 1958, 337-39.

Casey, Ruth. Review of *They Are People* and *Our Father's House*, edited by Mariella Gable, O.S.B. *Today*, May 1946.

*The Central Minnesota Counsellor Newsletter*, May 1972.

Cogley, John. Review of *Many-Colored Fleece*, edited by Mariella Gable, O.S.B. *Commonweal*, 22 December 1950.

Connelly, Francis X., S.J. Review of *Great Catholic Short Stories*, edited by Mariella Gable, O.S.B. *Catholic Book Club Newsletter*, November 1942.

Desmond, John F. "Catholicism in Contemporary American Fiction." *America*, 14 May 1994, 7-11.

Erskine, John. Review of *Great Modern Catholic Short Stories* edited by Mariella Gable, O.S.B. Chicago *Sun*. Vol. 1, no. 5 (1942).

Gable, Mariella, O.S.B. *Blind Man's Stick*. Boston: Bruce Humphries, 1938.

-----. Letters: 1918-1980. St. Joseph, Minnesota: St. Benedict's Convent Archives.

-----. Review of *Deschooling Society*, by Ivan Illich. *Benedictines*, Spring-Summer 1974.

-----. Review of *Flannery O'Connor, The Complete Stories*, edited by Robert Giroux. *Sisters Today*, April 1972.

-----. Review of *The Heart of the Matter*, by Peirre Teilhard de Chardin. *Spirituality Today*, March 1980.

-----. Thirteen essays on Catholic fiction. In *The Literature of Spiritual Values and Catholic Fiction*, edited by Nancy Hynes, O.S.B. Lanham, Maryland: University Press of America, 1996.

-----. "This is the New Pentecost." *The Catholic Messenger*, 29 July 1948; also *Catholic Digest* (October 1948).

Gandolfo, Anita. *Testing the Faith: The New Catholic Fiction in America*. New York: Greenwood Press, 1992.

Gardiner, Harold C., S.J. "The 'Dangers' of Literature. *America*, 13 December 1958, 335-36.

Gerhart, Mary. "Whatever Happened to the Catholic Novel? A Study in Genre." *Morphologies of Faith: Essays on Religion and Culture*. Ed. Mary Gerhart and Anthony Yu. Atlanta, Georgia: Scholars Press, 1990.

Giles, Peter. *American Catholic Arts and Fictions*. Cambridge: Cambridge University Press, 1992.

Greeley, Andrew. "The Catholic Novels of Jon Hassler," *America*, 17 November 1990, 366-67, 382.

Harriott, John X. "The Nun's Tales." *The Tablet*, 12 August 1989.

H.R. Review of *This is Catholic Fiction*, edited by Mariella Gable, O.S.B. *Friar's Bookshelf*, September 1949.

Hughes, Riley. Review of *Many-Colored Fleece*, edited by Mariella Gable, O.S.B. *Renascence*, Spring 1950.

Hynes, Joseph. "The Novels of Jon Hassler." *Commonweal*, 3 November 1995, 8-12.

Kennedy, John S.  Review of *Our Father's House*, edited by Mariella Gable, O.S.B.  *The New York Times*, 13 January 1946.

MacMahon, Bryan.  Interview by Kristin Malloy, O.S.B., Tralee, County Kerry, May, 1983.

Malloy, Kristin, O.S.B.  Interview by Nancy Hynes, O.S.B., St. Benedict's Convent, St. Joseph, Minnesota, 7 July 1995.

-----.  Eulogy for Mariella Gable, O.S.B., St. Benedict's Convent, St. Joseph, Minnesota, 24 March 1985.

-----.  "Toast of the Month."  *The Marianist*, October 1950.

McDonald, Grace, O.S.B.  *With Lamps Burning*.  St. Joseph, Minnesota: St. Benedict's Priory Press, 1957.

Menendez, Albert J.  *The Catholic Novel: An Annotated Bibliography*.  New York: Garland, 1988.

O'Connor, Flannery.  *The Habit of Being: Letters of Flannery O'Connor*.  Edited by Sally Fitzgerald.  New York: Farrar, Straus, Giroux, 1979.

Powers, J.F.  Interview by Nancy Hynes, O.S.B.  Collegeville, Minnesota, June 1994.

Review of *Great Modern Catholic Short Stories*, edited by Mariella Gable, O.S.B.  *The New York Times*, 22 November 1942.

Scallan, E.B.  *A Competent Censorship or Else Chaos*.  New Orleans: Catholic Herald Press, 1943.

Sparr, Arnold.  *To Promote, Defend, And Redeem: The Catholic Literary Revival and the Cultural Transformation of American Catholicism, 1920-1960*.  New York: Greenwood, 1990.

Tynan, Daniel, ed.  *Biographical Dictionary of Contemporary Catholic American Writing*.  New York: Greenwood, 1989.

Woodman, Thomas. *Faithful Fictions: The Catholic Novel in British Literature.* Philadelphia: Open University Press, 1991.

Wyatt, E.V.R. Review of *Our Father's House*, edited by Mariella Gable, O.S.B. *Commonweal*, 23 November 1945.

Yzermans, Vincent A. *Journeys.* Waite Park, Minnesota: Park Press, 1994.

# INDEX

*Index*

268                                    *Index*

26                                  *Index*

68                                    *Index*

Humanities teachers, xxxvii
Humor, 129-31, 147, 177-78
Hunt, Ignatius, 171, 195
Huxley, Aldous, 10, 62, 123, 143-50, 153, 162
Huysmans, Joris-Karl, 63, 93
*The Hymn of the Universe*, 205, 208
*Hymns*, 2
Hynes, Arleen, xviii
Hynes, Joseph, xl
Hynes, Nancy, "Introduction," xvii-xlviii

*The Idea of a University*, 11, 55
*The Idiot*, 66, 85
Illich, Ivan, xxxvi
Imprimaturs, xxv-xxvi, xliii*n.* 45
*In the Beginning*, 143
Incarnational world view: xl, 53-54, 58, 231, 233; O'Connor, Flannery, 170-71, 194, 243-44; Teilhard de Chardin, Pierre, 209, 215
Inclusive language, xxxviii
Individual integrity, xxxiii
Industrialism, 145, 202
*Inferno*, 35-36, 206-07
Institute of International Education, xxxiv
*Integrity*, 40
Interfaith Sexual Trauma Institute, xviii
Irish writers, 44, 130
Irony, 172, 240
Irving, Washington, 17
*Island Priest*, 73, 102
Italian literature, 63
"I Took Thee, Constance," 46

Jaeger, Werner, 8
Jansenism, xxvi, xxxix, 73
Jarrell, Randall, 62, 93, 110, 146
Jesuits, xxxiii, 60
Jewish writers, xxxix, 54, 64-65, 166
"The Jilting of Granny Weatherall," 47
Jim Crowism, 46
Joan of Arc, St., 121
John of the Cross, St., 7-8
John, St., 208, 210
John XXIII, Pope, 169, 203
Johnson, Ben, 129
*Journeys*, xliii*n.* 38
*Joy*, 69, 80, 118-23
Joyce, James, xxxii, xxxviii, 4-5, 13, 52
Judas, 121
Judeo-Christian heritage, 165, 171, 180, 196, 204
Justinian, Roman Emperor, 214

Kearns, F.E., 197
Kennedy, John S., xliv*n.* 56
Kessler, Martin, 145
*The Keys of the Kingdom*, 57, 84-85
Khayyam, Omar, 142
Kierkegaard, Soren, 35
"The Knife," xxix, 23, 46
Knopf, Alfred, 161
Kraft, Katherine, xlvii*n.* 89
Kremer, Michael, xxii
*Kristin Lavransdatter*, xxxviii, 3, 6, 116, 63-64, 67-68, 108, 162-63
*Kubla Khan*, 17

"The Spy," xx
*Stage of Fools*, 65, 81, 163
St. Benedict's Academy, xx
St. Benedict's Convent, xxx-xxxi, xxxvi
St. Benedict's Hospital, xxix
St. Cloud State University, xxxiv
St. John's Abbey, xviii, xxxv
St. John's University, xxxiii-xxxv
St. Joseph Convent, xliin. 24
St. Joseph, MN, xx
St. Joseph's College, xxvii
St. Martin's College, xxxvi
St. Mary's High School, xx
St. Scholastica Convent, xxxvi
St. Teresa's College, xxxiii
*The Star of Satan*, xxxviii, 5, 21, 79-80, 118
Stegman, Basil, xxv
Steinbeck, John, "The Miracle of Tepayac," 46
Steinmetz, Charles, 31
Stolpe, Sven, 52, 61, 67, 73, 106-07
Stream-of-consciousness, 4-5
Strong, L.A.G., "The English Captain," 9
*The Stumbling Stone*, 147-48
Suffering, 120, 212-13
Suhard, Emmanuel, Cardinal, 40
Sullivan, Richard: 44, 68, 107; "Night in August," 22; "Saturday Nocturne," 46
*Summa Theologica*, 6
"The Surgeon and the Nun," 12-14
Swift, Jonathan, 118
Sylvester, Harry, 11
Symbols, 54, 56-58, 131

"A Table Before Me," 40, 46

"The Tables Turned," 19
*Tablet*, xix
Talbot, Francis, xx
Tate, Allen, 53, 88, 110
"Teaching 'Dirty Books' in College," xxxii
Technology. *See* Science.
Teilhard, Pierre de Chardin: xxxiv-vii; Christogenesis, 208-09, 215-16, 219n. 63; cosmic view, 202; diminishment, 213; discontinuities, 202; *The Divine Milieu*, 212; education of, 203; *The Heart of the Matter*, xlviin. 91; noosphere, 59; omega point, 210; *The Phenomenon of Man*, xlviin. 90, 58; Pleroma, 211, 215-16; stature of, 202-03; work, 205-08; Dante and Teilhard, 215
Teresa, St., 7-8, 18
*Tess of the D'Urbervilles*, 17
*Testing the Faith*, xxxix, xlviin. 101
"That Heathen Alonzo," 22
"That One Talent," xliiin. 46
*That Uncertain Feeling*, 151
Theologian critic, 137-39
Theology and fiction, 136-37, 139, 147
*Theology and Modern Literature*, 147
*Theology and Sanity*, 136
Theology of weakness, 72-73
"These Gentle Communists," xliiin. 46
"They Also Serve," xliiin. 46
*They Are People*: xxiv, 47; Flemish edition, xlivn. 54; "Introduction" to *Great Modern Catholic Short Stories*, 9-14; writers and religious experience, 40-41

Sister Mariella Gable was chair of the English department at the College of St. Benedict in St. Joseph, Minnesota (1934-58), English professor (1928-58; 1962-73), editor of three anthologies—*Great Modern Catholic Short Stories* (1942; re-issued and re-titled *They Are People* in 1944), *Our Father's House* (1945), and *Many-Colored Fleece* (1950). Her essays defining Catholic fiction are in *This is Catholic Fiction* (1948) and her poetry is published in *Blind Man's Stick* (Bruce Humphries, 1938; Brandon Press, 1966). She published thirty-two essays and more than forty book reviews in books and periodicals. Receiving her Ph.D. from Cornell University in 1934, Gable earned a B.A. in English from the College of St. Benedict (1925) and an M.A. in English from the University of Minnesota (1929). She also studied at Columbia University and Oxford University and was Visiting Professor at Mt. Angel College, Oregon; Marillac College, Missouri; Marygrove College, Michigan; St. Martin's College, Washington; Marylhurst College, Oregon; Loretto College, Colorado; Mt. St. Scholastica College (Benedictine College), Kansas; University of Portland, Oregon.

Listings for Gable: *Directory of International Biography, World's Who's Who for Women in Education, Who's Who in American Education, Directory of American Scholars, International Who's Who, Personalities of the West and Midwest, American Catholic Who's Who*, vol. 9, *Guide to Catholic Literature, I, II, III, IV, Gallery of Living Catholic Authors* (Webster Grove, Missouri, 1946), *Book of Catholic Authors* (4th series), International Biographical Centre (Cambridge, England), American Biographical Institute, *The Encyclopedia of American Catholic History*.

Nancy Hynes, O.S.B., is Professor of English at the College of St. Benedict, St. Joseph, Minnesota.